BOOKS BY J. ALVAREZ DEL VAYO

Freedom's Battle

The Last Optimist

Give Me Combat

GIVE ME COMBAT

GIVE ME COMBAT
The Memoirs
of Julio Alvarez del Vayo

FOREWORD
BY BARBARA W. TUCHMAN

Translation From the Spanish
By Donald D. Walsh

Little, Brown and Company — Boston — Toronto

FIRST EDITION

T 08/73

Library of Congress Cataloging in Publication Data

Alvarez del Vayo, Julio, 1891-
  Give me combat; the memoirs of Julio Alvarez del
Vayo.

  1. Alvarez del Vayo, Julio, 1891-   I. Title.
DP264.A423A3   946.081'092'4 [B]   73-1213
ISBN 0-316-17983-3

Published simultaneously in Canada
by Little, Brown & Company (Canada) Limited

PRINTED IN THE UNITED STATES OF AMERICA

To the people of Spain in their fight for freedom

Foreword

Del Vayo has remained a contemporary man — a contemporary political man — a contemporary political socialist man — in whatever decade he has functioned. His concerns are as up to the minute in the '70s as they were in the '30s when he served as the last foreign minister of the Spanish Republic, or in 1914 when he felt the heartbreak of the ardent young socialist at the murder of Jean Jaurès and knew it to be the herald of war.

Although the cause closest to him, the retrieval of political freedom for Spain, does not have the immediacy of the front page for most Americans, it has for del Vayo the freshness of a battle lost yesterday. Because he sees it as part of a single fabric with the struggle for social justice everywhere it has kept him in the front line of that struggle at all times. If "Next year in Jerusalem" can come true in our lifetime for one exiled people, del Vayo can say with that much more conviction, "Tomorrow in Madrid."

It is significant that the first sentence of his earlier autobiographical book, *The Last Optimist*, contains the word "rebel" and the first sentence of this book the word "joy." Both are enduring elements of del Vayo's character. Since he was born of aristocratic lineage to a father who was a general and a mother who was a marchioness, his origins as a social revolutionary are plainly a matter of temperament rather than circumstance. He belongs to the kind of Prince Kropotkin, the Comte de Mirabeau or Chou En-lai — who are moved to fight the oppression of the ruling class into which they were born.

It is thirty-four years now — a whole generation — since the Spanish Republic was crushed, the last victim of appeasement. But in del Vayo's case hope deferred has not made his heart sick because sickness of that kind is simply excluded from his character. It is not in him to give up, partly I think, because he loves political battle. He is in it up to his chin; he swims in it like a fish. Like FDR he is the happy warrior. The corpuscles of his blood are composed of equal parts enthusiasm and optimism. He enjoys what he does, with all the confidence and belief in the future that that fortunate personality bestows.

Yet there must be iron in such a temperament if it is to stand up to failure, and underneath Vayo's optimism is the iron of persistence. He learned its value from two great models: Rosa Luxemburg and Fridtjof Nansen. Rosa was his teacher in her ardor, her humanizing of Marxist ideology, her "lack of concern at being isolated" and above all her incomparable morale, her refusal to be discouraged by repeated setbacks or ever to acknowledge defeat. "Never give up! Never!", even when the situation seems desperate: this, in memory of Rosa Luxemburg, became del Vayo's rule during the Spanish War, as it has been since. That it led Rosa to assassination typically does not deter him.

From Nansen, whom del Vayo accompanied on his relief expedition to Russia in 1922, he learned in person how the agony of the journey to the North Pole, close to starvation and given up for lost, had taught the explorer "not to despair about the final outcome of a great venture . . . Nansen had learned that when one struggles stubbornly for a noble idea, the skepticism of the overly intelligent who are incapable of risking anything for fear of failure cannot stand up against a wholehearted persistence." It is not only Nansen he is writing about here.

Del Vayo is today the outstanding living representative on the Republican side of the Spanish Civil War, the cause that gripped the West as the clarifying issue of the age of fascism. Through the encounters in this book with the men who have molded our time, the great and the puny, the good and the weak and the wicked, the reader will come to know the Spaniard at the center in the course of his several and often simultaneous careers as foreign correspondent, agitator and statesman. They will discover a man of cultivated mind, as open to art as to politics. They will find him at home in every capital from Madrid to Geneva, from Moscow to New York, from Paris to Peking. They will find themselves becoming his friend because, as I have found through an acquaintance that began in that year of despair, 1939, it is impossible not to be his friend.

One is drawn to del Vayo, I think, because one loves in him the thing many of us lack: belief in and unquenchable devotion to a goal. One loves him for his tremendous appetite for experience, as when he writes of his first visit to Moscow, "We were to be there only a few days but I wanted to see everything." One loves him not least for that vital and indispensable half of the del Vayo factor, his wife, Luisa.

While I would not expect to be on the opposite side of del Vayo on any fundamental issue, my reading of history is different from his. I do not believe history is unrolled by any categorical imperative, Marxist or otherwise; nor that the masses are its engine, nor their triumph its ultimate purpose. I am not sure I believe history has an ultimate purpose. If I am an observer, del Vayo is an *engagé*. He is committed, and will be till the day he dies.

BARBARA W. TUCHMAN

Contents

Illustrations

ONE

The Story Begins in London

When I first left Spain for the outer world I experienced a joy in traveling that I have never lost. An unlikely award — I was one of the worst students who ever attended the University of Madrid — took me to London. I had obtained a scholarship from the Junta de Ampliación de Estudios, established by the greatest educator of modern Spain, Don Francisco Giner de los Ríos, a man who was a combination of saint and reformer. The grant was for the purpose of studying the budget of Lloyd George and the British economic and social currents during the period before the First World War. I had written an essay on Lloyd George in Madrid; although it lacked any on-the-spot knowledge, the essay had interested the secretary of the junta, and resulted in my scholarship to London. Ten years later, when I tried during a Geneva conference to arrange an interview with Lloyd George, who had become prime minister, I told him, to curry favor with him, that I owed my career to him. Out of that first meeting grew a friendship that lasted through the Spanish Civil War.

From my first visit, London fascinated me. I already knew about it through some novels, including those of Pío Baroja, an arbitrary but original writer, very Spanish and very Basque, for whom the mystery of London had a constant attraction. One day, when I was a student in Madrid, I timidly approached a café where Baroja was holding forth and there I heard him talk about the charm of a foggy London day. It was enough to stir every fantasy of the imagination. London became for me a revelation in every way. Only a Spaniard of my generation, not a Spaniard of the so-called modernized and sophisticated and mini-skirted Spain, can sense the importance of being able to take a respectable English girl to the movies or on a walk through Hyde Park without a chaperon.

Hyde Park was a sensation all by itself, if just to see people lying on a grass that was green in a way only English grass can be, and to hear the soap-box orators debating everything — even religion and politics — with the crowd, without a single disturbance. Both experiences, the grass and the debates, were unlikely in the Spain that I had just left.

The boardinghouse where I stayed, in the Bayswater section, was in its way another center of my training. I learned to talk in a low voice instead of in a Spanish shout. There were a number of colonial ladies who came to spend a season in London while their husbands stayed in India or other British possessions in the service of the British Empire. At night, in the parlor, facing the fireplace, they exchanged their impressions of the day. They were the only boarders who allowed themselves such familiarity. The rest of us either ignored one another or whispered "lovely day," when the sun ventured forth to enrich our lives. For a Spaniard surfeited with sunshine, the tribute paid to its rare appearance had a comic sound. I never dreamed then that the Spanish sun, which at that time seemed so unimportant to my life, was going to save a Fascist dictatorship in my country by bestowing upon it thirty-one million tourists a year.

Sitting in one of those English armchairs that are the national symbol of comfort, pretending to read a book, I would frequently listen at night to the conversation of the colonial ladies. It was a way of learning English and at the same time feeling their sense of pride in belonging to so great an empire. Remembering some of those conversations as clearly as if it were yesterday and returning to present-day England, stripped of her former glory, with her colonial power entirely liquidated, one has the impression of having lived not one century but two. I have to admit, however, that as a personage, sure of himself and looking abroad with a sense of superiority hidden behind the best imaginable manners, today's Englishman continues to be fundamentally himself. This is his strength and it will continue to be so even if one day all England may be reduced to the single city of London.

The ladies to whom I listened in 1912 had more than enough reason for pride as they extolled the brilliance of imperial society, above all the royal family. The ladies were faithful readers of the *Daily Mail*. And through it they were informed of the slightest movements at court. When one of them was lucky enough to see the king or the queen in the royal carriage, she was assured of being the center of attention at the gathering that night. The smiles, the costume, everything had been minutely observed in order to be transmitted to those who had not been so fortunate. Just to be close to some lady-in-waiting at a charitable event was to have the feeling of being to some extent a member of the upper classes. All these ladies were Conservatives and detested Lloyd George.

The only exception to this hatred was a very elderly lady, not from the colonies but from the provinces. She was quite lively and she took a great fancy to me. I used to go with her on Sunday to churches where the preacher was a Socialist or a leftist Liberal. She scorned the ladies who took part in the nightly gatherings. She was extraordinarily alert, with a great sense of humor and a prodigious memory.

She was already a young woman deeply interested in politics when Gladstone injected into the Liberals of his time a healthy desire to break with the prejudices of the aristocracy and rely on the masses to impose the introduction of certain social reforms judged indispensable. She told me how the politics of the last third of the nineteenth century had been dominated by two strong personalities alternating the political power, Gladstone for the Liberals and Disraeli for the Conservatives. She had known them both. They differed in more than political philosophy. They were physically different. Gladstone was a big man, very confident of the effect produced by his presence. She described Disraeli so vividly that the biographies that I later read about the great Tory leader showed no greater insight into his personality. Disraeli, Jewish, very shrewd, knew how to win the favor of Queen Victoria by multiplying monuments and homages to the prince consort, the German Albert of Saxe-Coburg-Gotha, her lifelong love, and by adding to her crown the title of Empress of India.

Those two great politicians detested each other cordially. Disraeli said that Gladstone "was drunk on his own verbosity." And Gladstone returned the compliment by saying that the mere sight of Disraeli made him gnash his teeth.

This enchanting old lady, who could have been my great-grand-mother and who grew up in the tradition of the Liberal party, believed that Lloyd George was following the path traced by Gladstone. Since the reason for my being in London had to do with Lloyd George, I naturally spent a good deal of time studying this politician who inspired such contrary passions. At that time he was Chancellor of the Exchequer. He was extraordinarily intelligent and human. Recently the British historian and critic A. J. P. Taylor wrote of him: "David Lloyd George remains the most fascinating, because the most elusive, of twentieth-century British statesmen." I have heard eminent Britons say that Lloyd George was superior to Churchill.

The first time that I heard Lloyd George speak I found him very different from the Englishmen that I had heard up to then. He had nothing of that hesitation in going from one word to another that at times breaks the fluency of an Anglo-Saxon orator. He sounded rather like a Latin orator, Spanish, Italian, or French. He was by far the best speaker in the House of Commons. This Welshman, full of temperament and passion, was capable of understanding and communicating easily to others a complicated technical problem. He let himself be counseled by the technocrats of his time but he never let them control him.

From his youth, Lloyd George's ambition was to be a great orator

David Lloyd George, Chancellor of the Exchequer, 1912

rather than a great politician or statesman. But he was great in all three categories. He wanted to be a great orator because that was the best way of getting close to the public. He felt himself a part of that public. "It is not that I have taken on the cause of the people but that I am one of them." And his humanitarian disposition was strengthened by his reading. Hugo's *Les Misérables* led him to interest himself more deeply in the fate of the poor, and the plays of Ibsen led him to women's rights.

Lloyd George knew how to communicate his emotions. One of the leaders in the House of Commons confessed that he had wept during a speech of Lloyd George on the budget, a budget that bore the fighting title "The People's Budget." It was in this spirit that he plunged into the great battles of Parliament and of the people — fiscal reform, Ireland, limiting the powers of the House of Lords — which were the burning issues during my time in London.

When I heard Lloyd George and followed all the public controversy around him, I felt for the first time that a Progressive who does not claim to be a Socialist, and even at times an intelligent Conservative, can be more influential in creating a better society than a Social Democrat and, in the case of Great Britain, a Laborite. None of the English Socialists of that time, except the fighting Keir Hardie, equalled Lloyd George in his ardor to defend the cause in which he believed. He was careful to document himself well on any question under discussion, never leaving it to improvisation or eloquence; but once his files were complete, he attacked fearlessly.

When the members of the House of Lords had let themselves slip into the untenable — because unconstitutional — position of trying to reject his budget, Lloyd George exclaimed happily, "We've got them!" It was not within the prerogatives of the Lords to veto any measure of a fiscal nature. Lloyd George defied them to do so, saying that it would be seen whether a handful of idle aristocrats, moved only by personal interests, were going to prevail over the votes of millions of workers who had, during the elections, come out in favor of reform. Many of the Lords were great landowners and therefore opposed to Lloyd George's egalitarian recommendations with regard to the exploitation of the land.

His adversaries accused Lloyd George of being an opportunist. Perhaps; but he was also a man of principle and he could stand firm even though his stand was unpopular. His only interest was politics. He was not especially interested in social life. He had no interest in mingling with a class of people that he considered his enemies, because they were the target of his financial and budgetary policies, which were egalitarian. But perhaps there was another and more interesting side to his personality and temperament, warmer than those of the average British politician, for he had a strong attraction for the opposite sex. His secretary was the love of his life and an invaluable guide in the midst of

7

the numerous difficulties of his career. Indeed, on the death of his wife she became Countess Lloyd George.

Writing fascinated Lloyd George and several times he was on the point of forsaking politics to become a novelist or a journalist. The temptation was temporary. Politics always won out in the end. He was more loyal to his friends than some of his critics thought. He resisted all suggestions that he try to drive Herbert Asquith from power in order to succeed him as prime minister, even though he did not always agree with him. But Asquith was the prime minister, his chief, and he always defended him in public. Only the urgent need to win the First World War led Lloyd George to consent to be head of the Government, though he was clearly the most adequate figure to assume such a great responsibility.

During Lloyd George's passionate campaign for his budget and for his general policy of bringing about a more just society, I seldom saw him fall into demagogic excesses. But he did capitalize on the spirit of revolt that in those days was felt in the streets. The English working class had abandoned the attitude of unconditional submission to the upper classes. The class struggle was a reality even before Marx converted it into one of the bases of his socialist theory. Nineteenth-century England had developed amid the contradiction of advancing its industrial status while trying to hold back the working class created by this economic progress. This was one of the themes of my studies in London. The Industrial Revolution had brought about a population growth without parallel in history. The lives of simple people were thereby made very difficult. In the first period of the Industrial Revolution the condition of the British worker was miserable. The factory owners were getting increasingly rich; they thought themselves very Christian, but they were hypocrites — insensitive to the wages of hunger. Men were earning half a pound a week for working seventy-two hours and more. Women and children who formed a good part of the first workers' army of the Industrial Revolution, were getting less. And things went on that way for many years. Even in 1875 more than a hundred thousand children under thirteen were working in English textile mills.

A social agitation with aggressiveness unknown up to then was needed for the first Reform Act to be adopted in 1832. During the Victorian era, my elderly boardinghouse friend told me, the adoration of simple people for the queen had somewhat calmed the wave of working-class demands. Queen Victoria, with her irreproachable family life and her pride of empire, had been, on the whole, a sovereign of peace, after the Crimean War and the bombardment of Canton. But let us not speak of the English bourgeoisie, who considered themselves the world pioneers in technical progress and who led comfortable lives in houses that seemed to me horrible, crammed with furniture, with bibelots, and even at times with golden cages filled with parrots and other exotic birds. I used to visit one

8

of those bourgeois families because I was giving Spanish lessons to one of the sons. I was shocked by the bad taste in furnishings that people had, especially the men, who had quite good taste in clothes.

It was not only the bourgeoisie who revered the royal family. Talking with workers, I discovered their weakness for the monarchy and the aristocracy. Great Britain could go through all kinds of revolutions, but the monarchy would survive the spirit of revolt. Things have not changed much, for in a visit I made to London during the last General Election, I asked taxi drivers, newspaper vendors, construction workers, whom they were going to vote for, and most of them said they would vote for the Conservative Heath and not for the Laborite Wilson.

In the days when I was first in London the working class was not so tranquil. The trade unions were getting stronger and stronger. They had learned from the strike of the dockworkers at the end of the century that only through struggle could they better their situation. The years 1911 and 1912 saw widespread strikes that were the consequence of the deterioration in the economic situation. In 1911 it was the dockworkers again and the railroadmen. In 1912 it was the metalworkers. I attended their meetings and mingled with the workers, thus giving my political education a sense of direct experience. There was also the battle for women's rights, the famous suffragettes like the Pankhursts — Emmeline, Christabel, and Sylvia — who amused the cartoonists by chaining themselves to the railings of Buckingham Palace, going on hunger strikes, and generally making fantastic scandals.

All this created a climate of protest that was very helpful to the cause of Lloyd George. It placed in his hands a decisive argument against the Tories. The choice was between an orderly revolution by means of reforms that, however radical they were, left the capitalist system intact, and the alternative, revolution in the street.

Lloyd George was a leader of outstanding ability. The number of contemporary politicians who could be compared with him was very limited. Arthur James Balfour, very sharp, cultivated, a mixture of philosopher and politician, was prime minister when Lloyd George first entered Parliament, and Lloyd George considered it a great honor to be noticed by him. He was in Balfour's cabinet. Lord Curzon, imperialistic and dominating, later viceroy of India; Winston Churchill, youthful, bellicose, trying to attract attention, but feeling for Lloyd George an esteem that was reciprocated; Bonar Law, chief of the Conservative party, of whom Herbert Asquith said that "he had not the brains of a Glasgow baillie." Although Bonar Law was completely opposed to Lloyd George, he lacked the courage to defend his ideas, which were more liberal than those of most Tories. Lloyd George used to say that the Tories believed that it was the duty of the workers to sacrifice themselves for the nation, but that the Tories were in no hurry to imitate them. "As soon as the

Beatrice Webb: brains, charm, and beauty

(*Below*) Sidney and Beatrice Webb, founders of the Fabian Society

suggestion is made that their rents should be controlled, they say: 'Perish the British Empire! We will not have our rents touched.'"

Lloyd George was a central topic of discussion in the London School of Economics, which was the center of my formal studies and it was there that I learned to study seriously. There was a very stimulating atmosphere, with a first-class faculty: Bernard Shaw, H. G. Wells, Hilaire Belloc, the luminaries of the British intelligentsia, gave lectures there. A woman of exceptional quality who enlivened it all with her brains and her charm was Beatrice Webb. At present there is a new current in European syndicalist circles to redirect attention to the Webbs, who were the authors of the best history of British trade unionism. In my time, Beatrice was the person most admired by those who were taking courses at the London School of Economics, and also by the habitués of the Fabian Society, of which she was a founder. It was not only the young people, I and others, who felt the magic power of her personality. Bernard Shaw, who was on intimate terms with almost no one, made an exception of her.

Perhaps Shaw had an influence on Beatrice Webb's evolution toward radicalism. Shaw had the courage to write to his scandalized compatriots: "I have advised the nations to adopt Communism and have carefully explained how they can do it without cutting one another's throats. But if they prefer to do it by cutting one another's throats, I am not less a Communist. Communism will be good even for Yahoos." Among the majority of my fellow students at the School, Shaw was the favorite writer, and next to him, Beatrice Webb.

When I met her, Beatrice Webb had already evolved from a kind of Quaker attitude, a humanitarian emotion, a sympathy for the underdog, toward socialism. Born Beatrice Potter of a rich family, she went with her father to the United States at the age of fifteen. Her father was going to add the presidency of American railroad companies to that which he already had in the Great Western Railway of Britain. England was then at the apex of its industrial and naval power, but the penetrating gaze of Beatrice already discovered in the United States the power that was going to replace Great Britain in world dominion. She also discovered the contrast between the rich and the poor that was already beginning to appear in the United States, although with less intensity than in England. She would never forget that visit.

When I knew her she was already a fully formed woman, but a mental discipline as arid as the economy had not affected her beauty, upon which age had had no effect. When she died in her mid-eighties Kingsley Martin, then editor of the *New Statesman*, wrote that Rembrandt would have enjoyed painting her at that last moment of her life.

She told us how she went from charity work to socialism. I frequented in London some of the places that had contributed to her change in attitude. When my classes and research at the school were over, I would go to the East End, one of the poorest sections of the city, and would talk with the people. The women were more outspoken than the men in describing their misery. How sharp a contrast to the society women attending the theater, so expensively dressed, covered with jewels, and surely ignorant of, or at least indifferent to, the lives of the other women.

But the reason for the shift of the admirable Beatrice Webb toward socialism had a more solid base. She had specialized in research and she was going to be, with her husband, Sidney Webb, an authority on gathering and interpreting facts. Social investigation had led her to dig deep into the causes of inequality, which wounded her noble character. Her activities in the charity organizations made her see clearly that it was not a question of generosity or of personal egoism but the inseparable phenomenon of a system, the capitalist system, based on the exploitation of some men by other men.

Her studies in the life of the London East End strengthened her feeling that persuading the rich to ease their consciences by giving a few hundred pounds to the organizations for which she worked did not solve the problem. She saw the swarming East End; the physical misery and the moral debasement that followed in the track of the rack-renting landlord and the capitalist profit maker — this pushed her toward socialism.

To her intelligence, fineness, sensibility, were joined an extraordinary courage to face the social milieu from which she had emerged and not to fear, with time, being classified as an irresponsible Red. In the days of Stalin she wrote an indignant letter to the *New Statesman* because of a criticism of Russia that had appeared in that leftist weekly. The reluctance of certain intellectuals to take a courageous stand exasperated her, and she maintained that, however unattractive Stalin was personally, he had saved the revolution. If Trotsky, with all his genius, had won out in his struggle against Stalin, Soviet Russia would not have survived her internal and external conflicts. This was later essentially the opinion of two of Stalin's sternest critics, Isaac Deutscher and Georg Lukàcs. They both felt that one had to give Stalin credit for having kept Russia in a strong enough position to repel Hitler's assault.

For Beatrice Webb, the Cooperative Movement at first meant a step forward, an advance between the pure humanitarian position that appealed to her youthful nobility of character and the definitive acceptance of socialism as the only road to assure the liberation and the independence of the working class. She explained it more or less this way: "To one who has been bred in a stronghold of capitalism, the Consumers Cooperative Movement seemed a unique romance in the industrial history of the world. Throughout my study of the Cooperative Movement I had in fact been watching the very process of trial and error by which

12

this community of working men was establishing a 'New Social Order.' It became clear to me that the existence of strong trade unions, enforcing standard rates and the normal working day, and protecting the individual from arbitrary fines and capricious dismissal, was essential . . ." to the redemption of the proletariat from its long position of servitude.

The word "proletariat," as defined by Beatrice Webb, attracted me. In typically Spanish fashion I believed that I knew all about socialism when in fact I had read only a couple of books on the subject. I thought that one day I would write a book entitled *A New Theory of the Proletariat.* But as I began to read Marx and Engels, after studying David Ricardo, the starting point for Marx, my youthful enthusiasm was somewhat restrained.*

In the London School of Economics I learned to be a Socialist. *My Apprenticeship* is the title of one of the books of Beatrice Webb. I owe my apprenticeship in part to her. I also learned in that school, as I once said to Harold Laski, its former director, the art of combining a firm and consistent political conviction with a realistic position.

In the school we had organized, as an exercise in politics, a miniature of the House of Commons. We foreign students could participate in it, as could the British students. At the same time, and as a way of disciplining my activities, I carried out a research project on the treatment given to Spanish miners by the British Río Tinto Company.

While the Spanish university had been only a place through which to pass as quickly as possible in order to get a degree, the London School of Economics had taken possession of me. I spent almost every day of the week there, taking courses, studying in the library, or arguing with the other students. Only Sundays I spent admiring the English beauties in Hyde Park. I had a Spanish friend, a good poet, Ramón Basterra, later a diplomat, who half seriously had decided to imitate the London swells and who turned up in Hyde Park on Sundays in a cutaway and top hat. He wanted me to dress up the same way. I firmly refused, first, because that would not go well with my Socialist inclinations; second, because the little money I had left after paying tuition and boardinghouse expenses I preferred to spend going to hear musicians like Pablo Casals, who even then, sixty years ago, was a sensation, and who continues to be a sensation, celebrating his ninety-fifth birthday on December 27, 1971, by giv-

---

* When I was discussing one day with the late Joseph Barnes of Simon and Schuster the title of a new book of mine, I thought back on those student days in London. I suggested *The March of the Proletariat.* Barnes, somewhat disillusioned from the revolutionary experiences in which he had taken part, said to me ironically: " 'Proletariat?' That doesn't exist anymore." I answered: "If you're thinking of George Meany and the movement over which he presides, which instead of fighting against the war in Vietnam gives it support, your observation is correct. But outside of the United States the proletariat still has some meaning in almost all countries." But I finally agreed that a better title was *The March of Socialism.*

ing a concert. Or I would go to watch Anna Pavlova dance; she was my introduction to the Russian ballet.

An English poet called the Thames River "the dream of London" and I used to go there to enjoy the view and to admire *The Discovery*, the ship that was used by Captain Scott on his sensational voyages. Scott had created a lot of talk about himself that year when he reached the South Pole immediately after the Norwegian explorer Roald Amundsen. Captain Scott was the hero of my boardinghouse ladies, one of whose favorite conversational topics was the diabolical attempt of Kaiser Wilhelm II to vie with Great Britain for control of the high seas.

Beyond London Bridge I invariably went toward the Tower of London, one of the richly historic sights of the city, the royal jail and residence for political prisoners, a jail honored by the presence of kings, queens, princes, and bishops, and, according to Lord Macaulay, "the saddest place on earth." But every jail has an effect of repulsion and interest. In France, at the time of the Great Revolution, the Conciergerie was as fascinating as the Trianon. In Petersburg the fortress of Peter and Paul was the scene of some of the most compelling passages in Russian literature.

My attention was focused especially on Joseph Conrad, whose lectures I attended regularly. Here was the incredible case of a writer who, having been born and raised in Poland, had begun only as an adult to master English and yet became one of the best British writers of his time. For me English was the ideal language to express concretely what one felt, and it was ideal in any case for journalism, which was what most attracted me. The virtue of Conrad was in the way that he had learned English, as a sailor practicing it on ship and in ports; on schooners, because he hated motors — and a steamship, even though small, seemed to him a locomotive. As soon as he saved a few shillings, he bought a volume of the complete works of Shakespeare and in this extraordinarily difficult way he perfected his English and discovered his gift as a writer.

From a sailor he got to be a captain. Captain Teodor Jozef Konrad Korzeniowski sailed the world and from his vision, through his great black eyes, emerged the material that would give great enchantment to his novels. It was as the result of a voyage to the Congo that Conrad the novelist was born. John Galsworthy said of such a voyage that it had given him simultaneously a fever and an urge to write. After twenty years as a sailor, Conrad became a fabulous and famous novelist through his *Lord Jim*.

This work was clearly the one that best displayed his originality. With his Slavic sensibility, which was nevertheless so Western, he was happy to learn that he was being read in French whose authors, Balzac, Flaubert, Stendhal, he greatly admired. At times there was something of

Dostoevski in him, although he, as a Pole, hated Russia so deeply that he emigrated from a Russian-controlled Poland. His character Marlow, an adventurer, a man of the world and the sea, the central figure in *Youth*, is in many ways Conrad himself. He had a strong sense of the moral and the aesthetic.

Conrad was a writer whose beginnings were especially painful not because of his difficulties with English but because of what he demanded of himself. According to his own confession, it took him a hundred and three manuscript pages to relate the events of twelve hours. But he had an iron will to succeed. He was not disheartened when the bank that was helping him went bankrupt or even when his wife hurt herself so badly in a fall that she was a semi-invalid for life. Nor was he disheartened that it took his own publisher, who printed his novels because they sold well, a dozen years to discover that Conrad was a great novelist. He would spend his days writing *Nostromo* and his nights dictating the outline of his next novel. As a sailor he got accustomed to sleeping little and to spending his nights looking at the stars.

In spite of the difference in our ages, we had a friend in common, another writer, Cunninghame Graham, who looked and acted like an Argentine cowboy and who was always talking to me about Conrad. I benefited from the friendship of Cunninghame Graham and from his pocketbook, for he paid me most generously to translate into Spanish a biography of Saint Teresa de Jesús that his wife had written. Not knowing how else to get rid of her, he had sent her to Avila to write a life of the great Spanish mystic.

London had begun to shape me. My scholarship was renewed, and with the money from the translation I went to Leipzig. The university there had a course that interested me greatly: The History of Communism, Socialism, and Anarchism. And at the same time I wanted to see at close hand those Germans, who were beginning seriously to worry the British. It was one year before the beginning of the First World War.

TWO

Eternal Germany

I found Germany in 1913 much less receptive and more disagreeable than England. Compared with London, Leipzig seemed to me boisterous, superficially gay, but less civilized, in spite of the fact that the German language was considered to be the supreme expression of civilization and *Kultur*. I swiftly discovered that between the student at the University of Leipzig and the student at the London School of Economics there was a profound difference in attitude. I was shocked by the air of superiority of the German student. In him I could sense that there was already something of the future soldier. With his dueling scars, with the caps of his various associations and clubs, the impression that the student was a member of a separate and superior social group was much clearer than in England.

That impression of a predominantly military nation was evident at the table where I went every day for luncheon. I went there for two reasons: it was cheaper than in a restaurant and I could practice my German. I had luncheon in the home of a ruined soldier and aristocrat. He took in boarders to help his son, a Lieutenant von Stein, maintain a social life worthy of his rank. The von Stein household was a Germany in miniature in which the cult of the military was shared by most of the guests, people of varied occupations — bureaucrats, university graduates hoping for a position, or a lady librarian attracted by the presence of the heir, who occasionally deigned to appear at the table. This was for me an excellent introduction to German society.

As the youngest person at the table, I adopted an attitude of modesty and discretion. I did more listening than talking, offering as an excuse my limited command of the language. I did, however, take advantage of one opportunity to tell the senior von Stein that my father was a general in the Spanish army and that my mother had been a marchioness. From that day on my respectability was established.

The arrival of the kaiser in Leipzig to celebrate the centenary of a victorious battle was discussed at length at the table. It was cause for joy and satisfaction. It gave rise to a very exalted discussion of the irresistible force of Germany. "Discussion" was not really the right word. Everyone agreed that the kaiser's wishes were law in Europe. Everyone but me; I kept my silence.

As I became familiar with the classic German authors, I realized that the ideas that enimated the von Steins were the very same ideas held by the great espousers of German culture: poets, philosophers and historians who had a vision of a Germany that militarily, politically, and intellectually had to be the first nation in the world. If Goethe said: "We Germans were not born yesterday. But centuries will have to pass before our compatriots acquire enough spirit and high culture so that it may be said that they emerged from barbarity some time ago," he was talking to the individual German, not to the German nation as a whole, which he considered superior to all other nations.

For Lamprecht, whose history courses I took, the glorious period was from 1800 to 1870, the same period glorified by the former chancellor, Prince Bernhard von Bülow, whose latest book, *The Future of Germany*, was a great success. Germany without an emperor had seen her fields devastated, her cities sacked, her towns constantly threatened by foreign domination. But from 1800 to 1870 each step toward the reestablishment of imperial unity signified a step forward toward the prosperity of the nation. For the first time in history the Hohenzollern Empire had succeeded in creating a means of communication among the different components of the Germanic corpus that it never had in the past.

The passage of time brought about the consolidation of a transportation system equally beneficial in times of peace or war. In times of peace the military empire put into practice at a very efficient level its devices and mobilization regulations. For this it had at its disposal a railroad system in which discipline and punctuality were the amazement of the other European countries. A station in Leipzig was one of my regular walking goals. Twenty-six tracks bordered by fourteen platforms, with another adjacent station for freight. From that station, in the summer of 1914, I saw young Germans going off to war, singing.

To understand the Germans in the year before the First World War, one had to go back to the true point of departure, the creation of German unity, and to the principal architect of this unity, Prince Otto von Bismarck, an imposing figure and a virtuoso of realism in politics, a person who is much admired today by Henry Kissinger. As long as Bismarck was chancellor, he made all the decisions. But in time his powers became excessive and intolerable to Wilhelm II and this was the cause of their rupture.

I therefore began to study Bismarck. Before his time the German nation was a collection of semi-independent principalities dominated by princes. The life of the country was disorganized and erratic. Napoleon was adored by the Germans to a greater extent than by any other people, but his domination of Germany finally roused her. It was through war, the Franco-Prussian War, 1870–1871, that the unity of Germany was achieved. Born out of war, she carries about her an aura of war.

The center of the new united Germany was Prussia, and Prussia had a decidedly military bent. On January 18, 1871, in the Hall of Mirrors of Versailles, when the cry "Long live Kaiser Wilhelm!" was heard, it was the king of Prussia who was designated as the all-powerful right arm of a people whose religion was violence and pride, a people who could not conceive of a peaceful growth or a normal existence, a people which would either destroy everything or possess everything. There was about the Germans the grandioseness and vulgarity of Wagner.

I noted one of the phrases of Prince von Bülow: "The German question can be settled only by war. It is the price that we must pay to keep the German nation united and great." Bismarck believed in the cult of force. But his political genius added astuteness to force. His critics found it strange that a man of his talents should give importance to the dual treaty that he signed with the czar behind everyone's back. But in that apparently empty gesture could be glimpsed a policy of rapprochement with Russia that would be of use to Germany in her periods of crisis or defeat.

Bismarck thought that, even though they despised one another or hated one another, Germans and Russians somehow complemented one another. After all, Friedrich II had been saved by Peter III of Russia and it had been Alexander I who had come forward to assure the reestablishment of Prussia. Later it was evident that each collapse of Germany was followed by an understanding with Russia which provided a basis for the resurgence of Germany's international power. And this is true even today.

In the field of domestic politics the enemy, for Bismarck, was any force opposed to the total hegemony of Prussia. The *Kulturkampf*, carried on by Bismarck with a vigor worthy of the Iron Chancellor, had as a target the *Zentrum*, the political expression of German Catholicism. The anti-Socialist laws persecuted a movement that has always boasted of its international character.

On accepting the idea of a democratic Chamber, as a counterbalance to the capricious powers of the princes, Bismarck was far from wishing to give the regime a genuinely parliamentary regime. From the beginning the Reichstag had its claws trimmed by means of a calculated regulation that severely restricted its prerogatives. Whereas we noted that the British sovereign possessed all powers in theory but in practice exercised almost none of them, the truth in the case of the German Empire was quite the opposite.

By means of the Upper Chamber, the *Bundesrat*, the king-emperor, the king of Prussia, had an indirect veto power. Since Prussia had a majority of the votes in the Federal Council, on all essential questions — dealing with the army, navy, taxes, and customs duties — nothing could be done against the will of the emperor.

That was the Germany that I found when I reached Leipzig: an all-powerful empire and an emperor, Wilhelm II, obsessed by a desire to challenge England's control of the seas, a desire that would inevitably lead to war. The proclamation of Wilhelm II on the very day of his father's death, addressed to the army, was already asking for God's blessing "on days of calm as well as on days of storm." He was getting ready for the storm with his ill-timed interventions in Africa, with his expansionist frenzy in the search for new colonies, but above all with his defiance of England on the seas.

I took flying visits to other German cities to round out my view of the country, which would have been too limited if focused on a predominantly commercial city like Leipzig. I had the greatest sense of the disquieting power of Germany in the city of Hamburg. In speaking of its steady growth, the Germans, proud of their new maritime power, had only one word to describe Hamburg: *Kolossal!* Its docks and the bustle of its port bore witness to the imperial ambition to wrest from the hands of the English a world position that they would not relinquish without a fight. In the course of three decades Germany had spent four hundred billion *deutsche marks* to build a great merchant fleet and a great war fleet.

As a port, Hamburg had already left Le Havre, Antwerp, and Naples far behind. Its object at the time was to move ahead of Liverpool. When I would talk with my fellow students in Leipzig about the danger of war that all this activity implied, they would laugh. "These English," they would say, "we're going to get them down off their pedestals. And if they get fresh, we'll squash them." I would answer with some irritation that one of Germany's greatnesses was the art of imitation. In past centuries she had imitated France in the building of cathedrals and castles. Now she was imitating England in the building of ships and imitating the United States in the creation of an imperial industrial combine the size of the Krupp Syndicate. But the main thing was the ships. "If we wish to advance upon the markets of the world," said the kaiser to the citizens of Bremen, "let us remember the motto of the Hanseatic League: 'It is not essential to live or to eat but it *is* essential to sail.'"

In fact the Germans were not eating at all badly. Since 1910 they had been eating abundantly. Hunger was a thing of the past. Whether the year was a good one or a bad one, Germany slaughtered twenty-three million pigs and suckling pigs and drank sixty-seven million hogsheads of beer. In the beer halls the atmosphere was gay and exuberant, with the maître d'hôtel walking up and down ceremoniously bowing, and with groups of students shouting heavy jokes from table to table, jokes that later might be the excuse for a duel. The ladies, who were admired for their plumpness, spent the afternoons in pastry shops adding weight to their graces.

In the Germany of 1913 there was no lack of potatoes, *charcuterie,* or beer. But the Germans could not enjoy, for example, the exquisite hand-work of the French artisan. That was one of the reasons why they strove for *Lebensraum.* Among the caricaturists who delighted in torturing a certain type of German, Georg Grosz became famous by mirroring the wealthy society, the *Schiebers,* in the period immediately following the First World War. But the prototypical German of my days in Leipzig was best captured by a compatriot of mine, Luis Bagaría. If he had been an American, Luis would have become rich. In Spain he barely earned enough money to pay for the alcohol that sustained him as he spent the early hours of the morning going from one bar to another expounding his philosophy of the world.

Bagaría sketched the German with the spike of his military helmet coming right out of the top of his head. It was a perfect psychological portrait of the students with whom I used to argue at the university when I heard them constantly saying that the day when the German army went on the march, nobody and nothing would stop them.

In the university there was, fortunately, a group of Russian students with whom I got along very well. I didn't always agree with all of them, but we had an identical reaction to the chauvinism of the German students. Mixing with the Russians meant a change in my sleeping habits. Russians are capable of talking for hours and hours, far into the night. The group of Russian students represented the principal political tendencies that existed in their country immediately before the war. The Marxist tendency prevailed, and it had increased since 1912, when the strikes led to the murder of the workers in the Lena Goldfields mines. Two hundred and seventy-five miners perished because they refused to eat the rotten food that the staff served to them. The Marxists were divided into the Bolsheviks, or Leftist Socialists, and the Reform Socialists, like those who were in the first Duma, the Czarist Parliament that was dissolved as soon as it dared to proclaim the need for agrarian reform and that had to move to Vyborg in Finland.

Ideologically I was already on the side of the Marxists — but personally I was enchanted by the fieriness of one socialist-revolutionary student, a supporter of Bakunin and Prince Kropotkin and of their terrorist tactics. She was very knowledgeable about the history of the Russian

Revolution, and to hear her arguing with the Socialists, especially those with rightist views, was very informative and at times very amusing.

Her name was Aglaya Filipovna and she combined in it the family names of the two rival heroines of Dostoevski's *The Idiot*, Aglaya Iva-novna and Natasha Filipovna, both in love with Prince Myshkin. She was very pretty and I told her jokingly that I would be happy to be another idiot if she would favor me with a little of her tenderness. But she told me over and over that her only love was the revolution.

Aglaya's love of the revolution was matched by her hatred of the po-lice. She was writing her thesis — not sure that it would be accepted by her professor — on the history of the Russian secret police from the earliest times. She began with the reign of Ivan the Terrible, with his "Oprichnina," planned especially to break the intrigues and ambitions of the *boyars*, the nobles of that time. She then dealt with the "Preobajen-ski Prikaz" under Peter the Great, notable in the "War of the Beards," the hunting down of beard wearers — the officials who criticized the czar because he didn't wear a beard. She ended with the "Okhrana," the Russian secret police of our student days in Leipzig.

The "Okhrana" were less active in persecuting the Russian revolution-aries who were living in exile in Germany and Switzerland than they were in moving against the revolutionaries in Paris, where the Russian embassy was their headquarters. After the successful attempt against Alexander II the Russian secret police had concentrated their attention on France. Germany was largely ignored by them, and Aglaya Filipovna, who was a militant of the "Narodniki" faction, the populists, the heirs of the famous "People and Liberty," had chosen to come to Leipzig.

She was of noble origin and the prototype of the Russian revolutionary. She could have led a luxurious life but she preferred to risk prison and even death within Russia or the alternative miseries of exile to be able to study and prepare herself for the coming struggles.

In Russia the secret police were mightier than the government. Aglaya told me that the first document that Nicholas II received on mounting the throne was the report of Plehve, the chief of police. Plehve was of German origin but he wanted to be more Russian than the Russians and to defend autocracy against all liberal efforts, even the feeblest ones. His obsession was to pursue the revolutionaries in their "foreign fortresses" and to infiltrate their ranks with secret agents.

One of these secret agents, famous in the history of the "Okhrana," was a man named Hechelmann from a Jewish family in Minsk, who had studied in Lieja, where he joined a circle of Russian populists and there became an expert in the manufacture of bombs. A complete adventurer, he made contact with the secret police section of the Russian embassy in Paris and acted for years as an *agent provocateur*. But his Jewish origin was no discredit in the eyes of my friend Aglaya, who considered anti-Semitism, in Germany or in Russia, a reactionary and despicable weapon.

In order to be more effective as an *agent provocateur* Hechelmann became a convert to the Orthodox Church during one of his stays in Germany and he changed his name to Harting. "If we had a dozen Hartings in the Okhrana," Plehve told the czar, "the empire would have nothing to fear."

Another famous *agent provocateur*, even more famous than Harting, was Ivan Azev, on the surface an enthusiastic terrorist who even offered to help create a new revolutionary socialist group called, if I remember correctly, the Combat Organization. Azev made such an impression on the comrades that he was put in charge of uniting all the subversive groups into his organization. It was no coincidence that the most valuable members of all these groups mysteriously fell into the hands of the secret police.

No one could have any doubts about Azev or his activities as an informer because it was known that he was in touch with the best European specialists in the manufacture of dynamite and that he had set up a whole machinery for the production of false passports. His cynicism was limitless. At the funeral of one of the great exiled socialist revolutionary leaders whom he had betrayed, Azev presided at the rites. The dead man had confided to a friend: "I can die at ease. Ivan Azev will carry on the work better than I, and on the day of victory he will speak to the masses in my name." Azev was quite capable of doing this. When he was finally caught the revolutionaries tried to kill him but he escaped. Plehve, however, was destroyed in 1904 by a bomb tossed by a member of the group to which Aglaya Filipovna belonged.

As my stay in Leipzig lengthened I gradually came to a more balanced appraisal of Germany. I yielded to no one in my aversion to the chauvinistic students and to a bourgeoisie whose arrogance and vulgarity repelled me. But in time I found out about the romantic revolutionaries of 1848, many of whom emigrated to the United States after their defeat. And I learned about Schiller and Heine and dramatists like Gerhart Hauptmann and Wedekind, who were, for their times, very rebellious in technique and ideas.

Leipzig was a very bookish city; living there was an invitation to reading. It was also a first-rate musical center, thanks especially to the presence of Nikich, the great conductor. And I even became reconciled to the university. The seminar workshop, a very German institution, taught one to study with an intellectual rigor hard to equal. It taught one to replace improvisation and supposed originality by a disciplined habit of serious research that went to the bottom of each problem.

Leipzig helped me to know the Germans at a crucial moment in their history. It was an experience that was to be very useful to me whenever —

including now in 1972 — the rapid shifts in German foreign policy disconcert and bewilder many of the alleged experts in international affairs.

My Leipzig period also gave me a very valuable tool, the German language, difficult, as I have said, for a Latin to learn. I finally learned it better than French or English. And I learned to write it, quite an accomplishment with its constructions so different from those of Spanish. The German verbs always are at the end of the long sentences and the paragraphs are interminable.

While I was taking the special course in the history of communism, socialism, and anarchism, I spent quite a bit of time familiarizing myself with the German Social Democratic party. I already considered myself a Socialist not merely ideologically but technically, because when I was in London I had received from the creator and leader of Spanish socialism, the great Pablo Iglesias, a handwritten letter granting my request to enter the party. With this letter and with some audacity, I went as a newspaperman who hadn't yet any newspaper to one of the principal party congresses in which the two currents, right and left, opposed each other, with the first one numerically dominant.

As a party, German Social Democracy was an impressively organized force. With a leader of the stature of August Bebel and with an aggressive position in opposition to the old German Conservative party, whose motto was "Authority, not Liberty," Social Democracy was the strongest party in the Reichstag.

The Conservative party's newspaper was the *Kreuzzeitung*, edited for a time by the famous Baron von Hammerstein. I considered it my duty to read it regularly because the first rule in politics is to get to know the enemy well. The Conservative party strength was naturally in Prussia, in the provinces of Brandenburg, Pomerania, and East Prussia. It monopolized the cult of the throne and Protestant orthodoxy. It included aristocrats, sectarians, anti-Semites, great landowners and consequently sworn enemies of any attempt at land reform. Social Democracy, on the other hand, recruited its followers in the industrial centers and each election brought the party new votes. These votes, in 1912, came to more than four million. They snatched from the Conservatives the old city of the kings of Prussia, Potsdam, a victory which inspired a jubilant headline in *Vorwärts*, the Socialist organ: "Potsdam has seen the Red flag hoisted!"

I lived through the period when German socialism was very confident of its strength. But I did not share that confidence. I admired the party's doctrinal profundity, very superior to that of the British Labor party. Its two outstanding thinkers at that time were Karl Kautsky on the left and Eduard Bernstein on the right. I got to know them both quite well, and also Louise Kautsky, a wonderful human being.

As a Marxist theoretician, Kautsky enjoyed in those days an undisputed authority. All over the country Socialists would wait eagerly for the appearance of each issue of his review *Die neue Zeit*, which contained exceptionally valuable articles on international affairs, colonialism, socialism in a transitional period, and other equally important subjects.

Bernstein was the father of "revisionism," a word that is abundantly used today in Chinese-Soviet polemics. But Bernstein was even so a better Socialist than many of the present leaders of Socialist parties in or out of power. He greeted the fatal assault on Plehve as the heroic act of a new Wilhelm Tell and quoted Schiller on the occasion.

German Social Democracy had many attributes of a strong party. It was founded in 1875 as a compromise between the followers of Marx and Lassalle, the former a genius with his theory of class struggle, the latter more idealistic and romantic — he died in a duel over a love affair. But the party had other qualities that made me doubt its revolutionary effectiveness. Its parades, in which I took part, especially when the war got closer, were like military parades, with nobody allowed to break ranks. They lacked the popular emotionalism of similar parades in other European countries.

I saw German Social Democracy as too self-satisfied, too impressed with its solid parliamentary representation, with the backing of the unions that followed its political direction, with a great number of members who ought, in principle, in case of war, to declare a general strike and thereby erect a barrier that would stop the military. In principle, yes. But in practice? That was where my doubts began.

The doubts increased in the days after the assassination at Sarajevo of Archduke Franz Ferdinand, the heir of the weak and artificial Austro-Hungarian monarchy which, precisely because of its weakness, was irresponsible and tempted to indulge in warlike adventures.

The German chancellor at the time was Theobald von Bethmann-Hollweg, the grimmest of all the successors of Bismarck. His quality of mind was made clear in an incident that took place when I was in Leipzig. Some German officers in the garrison of Zabern, in Alsace, had mistreated civilians who had been a bit slow in making way for them on a town sidewalk, and then had arrested them. There was a great scandal, with foreseeable repercussions in France, still so sensitive about anything that involved the provinces that she had lost in the Franco-Prussian War. Bethmann was at first against the officers, but when he learned that the crown prince sympathized with them, he yielded at once.

I discussed the incident with some Social Democrat students at the university. They were indignant at the chancellor, but they were also indignant at their own party, whose reaction they found too prudent. The party voted against Bethmann-Hollweg in the Reichstag and he lost his majority, but this had no effect; he never thought for a moment of resigning. My friends insisted that the Socialists should have protested with greater energy. "What can you expect?" said one of my history classmates.

27

"Many of our Social Democrats are just as chauvinistic as the rest of the Germans. My father told me how the beginning of the twentieth century was greeted in Germany with joy, as the German century. The seventeenth century had been the French century, the nineteenth was the English century, and the twentieth was going to be the German century."

One could breathe in the air the expansionist design. It corresponded to the credo of Mommsen, the papal historian, who passed as a liberal. He maintained that in human history there were chosen peoples, called upon to lead, superior peoples. He did not feel it necessary to name Germany.

That summer of 1914, spent in Germany, remains one of the memories that have most deeply marked my political life. It may be said that the story has been told a thousand times. Very well, I have told it once more. There are very few witnesses of that demonstration of German militarism and of the collapse of the strongest Socialist party of its time, very few who are still alive and who can add a personal judgment to the story.

During the month of July events rushed ahead with frantic speed. Still many Germans believed that war would not come. But I was convinced that it would. The language of *Vorwärts* was one of retreat, of capitulation, despite its pretended loyalty to the cause of peace. When the news came of the murder in Paris of Jean Jaurès, that mighty voice against the war, we knew that all was lost.

I took part, with Russian students, with Social Democratic students, in a desperate attempt to demonstrate in the streets against the war on the occasion of the assassination of Jaurès. But the Social Democratic masses in general were listless. They had joined the war party. Only a few days later the Social Democratic faction in the Reichstag voted funds for the war. Wilhelm II said: "I recognize no Parties now. I recognize only Germans!"

The time had come for sad farewells. The Russians, my friends, men and women students, returned to Russia to continue the fight and to avoid being interned in Germany. I found myself more and more alone in the midst of a rising and suffocating tide of war. But one element of hope stood out, a formidable figure, a Socialist fighter who would never be a betrayer. Of her Lenin said: "An eagle." She was Rosa Luxemburg.

THREE

Rosa Luxemburg

When I first met Rosa Luxemburg she was engaged in a great campaign against war, which she saw approaching with a much keener sense of reality than that displayed by any of the other leaders in German Social Democracy. In spite of all that has been written about her, one had to know her well to realize the extraordinary personality of this woman, a woman whose brain was as big as her heart. Rosa was tiny but in her face was reflected all the greatness of an extraordinary fighter. Her eyes overflowed with intelligence and with tenderness. She was capable of arousing a great love passion and of responding to it. The great love of her life was Léon Jogichès, the undisputed leader of the Polish Party. Rosa continued to recognize his authority even after she had broken off her affair with him. Her correspondence with Jogichès shows to what an extent Rosa found it difficult to write to her former lover and to appear publicly at his side after breaking with him. It was an example of devotion to the cause and of intellectual discipline.

For me Rosa was a leader not only in socialism but also in journalism, which even when I was a student I sensed was going to be my profession. She wrote for *Gleichheit* out of love for it, and for the *Leipziger Volkszeitung* to earn her living. She had a sharp, clear style.

When I met her she was already a legendary figure in the Second International which, for all its weak sides, was noted for its freedom of expression. Three elements contributed to her fame: her personality; her interest in political action, which exceeded even her brilliance as a Marxist theoretician and scholar; her lack of concern at being isolated. I have recently read a book about Rosa, which does not deserve to be named. It is characteristic of the confusion, never sufficiently stressed, of certain intellectuals who, at some moment in their lives, embrace the cause of the revolution and later, as soon as it fails to satisfy their ideolog-

31

Rosa Luxemburg, heroine of the revolution, 1916

ical expectations or their sensibilities, disown it as if they were ashamed of having allowed themselves to be carried away by enthusiasm. And then the heroes of their passing revolutionary passion, whether they are named Lenin, Rosa Luxemburg, or Mao Tse-tung, are brought down from their pedestals and no longer found interesting.

Rosa's beginnings were not easy, as she herself told me. Among the obstacles she faced, although she never referred to it, was the fact of being Jewish. She was born into a liberal Jewish family in Zamoste, near Lublin in what was Russian Poland, on March 5, 1871, the year of the Paris Commune, a coincidence of which she was always most proud. She was a very intelligent child. At the age of five she submitted an article to a children's magazine, and as she grew up her intellectual curiosity was boundless. She studied biology, literature, economics. Her love of music was passionate and lifelong. She whiled away many an hour in jail singing Mozart arias.

Perhaps of all her multiple talents, her literary gift, if she had used it to the full, might have made her a great writer. This talent is clear in her letters, the famous letters to Sonia Liebknecht, translated into many languages, the less well-known letters to the Kautskys, and the ones that have just been published, *La Correspondance de Rosa Luxemburg et de Léon Jogichès*. And she talked as brilliantly as she wrote. What most delighted me was to hear her explain the most complicated Marxist doctrines in simple language to the workers who thronged to her evening classes.

It was to be expected that such an original personality would not get along well with the ponderous leaders of German Social Democracy, who found her strange, irritating, unbearable. In the congresses, it amused her to talk with Philipp Scheidemann, so pompous and solemn. Rosa used to tell him, quoting Goethe, that beyond the mind that he was capable of understanding he could not be found. Before Rosa broke with Kautsky she asked him: "Are we going to change the Communist Manifesto so that where it now reads 'Proletarians of all the world united' it will say: 'Proletarians united in peace time and cutting one another's throats in war time'?" This was her response to the tendency of the representatives of the most intransigent Marxism to think like Germans first and only second like internationalists.

At the time when Rosa began to be active, the revolutionary movements in Poland and Russia were going through a period of decline. The influence of the great Russian authors was in one respect effective, but in another, confusing. The mysticism of Dostoevski, the asceticism of Tolstoi, led many people to a passive attitude of nonresistance to evil. Rosa told us that the fault lay not with this or that great Russian genius but with those who sought an excuse for not fighting. She had always found in each great writer not the negative elements that others did but the happy moments in his activities when, even though fleetingly, he embraced the cause of the people.

At the age of fifteen Rosa was already linked, as a student in a Warsaw school, to "Proletariat," a revolutionary group equivalent to the Russian "Narodnaya Volia," and like it an advocate of terrorist action. And so, even though she was the best student in her class, she was denied, "for patriotic reasons," the gold medal that was the only honor that might have made it possible for her, a Jew, to enter the university. Fortunately this resulted in her moving to Zurich to work at its university. There she began to channel her limitless intellectual curiosity and to concentrate on a specific project, which resulted in an excellent doctoral thesis on industrialization in Poland.

The great future theoretician was beginning to take shape. Rosa was to impress even her opponents with works as fundamental as *The Accumulation of Capital*, published just when I was studying in Leipzig, and *Anticriticism*, of which the historian Franz Mehring, one of the most cultured members of the German Socialist party, said: "Simply inspired, truly great; nothing like it had appeared since the death of Marx." She was a Marxist. The Belgian socialist Emile Van der Velde, with whom I talked about Rosa during the Spanish War, called her "the Amazon of fighting Marxism." She did not think that every word of Marx, corresponding to each situation, should be taken strictly. When she wrote her famous essay, "The General Strike," based on the lessons offered by the Russian Revolution of 1905, she spoke out in favor of a revision of Marxist ideas on strikes.

This very important date in the history of the Russian Revolution, 1905, is the outburst that followed the bloody Sunday of February 9 of that year. The czar had ordered the shooting down of a peaceful demonstration — led by a priest with holy ikons — of workers asking for an improvement in their working conditions. Rosa foresaw the popular response that would swell and pass into history with the name of the Revolution of 1905. She could not stay quietly in Berlin awaiting the development of events. Using a false name, she went to Warsaw, was arrested, and narrowly escaped death. But she had seen the revolution close up and she was able to draw the right conclusion: for the first time in the history of the labor movement the idea of a general strike acquired a magnificent reality and passed from theory into practice.

Before the war Rosa talked to me about one of her favorite themes: the massive general strike. In her concept the massive strike was at once a symptom and a typical product of the revolutionary period. The first problem is to integrate it with the broadest course of the revolution. Her analysis started from her experiences in the Russian Revolution of 1905 and came to the conclusion that the general strike can succeed only in a revolutionary climate. That climate is its essential condition, even though

34

the revolution may not come the next day. She emphasized that in Russia the general strike was not carried out as a means of jumping into the social revolution through a *coup de théâtre*, avoiding the political struggle of the working class; it was rather the means of creating for the proletariat the fighting conditions to wrest from the autocrats the rights and the political conditions that would allow the working class to intervene one day in the destiny of the country. The general strike thus appeared to be the most powerful weapon for winning political rights. Rosa had learned a great deal from that first Russian Revolution. And more than once I heard her say, remembering 1905, that "the only teacher of the proletariat is history."

Returning to Germany, Rosa devoted all her energy to the task of injecting into Social Democracy some part of the revolutionary spirit that inspired her. Clara Zetkin, older than Rosa but carried away by her example of energy and courage, said: "To prepare for the revolution that would open the way for Socialism was the life work of Rosa Luxemburg and the only objective that the ambition of that unique woman ever knew." I was present at the final stage of the lengthy effort to make of German Social Democracy a true Socialist party. And I admired Rosa's determination and her realism; she had no illusion about carrying a lot of militants along with her, but she did see the best of them regroup around her, especially when the threat of war was beginning to be clearly seen.

Rosa's thinking about imperialism also bore her personal stamp. Others had written about imperialism with great profundity: John Atkinson Hobson, my teacher at the London School of Economics, Rudolf Hilferding, who later became my friend, and, during the War of Lenin, author of the classic *Imperialism: The Supreme Development of Capitalism*. Rosa began to interest herself in imperialism in 1900; precisely because of the looting of China by the great powers. She was indignant at the indifference with which German Social Democracy witnessed Germany's participation in that ignoble undertaking.

I heard Rosa lament that for most of her German comrades to talk of imperialism had become a routine habit, empty verbiage, especially at party congresses. Rosa humanized her doctrine, as she humanized everything. For her, every case of misery, of exploitation of the people subjugated by a great power, every movement of collective anger, became one more human argument with which to justify revolution.

With *Social Reform or Revolution* she had opened fire against the revisionism of Eduard Bernstein, author of *Problems of Civilization*. With characteristic clearness, she denied that social reform and revolution were incompatible. The fight for reform was the "means," the social revolution was the "end." If all of Bernstein's revisionism, Rosa explained, reduced itself to asserting that the transition from capitalism to socialism was slower than one ordinarily thought, there was nothing to be alarmed about. But Bernstein did not limit himself to raising questions about the rhythm and the rapidity of the march toward socialism. He cast doubts on the whole future of the proletariat.

Rosa Luxemburg thus placed herself on the side of Karl Kautsky in his controversy with Bernstein. She had praised the work of Kautsky on agrarian reform and had contributed regularly to his journal *Die neue Zeit*. She did not indulge in a devastating criticism of all the leadership of Social Democracy. She respected Bebel, and at the death of old Liebknecht, with whom she had been at times in disagreement, she spoke in praise of the strength and energy of his spirit.

Rosa was not at all anxious to spill the blood of her rightist opponents. On the contrary, she wrote: "The most pitiless revolutionary energy and the most generous humanity, the two together, that union is what inspired true socialism. A world has to be overthrown, but any tear shed that could have been wiped away and that wasn't is an accusation."

But after having sided with Kautsky against Bernstein, Rosa broke with him, for logically she could not accept centrism, and Kautsky's tendency to compromise and to opportunism ended by exasperating her and led to an open break.

Gradually, to the admiration of some and the hostility of others, the personality of Rosa impressed itself on the German movement. At the Jena Congress, in September 1913, I saw her round up, in support of an amendment of hers, 142 votes out of 475, not at all a negligible result for a minority position. It was an amendment mainly about the general strike. It proposed that the congress should congratulate itself on the interest shown by great sectors of the party on this question, and it insisted that the general strike was not susceptible to being "decreed" at the request of the party or the unions. It ought to emerge from a vast mass movement in which the struggle against economic and political injustice would reach its greatest possible intensity.

In Leipzig, in a hall shaken by the encounter of opposing factions, I heard Rosa maintain that the theory of just wars as opposed to unjust wars was only a pretext to avoid facing honestly the necessity for fighting against all war. There was a burst of applause at the end. That speech brought on her, at the Frankfurt trial in February 1914, the accusation that she was attacking the security of the state.

In the Frankfurt trial, she was also accused of insulting the army. She wrote a very sarcastic article against the "heroic" German officers in a small Alsatian town who had defended with their swords their privilege of walking on the right side of the sidewalks. Rosa was absolved.

Rosa was amused as she told us how the Public Prosecutor blushed when she took advantage of the trial to give him and the judges a lesson in Marxism. A resourceful debater, she knew how to take advantage of the contradictions in the accusation to score several points in her favor. She enlightened them on the inevitability that one day, sooner or later, the current social order would be eliminated and replaced by a socialist social order superior to it because it was more humane and more adequate to the demands for technical development. "Speaking of the army," Rosa continued, "I evoked the memorable personality of Bebel, our leader who had fought in the Reichstag against the ill treatment given to the soldiers. I rejected the Public Prosecutor's statement that it is the army that wages war. No! It is the whole people that wages war. And that is why we Socialists struggle to persuade the people not to wage war. For war is a barbarous act. Our agitation against militarism is not so weak or so simplistic as the Public Prosecutor imagines." And Rosa threw in his face: "The Public Prosecutor has devoted all his attention to my humble person. He has even stooped to cast doubts on my personal honor by suggesting that I would flee if I were condemned. Just in a single year, 1913, your colleagues, my Lords Justice, have caused members of our Socialist press to be condemned to a total of seventy months in prison. Has any one of our 'sinners' fled? In our position, you indeed would have fled. We do not flee and we laugh at your jail sentences. I have finished. You may sentence me."

Rosa's voice echoed with increasing authority in international congresses. She was firmly opposed to Socialist participation in bourgeois governments. In France such action had brought Millerand to power, followed by other Socialists, Briand and Viviani. This cooperation was due in part to the sympathy evoked by the intervention of all these notables in the Dreyfus Affair. Rosa said: "You claim that those 'Comrades' have saved the honor of the French Socialist party in the Dreyfus Affair. Well, I maintain that it was Guesde and Vaillant [opposed to the participation of Socialists in the government] who saved not only the honor of socialism but socialism itself."

Just as within German Social Democracy, in the international Socialist movement too, Rosa Luxemburg roused conflicting passions but never indifference. She knew how to attract people when she wanted to. Emile Van der Velde, referring to Rosa's first appearance at an international congress, spoke of "her magnetism and an oratorical power so convincing that she quickly dominated the congress."

The last meeting of the Socialist International that Rosa attended was in Brussels, on July 29, 1914. On the agenda was the struggle against war. It was a pathetic occasion. The war was already practically upon us and the International had not done a thing to stop it. When Rosa appeared, the audience acclaimed her. There were shouts demanding that she be given the floor. But she refused to make a speech. It was too late for speeches. She had already decided to fight against war in a more effective way than through mere verbal revolt.

The assassination of Juarès moved Rosa to tears. She had disagreed with him on several occasions, but she admired in the great French leader a culture and a finesse that she missed in the German leaders. With Juarès dead there were only three effective anti-war leaders: Luxemburg, Liebknecht, and Lenin. Her differences with Lenin have been exaggerated. It is true that they had disagreements on important questions, one of them being the whole concept of what the party ought to become. But what brought them together was much greater than what separated them. In the International Congress of Stuttgart, in 1907, Rosa signed with Lenin an amendment that indicated the line that the parties should follow in case of war: to take advantage of the chaotic condition created by the war to fight against the capitalist regime and to transform the war into the start of the revolution.

Rosa was imprisoned in the Zwickau Jail for her comment on a speech by Kaiser Wilhelm: "The Kaiser has spoken of the good working conditions of the German workers. This makes no sense at all." This was clearly not a ferocious attack. But in those days the person of the kaiser was untouchable, and Rosa's comment caused her to be accused of *lèse majesté*.

From the Breslau Prison, a women's prison and the most horrible one in Germany, Rosa wrote little before she was freed to plunge again into the battle that would cost her her life. But to "Loulie," Louise Kautsky, she did write: "Courage! We women will rise again to enjoy life for what little time we have left." In another of her letters from jail, Rosa repeated one of her favorite maxims: "One must be a candle burning at both ends." It was this ardor that she communicated as no one else could. Her years in prison did not weaken Rosa; they hardened her.

Rosa was in the fortress of Wronke from October 1916 to July 1917. From there she was taken to the Breslau Jail in which she passed the time, besides continuing her political letters and writings, in translating the autobiography of Vladimir Korolénko, *The History of My Contemporaries*. Rosa's friends had urged her to write a book on Tolstoi. But she had answered that everyone can read Tolstoi's books, and that what the books couldn't say for themselves she was not going to say. In one of her letters she asks: "Can one explain the music of Mozart?" On the other hand, Korolénko, less well-known, would fill for the German reader a gap in his knowledge of modern Russian literature.

Between one and another jail sentence Rosa wrote the pamphlet that she signed "Junius" and that she would have preferred to sign with her own name. The police seized most of the copies. How to get a copy out of the country? I found a delightful way. I smuggled one out in the diplomatic pouch of the Spanish ambassador, thus delighting his many enemies, for Polo de Bernabé was an enthusiastic admirer of Imperial Germany, perhaps, the most pro-German of all the diplomats in Berlin.

When the Russian Revolution broke out in October 1917, Rosa hailed it like a great world event. But she was later saddened to learn that the Bolsheviks had suppressed freedom of the press. "Without a free press uncontrolled by censorship, without freedom to gather, the role that the great mass of the people can play is negligible." Those and other reservations did not prevent her from expressing her "admiration for Lenin and for Trotsky, for the example that they have given to the whole world." Of Rosa's *The Russian Revolution* I have before me the German edition (with a prologue by our friend Paul Levi) published in 1922, three years after her death. The book has often been misinterpreted and used against Lenin by the very Social Democrats whom she had slashed without sparing a single cutting anathema.

Rosa's scorn for the Social Democrats appears in its full range in the last article she wrote. It is a classic document in the denunciation of the treachery of the Social Democrats. Its title is "Order Reigns in Berlin." " 'Order,' " wrote Rosa, " 'reigns in Warsaw.' So said Minister Sebastiani in the French Chambre when, after having launched their assault on the Warsaw suburb, the Russian soldiers penetrated into the Polish capital and began their executioners' tasks. 'Order reigns in Berlin,' proclaims the bourgeois press with shouts of triumph, as do Ebert and Noske, as do the officers of the 'victorious troops' that the petty bourgeois riffraff greet in the streets with fluttering handkerchiefs. Hurrah! In the face of world history, the glory and the honor of the German armies are safe. Those who were ignominiously defeated in Flanders and in the Argonne have restored their renown with a brilliant victory over the three hundred Sparticists of *Vorwärts*. 'Order reigns in Warsaw,' 'Order reigns in Paris,' 'Order reigns in Berlin!' Every half century the guardians of 'order' publish their victorious bulletins in the centers of the world struggle. But the whole history of revolutions and of socialism tells us that, though sown with circumstantial defeats, the road can ultimately be seen clearly ahead, the triumph of the peoples in revolt."

The honor of the German Army, satirized by Rosa Luxemburg in that article, was to be avenged a few days later by one of the officers of the Free Corps, Lieutenant Vogel, who gave her the *coup de grâce* with his pistol, after she had been attacked by a soldier named Runge whom his own fellow soldiers described as "degenerate, sadistic, and mentally backward." And on that same day they killed Karl Liebknecht, Rosa's inseparable fighting companion. A double assassination that should keep in the heart of every free man an eternal hatred of German militarism.

Rosa's whole style, her spirit, her grace, her sense of humor, were bound to irritate the dull German Comrades who spoke of Rosa among themselves as "the Russian," "the Pole," both meaning "the Slav." Her conversation, like her writing, overflowed with wit and vivacity.

During the war, the longest conversation that I had with Rosa was in

1916, on my return from the United States, before she was arrested because of the May Day demonstration. She emerged from one prison to enter another, from the Wronke Jail, where she had a certain degree of freedom of movement, to the Breslau Jail, strict, a severe test of the temperament of a fighter like her.

I told Rosa that I was convinced that Wilson would end up by bringing the United States into the War. In the spring of 1916 she was the heart of the opposition group called Spartacus. She had taken the offensive against the Social Democratic leadership of the German Socialist party. She was all for socialism, but would give nothing, not a cent or a man for a leadership that had betrayed socialism.

From these conversations with Rosa I learned that the first duty of a true Socialist is never to despair, or to give up the fight, even though everything seems to turn against one's goals. And not to worry if one is almost alone. Solitude will gradually be transformed into a new and fertile grouping if one maintains his perseverance, clarity, and enthusiasm. Not everything can be a success. Advances and retreats alternate until one sees the final realization of the ideal that has served as a guide and support.

From the beginning of January 1919 it was clear that the Ebert-Scheidemann Government, with the renegade Gustav Noske, the Social Democratic police agent stirring up hatred against Rosa and Liebknecht, had decided to eliminate the two of them physically, since it was impossible to suppress them politically. At first Rosa took few precautions. She delighted in roaming the streets, mingling anonymously with the crowds, "breathing the atmosphere of the Revolution." But Paul Levi persuaded her to take refuge in the home of Mathilde Jacob, where she found warmth and a delicious duck cooked by Mathilde's mother.

In the official Party press, in *Vorwärts*, there were incessant calls for the assassination of the two great leaders, and Rosa especially. In a wretched poem by Arthur Zickler, a regular contributor to *Vorwärts*, one could read: "The proletarians fall dead, but among the dead Rosa is missing."

On January 15 Rosa and Liebknecht were arrested by a troop of soldiers. The owner of the flat where they had gone for refuge afterwards described to Louise Kautsky the impression that Rosa had given to her in the hours that preceded their arrest: "Her sunken cheeks, her weary eyes showed the sleepless nights that she had spent, but her force of spirit was undiminished."

From the moment that Rosa fell into the hands of the military her assassination by them was certain. The military did not forgive her for having foreseen their defeat and for having mocked them when, after being conquered and repatriated, "they boasted of their bravery in killing German workers." The soldiers led Liebknecht and Rosa to the Eden

Hotel, headquarters for the cavalry guard. There Captain Pabst questioned them briefly. The precise, scornful, cutting answers of Rosa served only to increase the fury of the officials present.

They forced Liebknecht out of the hotel first to set up a simulated attempt at escape and to shoot him in the back. In the hall of the hotel, soldiers attacked and mistreated Rosa. A witness declared later: "I saw this poor woman knocked to the ground and dragged about." They carried her half-dead to a carriage. Lieutenant Kurt Vogel had merely to

EASTFOTO

Funeral procession of Rosa Luxemburg,
Berlin, June 13, 1919

thrust a revolver through the window and fire at her head to put an end to her life.

During the Geneva Conference, three years after Rosa's assassination, I spoke frequently about her with Christian Rakovski, who had been very close to her in international negotiations. Rakovski, a Rumanian landowner at one time, was Soviet ambassador to Paris but was dismissed during the Stalinist purges. I became a good friend of his and I saw him later in the Ukraine when he was back in power and I was there as a member of the Nansen Mission to help organize the fight against the hunger that was devastating Russia in the early twenties. He was a very attractive person and our common admiration for Rosa brought us even closer. Rakovski used to tell me how during international congresses Rosa's presence, which often infuriated many people, invariably enlivened the discussions.

I learned a lot from Rosa. And above all I learned the importance of keeping my morale high, even in a situation that seemed most desperate. Never give up! Never! That was my rule during the Spanish War and it is today, inspired by the unforgettable memory of Rosa Luxemburg.

FOUR

From Wilson to Lenin

Coming from a Germany flushed with victory in the fall of 1914 to the United States was like a fiesta, beginning with the emotion that we all felt as the American passengers sang the national anthem, which I heard for the first time. Gathered on deck, the Statue of Liberty barely in sight, the chorus lifted its voice with a feeling of joy at having escaped from a Europe in the clutches of war and at being home again in America. Some of the women mixed tears with their laughter. One of them held out her hand to me on seeing me so alone, a young defenseless foreigner, as if to help me enter the promised land.

The New York of fifty-nine years ago would seem almost provincial to a visitor of today. For me it was literally a new world. I spent the first days walking up and down its avenues, including the dazzling Fifth Avenue, gaping at its skyscrapers, casting a glance at the Public Library at Forty-second Street, which would be a favorite spot for me later on. I read more literature there than at any time since I had left Spain.

My life focused in three areas: the library, Fourteenth Street, where in those days there were groups of young Socialists, and Times Square, where I went to confront the agents of German propaganda who were trying to convince Americans of the justice of the German cause and to persuade Americans that no one could defeat Germany. With the authority that I acquired from having been in Leipzig when the war began, I became a very popular debater.

My love for New York dates from that first visit and from having lived there during most of my years of exile. In 1973 this sounds almost like a *boutade*, as the French would say. Most of my European colleagues who come to New York to cover the sessions of the United Nations Assembly find the city unendurable. I do not. I have had one problem. I used to walk back at night from the United Nations to the Hotel Tudor, only a few minutes away, and I had to look from left to right lest some drug addict emerge from the shadows anxious to acquire a few dollars by knocking me down. But apart from that, I have found New York vigorous and always impressive.

The American press was sharp and independent. It had abundant news, even though the New York *Times* in the 1910s didn't have the tonnage of the present Sunday edition. The journalism schools taught the cult of truth. To publish everything was the slogan of several papers. The observance of this admirable doctrine varied in practice. But the American reporter was trained to observe without prejudice and to tell what he had seen, without slanting the news in favor of anything or anyone, an attitude perhaps too mechanical, but one that created confidence. Not excessively embroidered like the French press. Just facts.

The American press and my friendship with some young journalists quickened my enthusiasm for a profession that still excites me today like no other. I became a reporter in New York during the First World War. And I was very proud to be named a correspondent of *El Liberal* of Madrid at a salary that, if I had not added to it by giving Spanish lessons, would scarcely have been enough to allow me to frequent any restaurant except the Automat next to the Public Library, where for one dollar one could obtain enough protein to work and read all day.

To Europeans in the 1910s, the United States had the reputation of being "the country of limitless possibilities." My experiences showed that this was not an exaggeration. After only a few weeks of working in Washington as a proofreader and as an occasional translator at meetings of the Pan American Union, I saved enough money to pay for my return trip to Europe in 1916 in order, not without some risk, to re-enter Germany, where the opposition to the war was beginning to be sizable.

Washington, "the city of conversation," as Henry James called it, gave me the opportunity, thanks to the Pan American Conference, to meet Woodrow Wilson, something that I had dreamed of ever since I arrived in the United States. He came to greet all the personnel of the Secretariat of the Conference and, as a reward for my tireless efforts (I had worked day and night), I was invited to the dinner offered to the delegations by the President of the United States.

It would be hard for an American progressive of today to imagine the admiration that President Wilson aroused among progressives throughout the world. Their main ambition was to see German militarism squashed forever. And their hope was Wilson.

I returned to Germany in 1916 and there in the cafés in the Kurfürstendamm were gathered the opponents of the war: the novelist Leonhard Frank, the poet Johann Becher, the philosopher Otto Buek, the Polish Deputy Korfanty, and some actors and actresses, all talking in hushed tones to avoid being overheard by the police spies. Whenever I appeared, everyone, knowing that I had been in America, wanted to know about

Woodrow Wilson with President Raymond Poincaré of
France, Paris, 1919

Clemenceau, Wilson, Lloyd George,
Paris, 1919

Wilson. Especially Frank, the author of *Man Is Good,* a title that he claimed I had suggested to him. He was the hero of the group ever since the day when, abandoning all discretion, he had punched in the face a man at the next table who was praising the torpedoing of the *Lusitania.* The United States was not yet at war, but all the intellectuals of the German opposition were convinced that Wilson would finally break with Germany and that it would be the United States that would finally determine the outcome of the conflict.

Upon progressive opinion throughout the world Wilson exerted an influence unequaled by that of any other American President, except perhaps Franklin Roosevelt during the Second World War. But Wilson's influence was even greater. When he landed in Europe in 1918, after the war was over, there was delirium. I was almost crushed to death on the Champs-Elysées by a crowd fighting for a glimpse of the American President. On the Arc de Triomphe one could read in letters of gold: "Glory to Wilson the Just!" That day Wilson eclipsed even Clemenceau, "the father of victory." A Frenchman beside me, his face purple from so much cheering for Wilson, said: "Clemenceau, yes, he won the war, but it is Wilson who is going to win the peace, and that is what matters now." A woman, defying the police, tossed a bouquet of violets into Wilson's carriage. That evening there were toasts to him in restaurants throughout the city.

While Wilson was winning the hearts of the French and of all the other Europeans, in his own country the isolationist intrigues were beginning that would finally bring about his defeat and his death. He went to the Versailles Conference confident of popular support but wary of the chiefs of state who were trying to win advantages for their countries. More than once Wilson had told his most intimate friend and counselor, Colonel House, that he was much more afraid of the struggles that would follow the war than he was of the war itself.

Wilson had attracted to himself the hopes of all the peoples that were awaiting the hour of peace to see realized their aspirations for national independence: Czechs, Poles, Albanians, everyone. On his study desk messages piled up from the leaders in the battle for freedom, telling him that they had faith only in him. It was a crushing responsibility and it was reflected in his face as the Versailles Conference developed amid the power struggles. He realized that, beginning with his own country, currents and countercurrents, impatience and confusion, made it almost impossible to construct a public opinion that knew what it really wanted, an opinion on which he could rely.

I had been a witness, in the United States, to that zigzag of reactions that had accompanied Wilson up to the moment when the country entered the war: contradictory feelings; a dangerous susceptibility. The same people who one day admired the audacity of the German Navy

48

were appalled two weeks later on seeing the President so calm and serene at the news of new outrages on the high seas. I remember well the explosion of anti-German feeling that followed the torpedoing of the *Lusitania*. Before cabling *El Liberal* I made a kind of public opinion poll on the street. The people were calling for a break with Germany. But Wilson replied: "A people can be conscious enough of its rights not to have to use force to convince other peoples." I heard many an American ask what he meant by that.

A businessman to whom I was giving Spanish lessons was irritated by all that philosophical talk. "What can you expect," he kept saying, "from a professor and the son of a preacher? Nothing will shake that man's balance!" But Wilson challenged his American critics to show in which of his books or speeches he had ever advocated pure and unresisting pacifism. As soon as he conceived the League of Nations he insisted on the need for sanctions and on the use of force in the service of the law. What he hated was the hysteria of rashness.

Wilson won almost unanimous support when he broke with Germany. A true explosion of patriotism ran through the United States, sprinkled with a few picturesque notes. The governor of Utah telegraphed to the President: "Ten thousand Navajo Indians are ready to leave for the Front and to fight Germany to the death." Wilson even got the support of those who had been ultra-pacifists only a few weeks before. Ex-President Taft, Chairman of the League to Enforce Peace, suddenly began making prowar speeches, asking if we were going to stand with folded arms in the face of the audacity of the German submarines. He called for the introduction of compulsory military service when only a month before he had shouted: "Down with armaments!"

The date of April 2, 1917, will remain forever in history. The photographs of the time show a hall bulging with people, all the beauties of Washington in evening dress in the galleries, the press gallery crammed with standing journalists who had come from all parts of the country, including Alaska, to report on this scene of limitless grandeur. President Wilson held in his hand the scraps of paper with the notes for his momentous speech: "What will be the choice of the American people?" The voice was quiet. It was not the volume but the content that was important. "This is one thing that we shall never do, that we are incapable of doing. We will not choose the path of submission. I urge the Congress to declare that the recent acts of Imperial Germany constitute nothing less than an act of war."

The word "war" was finally spoken but with the responsibility for the war thrown upon the kaiser. Strict logic did not abandon Wilson even in the most dramatic moment of his life. And on June 26 the first American contingent set foot on French soil.

In his attitudes toward peace and war Wilson went back to those of

49

Washington, the Founder, of whom Wilson had written a biography. His foriegn policy became a crusade for the ideals that were present in the origins of the United States. For Wilson, democracy was not a mere philosophical concept. It was the very essence of America, the lifeblood of the country. He drew inspiration from the memory of Mount Vernon, one of his favorite places — not only because his family came from Virginia, but because it was the cradle of the thinking of George Washington.

Starting from Washington and Jefferson, President Wilson sought to achieve freedom on a global scale. The pursuit of that ideal absolved him, in his eyes, from the apparent contradiction of a pacifist obliged to make war, but with the hope that, once the war was over, the people would accept the concept of a war without victory.

At first, on deciding to go to war, Wilson had the satisfaction of knowing that the whole nation understood him and supported him. No important American, much less the average citizen, would accuse him of hypocrisy when he shifted from peace to demanding from Congress troops, ships, and cannon. The difficulties came later. Wilson's allies had not been impressed by his address at Mount Vernon on July 18, the anniversary of the American Constitution, in which he pictured the United States as the guardian of ancient idealism. But when he tried to enforce his famous Fourteen Points and took a firm position against secret pacts, the other great powers objected that their alliances and commitments preceded America's entrance into the war.

Wilson complained that, even after America's entrance into the war, on the very eve of the Peace Conference and even during the conference, the odious practice of secret pacts continued. "Each minister," Wilson confided to his American staff, "dreams only of snatching from someone else a piece of territory which he can offer to his voters." And he lamented also that his most stubborn opponent among the allies, Clemenceau, hating as he did the Germans, should have borrowed the philosophy of the Prussian Karl von Clausewitz that peace is more than the corollary of war.

Wilson's cure for what he called international anarchy unchained by the war was international cooperation. As he outlined his plan for a League of Nations, he again had in mind the Founder, Washington, in the protection of human rights. This had been the subject of his inaugural address in 1911 as governor of New Jersey. His League of Nations was the universalization of the American tradition, a kind of continuation of the Union of American States.

Among his associates in the postwar period there was really only one who understood him. In Britain the dominant personality was Lloyd George. And though Wilson admired Lloyd George's brilliance, he feared his "elasticity." "In principle," Wilson commented, "nothing seemed easier than to have Lloyd George on my side. But then came the details. And there he always escaped me. And always laughing with his white teeth."

With an America more united behind him and counting, as he could, on the nationwide support of a majority of the workers, whom this former Princeton professor now called his "natural allies," the task of Wilson at Versailles might have been less thorny. But he felt himself abandoned by his compatriots. Even Lansing, his secretary of state, had turned against him. American opinion, manipulated by nationalist senators, accused him of endangering the Monroe Doctrine. And the new elections strengthened the position of Wilson's enemies in Congress.

Wilson did not let himself be intimidated at first by developments in his country. In September 1919 he said in Kansas City: "I have come out to fight a cause. That cause is greater than the Senate. It is as great as the cause of mankind, and I intend, in office or out, to fight that battle as long as I live."

Wilson's view of the future could not have been more correct at the time. "I can predict with absolute certainty that within another generation there will be another war if the nations of the world do not concert the method by which to prevent it." Wilson feared that once German militarism was defeated another kind of militarism would rise to imperil peace with an even more devastating war. Speaking in Denver on September 25, 1919, he said: "Stop for a moment to think about the next war, if there should be one . . . There were destructive gases, there were methods of explosive destruction unheard of even during this war, which were ready for use when the war ended, great projectiles that guided themselves and, shot into the heavens, went for a hundred miles and more and then burst tons of explosives upon helpless cities, something to which the guns with which the Germans bombarded Paris from a distance were not comparable . . . Ask any soldier if he wants to go through a hell like that again. The soldiers know what the next war would be like. They know what the inventions were that were just about to be used for the absolute destruction of Mankind."

Wilson was steeped in culture as few other American Presidents. In his notable *Leaders of Men* he stressed that "the strength of the true leader is not force but persuasion, not matter but spirit." He had a special competence to judge German *Kultur*. He said: "Germany has outlived herself among the nations because she has disregarded the sacred obligations of law and has made lynchers of her armies. And against this we can have only one answer: Force, force to the utmost, force without stint or limit, the righteous and triumphant force which shall make right the law of the world and cast every selfish dominion down in the dust." It is understandable that the Germans of the First World War hated Wilson. But their hatred was nothing compared with the loathing that the Nazis later felt for him.

In the light of all that has since happened, Wilson was completely right. The arguments of his detractors at that time, Lodge, Borah, remain as lamentable evidence of how easy it is, in certain circumstances, to lead the noble American people into a state of confusion with a few commonplaces. Wilson's failure was as awesome as his grandeur. "It was probably the most colossal and heroic failure of modern times," said Saul K. Padover, a Wilson expert who has stressed the fact that the ideas of Wilson, after more than a half century, have acquired an unquestionable contemporary importance.

The image that I carried to Germany from my meeting with Wilson in Washington was that of a man at the height of his intellectual and moral strength. He appeared at that time to be the prototype of the leader as the thinking man in action. Wilson had insisted, in his essays, on the perennial misunderstanding between the men who write and the men who act. He concluded that true leadership merges the two functions into one.

Before returning to Germany I stopped in Copenhagen to meet another of the strong personalities of the 1910s, the Danish literary critic Georg Brandes. I was eager to talk with the author of *Main Currents in Nineteenth-Century Literature,* the publication of which had caused a furor in literary circles and had prevented Brandes' appointment as a university professor. The first person to talk to me about Brandes was Miguel de Unamuno, when I was a student at the University of Salamanca. Both men shared an admiration for Sören Kierkegaard, precursor of Existentialism, which has had so much influence on Jean-Paul Sartre and others of our best contemporary writers. Between Brandes and Unamuno there had been an abundant correspondence. Brandes told me that, in his opinion, Unamuno was not only a very original and profound thinker but, from a strictly literary point of view, the greatest Spanish writer of his time, an opinion with which I was in thorough agreement.

Brandes himself was a writer who defied age and who, when he was well along in years, published a biography of Voltaire that was filled with youth and grace. I argued with him about the war and he accused me of not appreciating German culture enough. I said that all that great culture had not prevented the German intelligentsia, with few exceptions, from lining up on the side of the kaiser and from justifying all the crimes of German militarism. And as a consequence, that great culture, even if it should produce three more Goethes, was quite useless as far as I was concerned. The curious thing was that Georg Brandes was an enthusiast of French culture and was much influenced by Ernest Renan. But in those days his only interest was to crush Clemenceau, with whom he was carrying on a lively polemic on the causes of the war.

I had not met Clemenceau at that time. But even before our meeting I knew enough about the unbreakable French fighter to state my own arguments in opposition to those of the admirable Danish critic, who could have been my grandfather. For most people Clemenceau was unbearable. He had an immense pride and a limitless scorn for all French politicians, with a single exception, Jean Jaurès, already murdered. Clemenceau admired his loftiness of spirit and intellectual stature, even though he had at times differed sharply with him. Jaurès had been a supreme patriot who knew the Germans extremely well. Five years before the start of the war, in 1909 in Kiel, the kaiser confided to a friend that he considered Clemenceau to be a fearful enemy. For once the kaiser had clear vision.

Clemenceau was a supreme patriot. This atheist's God was his country. Certainly his polemical temper, his prodigious intellectual vitality that never abandoned him even when he was nearly ninety, turned his violent disputes into a savage game of wits.

When I met him in 1918, Clemenceau gave me the impression of the force of nature, square, massive, always ready to return two blows for one, wanting to live and die on his feet. He was a French patriot in the vein of Jeanne d'Arc and, a generation later, of that of General de Gaulle. I met him on a day when his patriotism was doubled by his indignation at seeing the cursed Germans commit the audacity of bombing his Paris.

It was in fact the first time that Big Bertha, the German long-range cannon, hurled its projectiles at the French capital. President Raymond Poincaré, whom Clemenceau had attacked ceaselessly since the beginning of the war, named him Premier. He indicated that his only governmental goal was victory. That day of the bombardment of Paris he said to us: "With or without Bertha we shall crush them." Whenever anyone spoke to him of the opposition to the war inside Germany, Clemenceau would snort: "Good Germans! There is no such thing."

Clemenceau was a man of war. He had made war all his life, in Parliament, in his paper, on the street. He was fascinated by the thought of the ragged soldiers of the Great French Revolution fighting victoriously against better armed and better trained soldiers. And that is why he was always a Jacobin. He was an orator of the first rank, but above all he was a man of action. He was an individualist, a nonconformist, a contester who fought against his adversaries and his followers, especially those who did not share his aggressiveness. He felt great scorn for people who preferred words to action.

Clemenceau was not a Party man, although he agreed to serve the party. But he never let himself be influenced by its calls to discipline. He heeded no external discipline, only the one that his conscience or his thinking dictated. Of bourgeois origin, a doctor and a doctor's son, he detested the bourgeoisie and all its artificial manners, its traditions, its Academies, its ceremonies. His legendary appearance, with sweeping

53

moustaches, crushed hat, cane, and gray gloves, made him unmistakable. But even more unmistakable was his determination to keep going until the day of his death. He was a man of great courage. At the start of the war, with the Germans close to Paris, when the suggestion was made to transfer the capital to Bordeaux, Clemenceau refused. When he was urged to abandon the capital, he replied: "If we leave Paris, we shall leave it for the Front. We are too far away from it."

Clemenceau was a man of war but not a militarist. He was a civilian who did not like the military. He showed this dislike at the time of the Dreyfus Affair. He could not tolerate the belief of the General Staff that it was entitled to the last word. He stood by Dreyfus in spite of "reasons of state," personified by the General Staff. "Reasons of state" were among the main enemies of Clemenceau. He believed that the military, like any other functionaries, should be at the service of the nation, not lording it over the nation. He refused to give any privileges to the military, even in the name of the national defense. If he had been an American, the Pentagon would hardly have found him a cooperative government official.

Educated in the strict school of Hobbes and Darwin, a follower of Pascal's thinking, he was very much a man of the eighteenth century, dominated by the French Revolution and Voltaire, passionately devoted to the idea of liberty, about which he wrote: "Liberty is the right to discipline oneself so that one may avoid being disciplined by others."

One of the reasons for his popularity was his ferocity. He would not send others into danger without leading them there. He was brave in action and in speech. He did not hesitate to say to diplomats: "You have lied!" At the end of the first period of danger and difficulty for France, he was planning to carry her to final victory with a determination that never faltered. He had begun his political career in a humiliated France. He was determined to end his career in a France that would be the most powerful nation in Europe.

That incisive attitude is what led him to his bitter controversy with Georg Brandes, who could not endure the voluntary ignorance of some German scientists and writers opposed to the war and hating the kaiser. For Clemenceau, a lifelong journalist and a master of polemics who had changed the name of his newspaper from *L'Homme libre* to *L'Homme enchaîné*, to insult the great Danish critic for his reverence for the great old German culture was a diversion.

An inseparable part of his attire, his gray gloves hid the pitiless claw accustomed to bring down ministries and that had earned him the name of Tiger. But if anyone dared to use the same freedom to attack his government, the "father of victory" stopped being paternal.

I talked a lot with Georg Brandes about literature. In my two years in New York I had considerably enlarged my knowledge of the novel and the theater. I read the latest plays and attended performances of the experimental theater of the Washington Square Players in the Village. I was planning to write a play about Saint-Just, a subject that later attracted André Malraux and that seemed to me more worthy of being staged than Danton, about whom there were already two classic plays.

The novel tempted me even more. But I wrote only one, *The Red Path*, whose protagonist was Rosa Luxemburg, and which was translated into Russian. It had, if I may say so, a great success in Spanish America and I have heard many Spanish Americans say that the novel had won them over to the cause of revolution.

I took leave of Georg Brandes to go to join the antiwar forces in Germany, an activity not without a certain danger, especially for a foreigner.

To return to a Germany at war after two years of absence was an adventure, since I had to flee from there in 1914 as a result of my antimilitary activities at the university. And I had written, over my signature, many anti-German articles in the Spanish press. But the visit was an extremely valuable experience. It began by proving that the Prussian police state, despite its reputation for being perfect, would eventually collapse. It was perhaps a sign of the deterioration of the general situation. The fact is that I presented my passport at the border without the slightest nervousness and slept that night at the Berlin Hotel am Zoo without being visited by the police. The next day, as a precaution, I moved to the house of a friend who had diplomatic privileges.

I managed to stay five months in Berlin. Thanks to the generosity of writers and other friends more or less involved in the antiwar movement that was rapidly developing, I solved my main difficulty, that of obtaining food stamps without having to make frequent appearances to obtain them at the police station.

Compared with the Germany certain of a quick victory that I had left two years before, this Germany in 1916 presented a quite different picture. There was no quick end in sight. In spite of their brilliant successes against Serbia in 1915 and against Rumania in 1916, the situation of the imperial armies was becoming more awkward with each passing month. Hindenburg and Ludendorff had to operate on immensely extended fronts and, as was soon evident, Verdun and the Somme were exhausting the German reserves. In spite of the secrecy that surrounded all military affairs, some leaks reached the opposition circles among which I moved.

I got a lot of practice in clandestine work and at times I acted as an intermediary between groups. They were German antiwar groups. They gathered in Berlin cafés frequented by artists. One of them was led by the painter Herstein, who years later, when I got married, made a portrait of Luisa, my wife. It was a picture that, with many others, stayed behind in Madrid when Franco's troops arrived. I did not want to take anything out of Madrid or out of Spain in order not to demoralize people by giving the impression that I judged our cause a lost one.

Another group gathered around a Miss Yesierska, a Pole who was very close to Rosa Luxemburg. In those groups there were young actresses who belonged to the opposition. I pretended to be courting them in order to cover up my political activities. What we would do was to hold a meeting in which, under pretext of talking about theater and literature, we would plan the distribution of leaflets to be relayed from hand to hand announcing a demonstration like the May Day one, or spreading the war news analyses from the Swiss or other neutral presses.

The opposition to the war was more active in literary circles than in labor circles. It was true that the workers were more and more attentive to the words of Rosa Luxemburg and Liebknecht and some of the "Independents," Socialists who had broken with the majority. But a lot of weight was still given to the attitude of resignation and obedience to authority recommended by the official Social Democratic leaders.

In literary circles the opposition grew with each passing month. Tilla Durieux was a famous actress who died at an advanced age only three years ago. Her husband Cassierer was an art dealer and so they could hold certain private meetings. At one of them Heinrich Mann, less famous as a novelist than his brother Thomas but a highly respected essayist, read us his essay on Zola, which was a brilliant denunciation of war.

All this could not in the long run go unnoticed by the police. One night as I was about to enter a café in the Kurfürstendamm, one of the young actresses came out to meet me. Taking me by the arm she warned me that the police were inside checking everyone's identification papers. Of course I did not go in. It was clear that if I didn't leave very soon I would be arrested.

I let a couple of days go by and decided to run the risk of going to police headquarters to ask for an exit visa for Switzerland, en route to Spain. They told me; Third floor, inspection. I thought this was the end. I hesitated on the stairway. There was the possibility of going back down and definitely entering a clandestine life, continuing to help the antiwar movement. But the war might last two years more and that was too much Berlin for me.

I went into the inspection room and watched calmly as a policeman checked the archives. Finally he stamped "approved" on the paper that they had given me downstairs. The visa was assured. Evidently the Leipzig police had not informed the Berlin police about the circumstances that had forced me to leave hastily for the United States in 1914. I took the first train for Switzerland and the next morning I arrived in Berne.

In Berne I immediately made contact with the exiled German opposition. A couple of months later, I met again Elsa Klossovska, wife of the painter Eric Klossovski and mother of two men who are famous today. I held them on my knees when they were babies; Balthus, the painter, whose pictures are worth a fortune, and Pierre, whom many think one of the best contemporary French writers and also an excellent painter. They were a family of painters. Elsa, who was called Muckie, was very attractive and she dreamed of being a second Ninon de Lenclos, who would be beautiful until she was at least eighty. She painted my portrait, which was left behind with the other pictures in Madrid.

In 1916 and 1917 Switzerland was a lively and exciting place, which was unusual for a country that was efficient from the point of view of organization and work but calm and sheltered from commotion. In Berne, the center for embassies and special services, I could follow the wild tales of the secret maneuvers of the Germans and the Allies. The city had the atmosphere of a suspense novel, with each important newcomer rousing the curiosity of the opposite side. One had to be on guard lest someone search the pockets of one's coat hanging on a hook in the café, in search of compromising documents. And of course there were the baggage rooms in the hotels.

After the execution of Mata Hari, the exotic dancer convicted by the French of being used by the German secret service, any attractive woman who appeared in a luxury hotel, even though she came only to escape from the restrictions of countries at war, set the secret service in motion. Fantasy was mixed with reality, but it was clear that Switzerland, which profited greatly from its neutrality, became with the advent of war a center of influence for both sides.

The Germans spent a lot of money to influence Swiss public opinion. But from the very beginning the task was not easy. The German treatment of Belgium, a small country, was deeply resented by Switzerland, also a small country. And it was precisely in German Switzerland that the feeling against Imperial Germany was strongest, even stronger than in French Switzerland.

The subterranean war of agents and spies was accompanied by the public war of the communiqués of the Swiss newspapers, pasted on the walls of the arcades in Berne as soon as any important political or military event took place. This was a war of bulletins stronger than the fear of a possible German invasion. The Swiss government increased its counsels of prudence to the newspaper editors, but the war had created an emotional climate hard to control. With the entry of the United States, Berne felt an increase of sympathy for the Allies and an increase in its conviction that the Germans no longer had the slightest chance of victory. The day after the announcement, someone in a German propaganda center blurted: "Now we are indeed lost." And the papers that were supporting the Allied cause became even more polemical in spite of all the official warnings.

At this time Zurich interested me because of the presence of Lenin, whose later activity would change the course of history. It was also the center of the most important literature of the German opposition; German writers and intellectuals flocked to Zurich month after month, like Leonhard Frank, Ludwig Rubiner, an imaginative essayist, the poet Ferdinand Hardekopf and, from other parts of Switzerland, René Schikele, the fine Alsatian writer, author of *Mein Freundin Lo*, the philosopher Otto Buek, and a large number of professors and pacifists who would have been in German jails if they had not chosen exile.

On the edge of that "respectable" intelligentsia were the young rebels with whom I coexisted — poets, painters, sculptors. They were the strength of the Dada movement. Through Hans Richter, the painter, I had made the acquaintance of one of the most amusing and eccentric backers of the group, Emmy Hennings, a Danish poet and creator of subversive couplets. Through her I managed to follow the development of one of the most discussed and least understood of literary movements. Dadaism was born in 1916; it wakened the interest of writers and artists who would later earn general recognition in the world of the arts: Louis Aragon, Hans Arp, Paul Eluard, Max Ernst, Francis Picabia, Erik Satie, and Tristan Tzara, its principal promoter, whom I used to see in Paris many years later, especially when he would come back from a visit to Picasso bringing greetings from him.

The greatest extravagance of Dada was its insistence that it had nothing to do with politics. But the mere fact that it was totally opposed to the war made it a political movement and every time that Emmy Hennings mounted a platform to sing an antiwar song the hall bulging with young people would burst into a thunder of applause. Tristan Tzara himself later denied the supposed unpolitical character of Dada. Speaking on "Post-War Surrealism," Tzara said: "In 1917, when Franz Platten returned to Zurich, bringing from Moscow details about the revolution, we Dadaists in Zurich — Hugo Ball, Serner, and I — welcomed the Russian Revolution because it was the only possible way to put an end to the war."

Officially (and how ill its official word became it), Dada proclaimed itself antiartistic, antiliterary, and antipoetic. It was equally opposed to futurism, expressionism, and cubism, but it acknowledged the individual worth of an Apollinaire or a Picasso. At the same time it declared that it would rather disappear than contribute to swell the Olympus of the Arts with new divinities. The ballet "Parade," whose authors were Satie, Cocteau, and Picasso, was appreciated by the Dadaists for its appeal to liberty and for having scandalized the bourgeoisie. Dada began as a literary review, *Cabaret Voltaire*, whose first issue had on its cover a very flashy drawing by Hans Arp. Its initial list of contributors included Hugo Ball, Blaise Cendrars, Emmy Hennings, Marcel Janco, Kandinsky, Picasso, and Tristan Tzara. Besides the review there was the Dada Gallery, where I saw an exhibition of the paintings of Paul Klee. The articles in the review were written in many languages and testified to the universal character of the movement. The gallery had exhibits by painters like Chirico, up to then unknown to the public.

On the stage at the Cabaret Voltaire everything was innovation. The Punch and Judy show was more audacious than any puppet show of today. The orchestra was replaced by the concerted noise of keys and tins and heel-tapping by the audience, and at times the noise sounded like a real stamping of protest. There was ballet in which well-known writers and painters parodied the formalism of the classic dance. There was imagination and spontaneity, rebellion against all formality, an insolent and provocative style. The audience was at times disconcerted, at times receptive, through snobbery, and at times infuriated to the point of aggression. After one of the recitals of Emmy Hennings, at which I accompanied her, we were pummeled by a group of Germanophiles. In spite of my efforts to protect her, Emmy emerged from the encounter with a black eye.

The French expression "contestation" (debate), used today to refer to the student movements in the Western countries against society's asphyxiation, was well applied to Dada. For its adherents the accepted literary criticism was nothing but empty petulance. The professional critic was presented as a failure, incapable of producing a work of his own, writing with a spiteful pen, soaked in frustration, yearning to destroy the work of true creators. Dada rejected schools and their pontiffs, in literature as well as in art. An exception was made of Romain Rolland, whom Dada respected less for his writings than for his denunciation of the war.

The Dadaist assault spared a few painters and sculptors, mentioned above.

Among the spared musicians was Edgard Varèse, whom I saw frequently many years later during the Second World War, when we were neighbors on Sullivan Street in Greenwich Village in Manhattan. Dada announced with great fanfare that Charlie Chaplin supported the movement. Its supporters multiplied everywhere. It was indirectly represented in the Salon of the Independents in New York in 1917, the first of its kind in the United States and marked on its first day by all kinds of incidents. Before an interested and brilliant audience that included some very distinguished ladies, an art critic who was to deliver a lecture on painting appeared onstage drunk as a lord and proceeded to take off his trousers to the dismay of most of his audience and to the hoots of laughter

Lenin in exile, 1914

of a few unfazable ladies. The police carried him offstage and he was saved from jail only because of the bond put up by a rich collector friend.

Dada was not afraid of scandal; it welcomed it. Even thirty years later in April 1947, Tristan Tzara, in a packed hall in the Sorbonne, defied with an ironic smile the fury of André Breton, the surrealist, who, surrounded by supporters and armed with a monocle, pointed an accusing finger at him. It was the clash between Dadaism and surrealism. Love, revolution, poetry, and dreams, the four essential postulates of surrealism, were defied by this truly militant debater. That day Breton was tumultuously supported by his admirers. To his unquestioned literary prestige he added the fame of his scorn for official honors and awards. He had rejected several prizes and in 1950 he rejected the coveted Prize of the City of Paris. But Tzara also had plenty of defenders, and it was finally Breton who left the hall in defeat.

In 1919, two years after I was in Zurich, I again met my Dada friends in a Berlin shaken by the struggle between the forces of the old reactionary regime and those of the left, shaken by the assassination of Rosa Luxemburg and Karl Liebknecht. The greatest Dadaist demonstration, and practically the last one of such size that I attended, took place in Berlin in June of 1920. Its theme was "International Dada Fair." The movement enlisted the services of Georg Grosz, a caricaturist with claws, implacable in his portrayal of the rich and rising bourgeoisie. Grosz was promoted to the rank of Marshal Dada.

There were several subsequent attempts to revive Dada. One was successful, thanks especially to Max Ernst, who illustrated *Dada au grand air*. There was a publication in German, *Der Sangerkrieg Intirol*, because it appeared in the Tyrol. But the atmosphere had become too tense and the political struggle too bitter to make shocking the bourgeois an adequate goal. The Germany of 1921 did not resemble at all the Germany of 1918. The triumph of a true revolution in Germany had been a possibility when the war ended. But that opportunity had been wasted. The bourgeoisie so savagely satirized by Dada had been clever enough to take advantage of the weaknesses of the working class, or at least the weaknesses of its leaders.

In Zurich the most important person was Lenin. But he was not important to the waiter in the café where he went once a week and which was frequented by a group of young students, writers, and painters. I was the only one in the group who knew who Lenin was. One day the waiter confided to us: "You see that fellow, the one with the little beard, sitting alone in the corner? Well, he's crazy. He claims that one day soon he'll return to Russia to start a revolution and that he'll win it!" This was a few months before Lenin's departure from Switzerland for Petersburg in the famous "sealed" train placed at his disposal by the Germans and which caused so much talk.

From the time of my arrival in Switzerland I followed Lenin, who was waging an implacable campaign against the "social patriots," the Socialists who in several countries had voted military credits or entered war governments, and against Kautsky, the pope of German Marxism, because he had once had a great reputation, but now seemed to Lenin one of the most dangerous representatives of Socialist confusion and abandonment.

Lenin spoke several foreign languages, and there was no problem of communication, especially for a young Socialist like me who came from Germany and who had been closely tied to the German antiwar movement.

Lenin had no tolerance or forgiveness for the renegade Socialists. He did not believe in the purge of the Second International. He considered it rotten; it would have to be replaced by a new International. This was the beginning of the Third International that was going to take shape soon after the triumph of the Russian Revolution in October.

He saw as clearly as anyone that in the hand of the Kerenskis of the first revolutionary phase the Russian Revolution was headed for certain failure. The news, received in Zurich, that on February 27, 1917, the red banner was hoisted over the Winter Palace in Petrograd filled Lenin with joy but also with worry. Lenin's great lesson for all the revolutionaries of yesterday, today, and tomorrow is that the most important thing is "to find the right political line." The number of those who adopt it at the beginning is secondary. Without a "right political line" there is no successful revolution. That was the source of his "April Theses," which brought him victory — the creation of the first proletarian state in history.

In his days in Switzerland, from the announcement of the February Revolution up to his departure from Switzerland, Lenin gove the final touches to the strategy that he proposed to follow. The task that awaited him was gigantic. It was nothing less than to win over peasants who wanted only "land and freedom," that is, a bourgeois revolution, to a revolution firmly oriented toward socialism.

When we recall what we heard about Lenin in Zurich and the course of his activity from the time that he set foot in Petrograd until the Bolsheviks took control, we realize to what an extent everything had been correctly planned and foreseen. Once again the cult of the personality. It is a fact that without Lenin there would not have been an October Revolution; certainly not a victorious revolution.

Of the three countries in which Lenin had lived in exile, England, France, and Switzerland, he preferred Switzerland, among other reasons because its libraries were essential to him. He and Krupskaya, his wife, lived like the poorest of the exiled Russians in Zurich. Their meals were unbelievably frugal. There was almost no money to buy books, and this made the public library so essential. In Switzerland readers were trusted. If a reader was going to be away from the city, the library would send him the books that he wanted, mailed in a returnable carton. Lenin could not have asked for more.

At that time Lenin was working on a book about the State. He was concerned about means for assuring that the government could function in a transitory period, between the outbreak of the revolution and its success. He was absorbed to such a degree by that problem that during his escape to Finland, before the Bolsheviks came into power, he worked feverishly to finish a manuscript originally entitled "Marxism and the State" and later published as *The State and the Revolution*. It became one of the classic texts of Leninism.

The outbreak of the revolution in Russia in February 1917 posed for Lenin an urgent and anguishing problem: how to get back as soon as possible to his country. He couldn't sleep. He invented a thousand ruses. One was to get hold of a Swedish passport that would be forged by a comrade from Stockholm, a passport of someone who looked like him. Since he didn't know any Swedish, he would pretend to be a deaf-mute. Meanwhile he was sending instructions to his friends in Russia. A month after the fall of the czar, they continued to be a very small minority compared with the supporters of the new government of Kerenski. "Our tactic," he wired them in March, "is complete lack of confidence in the new government. Let us above all be suspicious of Kerenski. The only true guarantees are the arming of the proletariat and immediate elections in Petrograd."

In a meeting that took place in Zurich soon after the news of the February Revolution was received, Lenin had already declared: "If the Russian Revolution does not manage to become a victorious Paris Commune, it will be stifled by reaction and the War." The problem of his return to Russia was finally solved. But not on the terms quoted by many commentators of that time and then later repeated by supposed historians of the Russian Revolution. Despite Lenin's impatience to board the train that was to carry him to Russia, he went only on certain conditions. The group of exiles that he led were to have the exclusive use of their railroad car, in order to avoid intruders or spies, and that stipulation gave rise to the legend of the "sealed car," in the best Prussian style. Lenin also insisted that the car have extraterritoriality. Its occupants would be exempt from the necessity of showing passports or passing through customs. The negotiator for these conditions, the Swiss Socialist Franz Platten, traveled with them as a guarantee that everything agreed on would be respected.

Apart from the preparations for the journey there were the preparations for what to do upon arrival. Those weeks in Zurich were decisive. Each hour was important. First, Lenin had to organize his own Russian comrades, with whom he had to establish the basis for what would become, on their arrival in Russia, his first great address before the Soviet, known in the history of the revolution as "The Theses of April." Lenin was a good listener. If he made a mistake, he was the first to recognize it and to acknowledge it. He would remark: "It seems to me that there I have written nonsense." He continued to make such remarks even when he was the undisputed leader of Russia.

Lenin could listen, he could discuss, but when he really felt himself on firm ground on an important point, he did not yield. Vera Zassulich, originally a terrorist, then a convert to Marxism, said of him, comparing him with Plekhanov, another great theoretician of Russian socialism:

Lenin and other Russian exiles, Stockholm,
1917 — back to Russia

"Plekhanov is a greyhound who catches his prey, tosses it, and then lets it go. Lenin is a bulldog. Once he has caught his prey, no one can pry it loose from his jaws."

The prey in those days was the First World War. Opposing the comrades who thought that it would be evil to make a pact with Imperial Germany and that they must carry on the war like the Jacobins in the French Revolution, Lenin, who had always considered himself a Jacobin, a supporter of Robespierre against Danton, raised the flag of peace. In his eyes, to continue the World War in Russia was to ruin the Russian Revolution. On the way back to Russia, Lenin kept murmuring and smiling to himself. When he was asked what he was muttering, he answered: "Peace and bread." It was the essence of his program.

Lenin had carefully weighed the pros and cons. He knew that, because he was traveling with the approval of the German authorities, he would be accused of being a German agent. And in fact he was widely accused of treachery. But what was essential was for him to be in Russia at the side of the Russian workers. He nevertheless took the precaution of having a group of well-known Socialists, including Loriot and Guilbeaux in France and Levi in Germany, sign a declaration that said: "The Russian internationalists who are entering Russia to serve the cause of the Revolution will help us to arouse the proletariats of all countries against their respective governments, especially Germany and Austria." The signature of Paul Levi, a friend of Rosa Luxemburg and me, was important. His influence on the German labor movement increased when he returned to Germany after the kaiser was deposed.

And so in Switzerland ended one of the most famous political exiles of all times. It began in Munich, with a very austere communal life and a group of exiles who saved every possible penny to be able to publish *Iskra*. Lenin was and is, for all political exiles of all times, an example of how to fight for one's country from the outside.

FIVE

The Nansen Mission

If it had not been for the blue eyes that revealed his Nordic origin, one would have taken Fridtjof Nansen for a Spanish *picador*, because of his wide hat with upturned brim and his erect carriage. His appearance was unmistakable among the starched shirts and the solemn airs of the personalities who, in the Geneva of the early 1920s, gave to the League of Nations its decorum and its promise. I went to Fridtjof Nansen each time a political or human problem shook the complicated international deliberations that followed the First World War.

Nansen by then had a fabulous past. He was by vocation a painter, and by a zest for knowledge and adventure an explorer. When I met him on the shore of Lake Geneva, so calm, sometimes alone, sometimes in the company of Lord Robert Cecil, whom I also admired for the strength of his pacifist ideas, I thought of the Nansen of legend, the Nansen of the polar ice floes.

On one trip he and five companions became the first men to cross Greenland on skis. One might say that Nansen was born on skis. His mother was a Norwegian ski champion. For Nansen his famous journey was significant not only for the discovery of places never before explored at a latitude of sixty-five degrees, but also for the discovery of an oppressed people, the Eskimos, about whom he wrote a moving account.

He understood the Eskimos, whose decline, according to him, began when the Westerners brought them Christianity and the fruits of their civilization. He felt a sense of injustice each time that one of them succumbed to the evils that the "civilized" had brought to them. His voice became passionate and accusing as he recalled the indifference with which the world watched Greenlanders and other indigenous peoples meet their tragic fate. And then he spoke of the civilizing claims of the missionaries, that attitude of superiority concealed in a false evangelical humility, their shocking behavior with respect to other civilizations which they did

Fritjof Nansen with H. H. Bryn,
Norwegian Minister to the United States

not understand but which, nevertheless, they claimed to educate. Nansen saw hope for the salvation of the Greenlanders only in the withdrawal of the Europeans.

Nansen's face lit up as he talked about the most dramatic episode of an expedition that made him famous, after he had been called a visionary and a madman: the moment when he decided to leave his boat almost immobilized on the ice and to set out on a sleigh, accompanied by only one of his men, Johansen, on his dramatic exploration toward the North. They wore wolf skins, the best protection against the cold, and carried deerskins to improvise a relatively endurable bed.

Nansen was an excellent hunter; he counted on his gun to replace the food rations carried in the sleigh which would not last indefinitely. He did get a few animals. But not enough. This animal lover had to endure the grief of letting his dogs be killed in order to stifle the pangs of hunger. Johansen has testified to the grief of Nansen. "Yesterday Pan was killed, and Kvik, who had ended by devouring the hide of his tent, was also sacrificed. He was the only one of our dogs who had come with us from Norway. I killed him with a knife thrust, without the poor animal knowing what I was doing. Nansen had brought him from his home in Norway, where he was loved by everyone. The night that Kvik died Nansen was a totally different man." And Nansen's faithful companion adds: "Our clothes, covered with dirt, stuck to our skin. Our hair and our beards grew; our face and hands were black and dirty. We had become real savages. It was real torture to be smothered under all that dirt and not to have a piece of paper with which to wipe our hands."

Nansen knew very well what hunger was when in 1922 he organized the expedition to Russia and invited me to be a member. He had heard of my "fame," if I may be permitted the word, as a correspondent of *La Nación* of Buenos Aires, and he thought that a report by me from the hunger zone might help to collect contributions in Argentina for his relief fund.

The experience of his journey to the North Pole had taught Nansen not to despair about the final outcome of a great venture. The same people who had joked about his expedition and who, after hearing no news of it for three years, had given it up for lost, welcomed him upon his return. Honors were heaped upon him. Universities in several countries granted him honorary degrees. And finally came the Nobel Prize. Nansen had learned that, when one struggles stubbornly for a noble idea, the skepticism of the overly intelligent who are incapable of risking anything for fear of failure cannot stand up against a wholehearted persistence. I, who as a child had followed, fascinated, the stories of Nansen's expeditions to the Pole, now followed him personally in Geneva in his efforts to give to the League of Nations his missionary zeal.

Of all the great men in Geneva Nansen was the only one who had the courage to fight for aid to Russia. The Western international atmosphere was infested by a current against anything that had to do with the Bolsheviks. Frustration merged with hostility. The Western intervention policy in Russia had failed miserably. In the midst of enormous difficulties Soviet power continued. In Geneva I heard: "And that Nansen still wants to help them escape starvation. Let them starve to death. And that Nansen, who is a Bolshevik at heart — if he weren't he wouldn't get along so well with Lenin — let him leave us alone with his proposals."

Nansen had no intention of leaving in peace all those Western diplomats who did not forgive the Bolsheviks for having defeated the generals and admirals financed and armed and ordered to put an end to the Russian Revolution. The language of Nansen was clear and cutting. When he received the Nobel Prize in Stockholm, he had said: "What do you understand by the words 'War never more'? This should mean not only 'No more world wars, no more wars about national honor.' This must say: Never more any kind of war! In the course of my life I have arrived at the conviction that to set great things and great ideas in motion one must not think about retreat. In the League of Nations governments must never think about turning back."

Nansen did not retreat. He always charged. He began by setting an example, turning over to aid for Russia the money that he had received with the Nobel Prize. The Hall of the League of Nations was silent when he rose to defy the icy hostility of the delegations who were insensible to the sufferings of the Russian people. "At this hour," said Nansen, "from twenty to thirty million people in Russia are exposed to hunger. If in the next two months we do not come to their aid, they are lost. Transportation is manageable, control is guaranteed. Do you wish to leave all the responsibility to private charity? It is paralyzed by all the prejudices that have been set up around this problem, by the arguments of those who fear that our aid may strengthen the Soviet regime. I am speaking not in political terms but in human terms. The governments declare that they cannot give five million pounds for this aid. But this is half what it costs to build a new battleship." And in another speech: "This is a struggle against the clock, against the winter that is descending from the north, silent and terrible. And I think I know what it is to struggle against winter. But the struggle that is now going on in western Russia is greater than anything that I could imagine."

Nansen had gone to Russia to get firsthand information. He found vast areas devastated by civil war and hunger, without trains or boats or clothing or disinfectants. He also found a justifiable suspicion on the part of the Russian authorities toward the League of Nations. Chicherin, commissar for foreign affairs, refused to recognize Nansen as an envoy of the league, but Nansen knew how to fight on two fronts. The man who was suspected in Geneva of being a Bolshevik stood up to Chicherin. He asked for a special train to return to the frontier in two hours. Of course he knew that he enjoyed the confidence of Lenin, who with great clairvoyance saw in Nansen the only person on the international scene who would fight to the bitter end to organize aid to Russia. Chicherin accepted a compromise: Nansen would speak on behalf of the individual nations.

Just as he had succeeded in carrying out the immense task of repatriating a half million European war prisoners left in Russia, Nansen overcame all the obstacles to his antihunger campaign. The commission for the relief of the starving Russian people was organized. It was through Nansen that I, as a member of the commission, achieved my dream of entering Russia.

It was the first of my ten trips there, and the most difficult, the most dramatic. It was difficult because we had to deal with local authorities overwhelmed by an enormous number of problems for some of which there was no possible solution. They were grateful for our presence but frequently irritated by the demands of our mission. And the trip was dramatic because we were in daily touch with death. In Warsaw they had supplied us with vaccine and emergency drugs. But against the exanthematic typhus, which was killing an incalculable number of Russians, there was at that time no effective vaccine. Our best defenses were to wear high boots to protect our ankles against the bites of the infecting louse and to keep the railway car in which we were traveling in the best possible state of cleanliness.

I had with me several books by Lenin and some Russian novels, especially those that described the landscape and the customs of the Ukraine, the zone in which the Nansen mission was going to operate. In the Volga Herbert Hoover's organization was making a parallel attack on the problem of hunger. As we approached the Ukrainian frontier, people kept getting off the train. No one was touring Russia in those days. We had already left behind us the old battlefields, theater of the German-Russian encounters, where the Northern nights, so short and so bright, had allowed us to see the traces of the great combats.

We had been sitting fourteen hours in an old and uncomfortable car, but in view of what we suspected lay ahead of us, we considered the trip a pleasure excursion. Polish patrols guarded the roads near the frontier. Their mission was more sanitary than military: to prevent typhus from spreading to Poland and the rest of Europe. The Polish sentinels looked at us in amazement. We must have seemed to them out of our minds to be going toward the land of the epidemics, a land thousands of Russian fugitives were trying to flee, outwitting the *cordon sanitaire* established by the Poles.

It was already night when the train, by slackening its pace, showed that we were approaching the Russian border. I looked with some emotion at the red flag of the little station where we stopped. Not all Russians were fleeing from their country. From the adjoining car that was transporting Russian prisoners repatriated from Czechoslovakia came shouts of joy and revolutionary songs as they entered their own territory.

At the Chepetovka station we got off the train and another kind of emotion overcame me. It was the first direct, brutal encounter with misery. Heaps of human beings, with starving faces, were piled on the platforms of the station and in the waiting room. They were accustomed to hoping without hope for the arrival of a relief train that would get them out of there. Our train for Kiev would not leave until twelve hours later. We had with us a Swiss interpreter who went to make sure that there would indeed be a train at or near midnight. Some members of the Commission made themselves comfortable in a corner that was cleared for them by the station authorities. I chose instead to venture into the heart of the city, accompanied by the interpreter and a Russian official, who had joined us either out of courtesy or for surveillance. First we saw the outskirts of the station: a real encampment, at every step an improvised hut. There were fugitives from the most remote parts of Russia, trying to get into Poland. Some had been there three months counting the minutes, endless minutes, until they could get to leave. There were about five thousand of them.

We approached the huts. Men, women, and children came from them, attracted by two men unusually dressed, and through the interpreter I began to talk with them. At first they hesitated, perhaps inhibited by the presence of the Bolshevik official. But their sufferings, and perhaps the illusion that we could help them, finally untied their tongues.

Their stories were horrifying. I wrote down in my notebook what they told me. It was the first authentic picture of starving Russia, and today, fifty years later, I can understand why most Western diplomats and politicians thought that Soviet Russia could not survive such a catastrophe. Some of the refugees had come from the Volga or the Caucasus, covering hundreds of miles on foot or traveling hidden on the platforms of trains. They told us horror stories of the situation in the Volga region, where American aid was not sufficient to restore a badly deteriorated situation.

One of them who, in spite of being clothed in rags, looked like a cultivated man, gave greater coherence to the story. He lamented: "We have been here for months. We have come from one cemetery to fall into another." And, looking at the Russian official: "Why won't they let us leave the Ukraine, since the Ukraine can't feed us?" The Russian official later told us: "Even though our government ought to lend all needed facilities, nothing would be solved because the Polish Government refuses to accept Russian emigrants." Among the huts I could see rough crosses, improvised tombs. Each day illness and hunger wreaked havoc among the fugitives. Meanwhile, at the station, the other members of the Commission were trying to convince the customs officers that all our baggage, including the food supplies and medicines, were included in the agreement on diplomatic immunity granted to our mission.

When we finally boarded the Kiev train, day was breaking. The train went faster than we had expected. We were privileged to have a whole car at our disposal. It would be coupled to other trains whenever their destination coincided with ours at the connecting stations. As I looked through the window, I saw dauntless secret travelers jumping onto nearby trains when they slowed down. Before they reached a station they would jump off and wait until the train started up again. They were clearly more afraid of the Red guards stationed on the platforms than of the railroad employees.

We crossed a great number of destroyed bridges only half rebuilt. From what the refugees from the Volga and the Caucasus told us it was the same all over Russia. It was the result of the invasions of recent years, the military adventures of Kolchak, Denikin, and Wrangel, Czarist admirals and generals, who had not been able to topple the Soviet regime but who had destroyed a great deal of Russian territory. They contributed materially to the ruin of the country, completing the devastation created by the German armies. Russian agriculture, already weakened when Lenin came into power, suffered enormously at the hands of undisciplined soldiers, who indulged in unbridled sacking. This was one of the causes of the starvation. There were in the Ukraine some parts, but very few, where the farmers' efforts had produced oases of relative normality. In the railroad stations the farmers were selling bread and milk, but at exorbitant prices. We finally reached Kiev, a beautiful city because of its monasteries and churches, but a city that had been terribly punished. Since 1917 Kiev had changed hands fifteen times; sometimes the Whites were in power, sometimes the Reds.

Of the three important cities in the Ukraine — Kiev, Kharkov, and Poltava — which I visited in the succeeding weeks, I found Poltava in the worst condition. It was not really in the area of starvation, but it was in the sector of the three districts of Constantinople, Kobelyaki, and Lublin, where the drought and the carnage had reached the most severe proportions in the preceding months. The children were clearly in need of help. But the adults needed it even more. At first, an understandable sentimental tenderness led the relief organizations, especially the Americans, to concentrate their efforts on the children. But the adults were dying in greater numbers.

In Poltava exanthematic typhus was killing people by the hundreds, in spite of the tropical heat. The few doctors on duty urged us to be extremely cautious, but if one wished to get anything done, he could not let himself be obsessed by the fear of contagion. That was one of the risks we knew we were running. More infuriating was the incompetence of certain railroad employees. In Poltava the stationmaster dispatched the train that we were to take without waiting for us to return from one of our visits to the city. His solution was to offer to couple our car to a cattle train, which was pressed into service in those days as a passenger train. One can imagine when we would have reached Kharkov. It was hellishly hot in the station. Our argument with the stationmaster attracted an enormous number of Russians astounded that anyone would dare to protest. Two of us cut brusquely through the interminable argument by asking to be taken to see the supreme authority in Poltava, the President of the Soviet Executive Committee. The idea was a good one, for it gave us the chance to meet Comrade Drobdnis. I shall never forget his name or his face.

In my different trips to Russia I have seen Russian farmers in the most varied situations of crisis, despair, and hope. Agriculture has always been the most difficult problem for the successive Soviet governments. They can launch ingenious and perfect spaceships to explore Venus, they can master a space technique that is the envy of all. But they are incapable of solving the problem of Russian agriculture. I have met Russian farmers in the bitterest periods of enforced collectivization under Stalin and I have seen their faces marked by impotence and rage. In 1961, I saw them during the course of the promising Seven-Year Plan sharing the euphoria of Khrushchev, who was then talking of outstripping the United States in the production of grain. I have seen the hundred-year-old peasants of the Caucasus, who are not only the object of sensational reports but are a very living and lively reality, younger and more active than men half their age in other parts of the world. I saw a country woman of a Kolkhoz who was over a hundred and five years old. She danced a popular rustic dance in our honor, and said that she would like to live another twenty years to see Russia become the most powerful nation on earth. But because Drobdnis was the first Russian farmer whom I met, he left a lasting impression on me.

He looked as if he had come out of a Russian novel. Very human, one of those people that one could imagine being both sentimental and tough. Bearded, laconic, but with a frank look. He received us in a room whose walls were covered with red draperies, with an enormous picture of Karl Marx between portraits of Lenin and Rakovski. I told him that I had seen Rakovski, months before, at the Geneva Conference, and that I hoped to see him again in Kharkov. But in order to do that we had to get to Kharkov. He found a solution at once. Our car would be coupled to the first train that passed through Poltava. But meanwhile, and to save us time, he would put at our disposal the only automobile he had. And he gave us dinner. We were extremely grateful for the meal, since we had been eighteen hours without touching food, not even a bite of bread.

To relate our excursion across the Ukrainian fields during the night in that car that looked like a dismantled tank would require a whole chapter. On impassable and impossible roads, with only one headlight, lurching across ruts and swamps, with a driver who kept singing so that he wouldn't fall asleep, it was a miracle that we didn't crash into something. From the villages great packs of dogs came running at us, and one couple wakened by the noise of the car shouted at us words that we didn't understand. I'm sure they were insults for the disturbers of their sleep. It took us twelve hours to cover about a hundred miles. The slightest injury to the car, to a wheel, would have been catastrophic. But the fantastic thing is that, in spite of the noise and the jolting, I slept for a good part of the trip.

Rakovski received me with the same cordiality that he had shown me in Geneva. "I didn't think that we were going to meet again here and so soon. The famine in the region is very serious. Unfortunately it has taken too long to recognize it. A quite natural feeling of solidarity persuaded us to send great amounts of grain to the Volga, so when famine appeared here, we lacked the means to cope with it. And then there was the miserable transportation situation. Here in the Ukraine alone there are nine hundred and fifty bridges destroyed by the counterrevolutionary troops." I got along very well with Rakovski, who was Rumanian, which is to say a Latin, and who spoke perfect French. When we told him what had happened to us in Poltava, he gave me a handwritten note requiring Ukrainian authorities to assist us in our mission. This was the last time I ever saw him. He was killed in the monstrous and insane purges of the thirties. He was a complete revolutionary, and infinitely nobler and more intelligent than the police, the organizers of repression.

In Alexandrovsk, capital of the Zaporozhe, there was desolation. I helped some people to cross the street, ignoring warnings not to get close to them. In the Alexandrovsk hospitals there were three hundred cases of cholera and of exanthematic typhus. In one of the hospitals I found a doctor, who, like the farmer in Poltava, seemed to have come out of a Russian novel. He had studied in Paris, was quite up on modern French literature, and when he spoke of the years he had spent in France his face lit up. "All that has ended for me. And all this is about to end for me. Four of the doctors who were working in this hospital have died of typhus. We scarcely have any towels, we have to ration soap like a treasure, and there is one thermometer for every thirty patients." When I left him he gave me his address. I promised to send him some books from Paris. "That would be the best present," he said, "if they arrive in time." When I left the hospital I found myself in a funeral procession, almost mechanically, scarcely knowing what I was doing. One began to get used to death, to lose one's fear of typhus, to sink into the general suffering.

And a few streets beyond there was the contrast. From a home came piano music, a Chopin sonata. I knocked on the door. A beautiful young Russian girl came to open it. She spoke French. "What can you expect? Our only consolation is music. It is wonderful that a foreigner like you should come to help us." I kissed her hand and gave her a chocolate bar from our ration. She smiled at me. I can not remember a sadder or more enchanting smile.

The only solution was to put on a show of strength and to see how we could organize our aid most efficiently. Captain John Gorvin, the English chief of the mission, patted me on the back: "Good nerves for a Latin!" And really good nerves were needed to watch the Ukrainian Red Cross sisters lift children from their beds to show us their warped bones, their swollen bellies, their wasted muscles. The food that they were getting was terrible. Their soup was salted water.

Captain Gorvin urged me to be more cautious. He said he did not want any more losses in our ranks. As a matter of fact, that winter, out of the Nansen group in Russia, a very limited group, eight delegates had died of typhus, among them the famous Doctor Farrar, who was in charge of the antiepidemic campaign. Doctor Farrar (I don't remember his first name) was famous for his research in the struggle against epidemics. Nansen was much interested in involving him in his mission and was terribly shocked to learn that Doctor Farrar was a victim of the epidemic that Nansen had gone to fight.

The railroad stations were centers of infection. I took care never to get off the train without high boots. Except once. It was an incident that caused a conflict outside and inside the commission. It was after dark and we had had supper in our car. As if they had smelled the food, a group of children had gathered under our window and were making signs, putting their hands to their mouths. They were begging for food. Two Russian soldiers moved toward them menacingly. I jumped down to the platform in slippers, without my boots. With a few words of Russian I indicated to the soldiers that they should stop threatening the children. I called our interpreter and asked him to tell the soldiers that if they mistreated a single child I would complain to Rakovski and I showed the paper that the president had given me. Most of the children ran away, but about five stayed there, with their little faces hungry and pleading. I went back into the car, got some of our food and gave it to them as they tried to kiss my hands.

Within the commission that action brought on a clash with one of its members, a compatriot of Nansen. Many years later he became famous, but his fame was quite distinct from that of Nansen. He was, in fact, Vidkun Quisling, *the* Quisling, the personification during the Second World War of treason and collaboration with the enemy. It was natural that even then we should detest each other. He was complaining because I had squandered part of our food on starving children.

When our mission was over, the Soviet Government, in a gesture of gratitude, invited us to spend a few days in Moscow. These were exciting days of relief and interest. I was lodged in the home of a former millionaire, Berg, the sugar magnate. The house had been in the news after the revolution because, when it was the temporary headquarters of the German Embassy, the ambassador, Count von Mirbach, had been murdered there. It was a most luxurious residence, although furnished in poor taste. Mr. Berg, aside from having his house and his paintings confiscated by the government, had suffered no further harm. He lived and worked in the country. A daughter of his had married a Bolshevik officer. The room that she and her husband had occupied in the palace might have been called the "hall of mirrors." Her closets must at one time have been filled with a stunning wardrobe. Now no doubt she dressed like all the other Russian women one saw on the streets, and if she had a private room for herself and her husband she could consider herself fortunate. I am sure she was.

I talked with several people who had had privileged positions before the revolution. They had adjusted easily to the change of regime. Some of them spoke with scorn of the White Russians who had gone abroad. It is true that most of the people with whom I talked were young, and the girls were especially spunky. They reminded me of the girl in the famine zone playing Chopin. The difference was that these girls were not starving.

In Moscow the food supply was adequate but fantastically expensive. The inflation was similar to that of a year later in Germany during the crisis of the deutsche mark. A bottle of beer cost a million rubles, the equivalent in those days of two hundred and fifty German marks, with which one could buy at that time a whole barrel of beer in Berlin. On the other hand caviar was cheap. You could buy it on the street served in paper cones, like roasted chestnuts in the winter.

We were going to be in Moscow for only a few days, and I wanted to see everything. The night that we arrived I went to see the Kremlin with its red star lit up. I had brought with me a thick volume of Russian history, so that it was easy for me to reconstruct the history of the building that even today sends forth alternating messages of peace and aggression, messages that keep world attention wondering about the thinking that goes on behind the walls of that marvelous heap of temples with piled-up treasures, official residences, and halls of congress. The Kremlin is impressive at all times, but especially so on Saturday afternoons, with the ringing of all the bells in its churches.

Lenin was still alive, although his activities were restricted. He had had an initial attack of arteriosclerosis, but according to reliable sources his mind was sound and his directives continued to be formulated with his customary genius. Some months had gone by since the introduction of the NEP, the New Economic Policy, which was unquestionably a retreat, but so opportune that it saved the revolution. European delegates who had been present when Lenin presented the policy told me of their reactions to his support of such a sweeping innovation in economic practice up to that time. The report was characteristic of Lenin: free of bluff, realistic, imaginative, and the essence of clarity. His oratorical style was as overwhelming as a locomotive. Communism at war left room for a certain transitional capitalism. Lenin did not like the expression "State Capitalism," which might discourage revolutionaries and encourage reformers, those Western Socialists who had never been in sympathy with the October Revolution and who had never stopped criticizing it, even though in their own countries they had never been able to create any kind of socialism.

There was still hope that Lenin would recover his health. But I heard conflicting stories about it. His iron constitution had enabled him to endure the grave wounds of the attack of August 1918, but early in 1921 the first symptoms of nervous strain appeared. He was opposed to any tapering off in his activities. It took a specific order from the Central Committee to get him to consent to take a rest in Gorki, the sumptuous residence of a former governor of Moscow. It was so sumptuous that it got on Lenin's nerves. The most powerful man in the New Russia continued to lead the same modest existence as when I knew him as an exile in Zurich. And he wore the same suit. The old Communist Clara Zetkin, the leader of the Third International and a good friend of Rosa Luxemburg and of mine, used to say: "I would have sworn that Lenin was wearing the same jacket, cleaned over and over, that he was wearing when I first met him in 1907." In Moscow there was a story that one day he had received a worker, who showed some embarrassment in his presence and kept looking at his suit and his shoes. On coming out of the interview the worker said to his comrades: "He received me like a brother, but when I saw his shoes I didn't dare to ask him for anything."

In spite of the brevity of our stay in Moscow I was able to visit the museums, go to the theater, and make contacts in literary and intellectual circles. The Marosov and Schubchukin Modern Art Galleries, formed from the private collections confiscated by the state, proved that to see the best in French painting, from Manet to Picasso, one has to go to Moscow. The rich industrialists of the czarist era vied with one another in buying up the best paintings that they could find abroad. The theaters were well attended by a public that years before could not afford the luxury of a ballet or a play by Chekhov. It was a mixed public, with a good percentage of workers, but also of women who were once in high society. Given the high cost of stockings, they wore socks, a custom that was later to become fashionable, but which was then an innovation not without a certain charm. At nighttime music was played in the gardens, and Moscow for a moment seemed unconcerned by the misery still so vivid in our minds.

I made a separate investigation of the intellectuals' physical hardships, planning to submit to the Nansen Commission a proposal to give them special aid. In Kharkov an aged university professor had told me: "You cannot imagine how we live. The salaries that should have been paid us in March we did not get until May, and there were many days when we had only bread and tea. But we suffered most from the lack of our working tools, books and journals." The artists were just as badly off. In Moscow I talked with a painter by the name of Konchalovski, a very interesting fellow, who was having a show with many pictures that had Spanish themes. He had spent some time in Spain and he recalled the Prado Museum with deep emotion. He complained less of money troubles than of the lack of materials — brushes, paints, canvases.

On the other hand, there was plenty of freedom of expression. Many of the thinkers and writers who had been considered quite conservative had welcomed the Revolution of February 1917. Nicolai Alexandrovich Berdyayev, an eminent philosopher and essayist, had publicly and openly rejoiced at the "fall of the Holy Russian Empire." At the head of the most enthusiastic supporters was Vladimir Mayakovski, who published in Gorki's review *The New Life* couplets that sailors would later sing as they attacked the Winter Palace. Sergei Essenin marched right by his side, while Alexander Blok, an excellent poet, sang to the renewal of the glories of Stenka Razin and Pugachev, the heroes of the peasant uprisings under the czars, hoping that "the magnificent rebellions of the past would be immortalized in voluntary musical waves." In two masterly poems, "The Twelve" and "The Scythes," Blok exhorted the intellectuals not to weep for the dead but to listen to the music of the future. Russia, he wrote, will emerge from her agonies revitalized. The real Russia, the Russia that Dostoevski saw, the Russia that Gogol compared with a rushing troika, Russia the hurricane.

But there were many dissidents, and they were tolerated. There was no official imposition of Marxism on writers. On the one hand were the leftist extremists, those who talked of bombing Pushkin and all the classics. On the other hand were those who, having supported the February Revolution, thought that the October Revolution had gone too far. They told me how, at the moment of major conflict, in 1918, in the immense hall of the Polytechnic Museum, conservatives, Tolstoians, anarchists, idealists, could all express themselves as they wished, arguing with the spokesmen for the October Revolution, speakers like Lunacharski, named University Professor in 1920, who held in his home a "Free Academy of Spiritual Culture," in which Berdyayev was allowed to develop his theses on Dostoevski's philosophy and the sense of history.

The authorities were eager to attract the intellectuals. Up until 1922, the date of our visit, the Pan-Russian Society of Poets and the Pan-Russian Union of Writers did not feel overly dependent on the official party line. Anna Akhmatova, a great poet, was not prevented from publishing her "Rosary."

Mayakovski had few rivals in revolutionary circles. He was the poet par excellence and the electrically charged propagandist for the "Socialist structure." To reach the masses he made use of everything: theater, poetry tournaments, literary pilgrimages. He preached and orated everywhere.

But the least orthodox writer could write without fear of getting into trouble with the authorities. The novelists Gladkov, Furmanov, and Tarassove Rodianov wrote novels that were, to be sure, revolutionary, but not rigidly orthodox. The Communist party, under the influence of Lenin and Gorki (who was at first against the October Revolution but later aligned himself with it), preferred to get along with the intellectuals, the "fellow travelers," hoping that they would end up by slowly absorbing the Communist ideology. The "Proletkult" enjoyed official support, but even the most "formalist" writers did not feel inhibited.

The discussions were exciting. To sound out how far tolerance would go, I championed Dostoevski, although Tolstoi had been from far back my favorite Russion novelist. Fedor Mikhailovich Dostoevski was certainly not in fashion. I brought up his past as a persecuted man, who had been implicated in a revolutionary plot, arrested in March 1849 and condemned to death in December, and who had spent the years 1850 to 1854 in exile. He died a year after the publication of *The Brothers Karamazov* in 1880 and had a funeral as massive and as emotional as that of Victor Hugo. The young Russian writers with whom I talked found in him a symbol of contradiction.

The important thing, however, is that we could feel free to disagree, and what I remember especially from that first trip to Moscow, which was to be followed by nine others, is that anything at all could be discussed.

SIX

Russia

In 1928 Yasnaya Polyana was the gathering place of writers from all over the world in a homage to Tolstoi on the centenary of his birth. I considered him (with Cervantes and Stendhal) one of the three greatest novelists of all times. The three Spanish writers invited to participate were Miguel de Unamuno, Ramón del Valle Inclán and me, because I had written two books on the New Russia. Neither Unamuno nor Valle Inclán could go, so the representative of Spanish letters at so memorable a centenary was the least deserving one.

Our host and intellectual guide in Yasnaya Polyana, Tolstoi's home, was Anatoli Vassilievich Lunacharski, Cultural Minister in the Soviet Government. My contacts with him were to continue until 1933, when, on the establishment of diplomatic relations between Spain and Russia, I, who was then ambassador to Mexico, was named the first Spanish ambassador to Moscow and Lunacharski was named the first Soviet ambassador to Madrid. Neither of us ever took his diplomatic post, for the replacement of the Azaña Government by one considerably to the right of it brusquely cut off the gesture of goodwill toward Soviet Russia.

Lunacharski was well acquainted with the literature and the art of my country. He agreed with me that our two countries should come closer spiritually, a hope that was strengthened during the Spanish War when Soviet experts came to help us in our struggle against international fascism. Some of the Russians, with their facility for languages, quickly learned Spanish. In those days in which the future of the world was at stake and in which world anti-Fascist forces were active, there was great sympathy between Spain and Russia. The affinities between our two countries extended even to the dance. Our flamenco dances had their counterparts in some Russian popular dances.

Lunacharski and I talked for many days about Tolstoi. I recalled how, when I was young, I had come upon a very bad translation of *Anna*

Karenina. I was fascinated by it and I swore that some day I too would be a writer. Lunacharski said that *Anna Karenina* really had to be read in Russian. Later it was *War and Peace* that made me see in the Russian woman a figure unique in the world and that prepared me to know her when, in the years before Lenin came to power and I was studying in various European universities, I met young Russian woman students who were already enlisted in the revolution.

Lunacharski and I shared an interest in the theater. In this field I was an "aficionado," an amateur. He was an authority, especially in all that concerned Russian dramatic art. He had written much on the theater before the October Revolution and before he became People's Commissar for Public Instruction. He was the author of a dozen books on the theater. His association with innovative figures in the Russian theater and cinema like Meyerhold, Mayakovski, and Eisenstein, quite apart from his own contributions, had already assured him, by the time that I knew him, a place in the front rank of the effort to unite the theater and the revolution.

Romain Rolland, himself the author of an essay, "Le Théâtre du peuple," whom Lunacharski met in Switzerland after the beginning of World War One, had a great influence on him. Rolland wanted to bring the theater to the masses. He never forgot the important role played by the spontaneous dramatic performances of the French Revolution during the height of Jacobin activity, the festive homages to Nature of which Robespierre was so fond.

Lunacharski was a devotee of art. When there was a rumor, at the beginning of the revolution, that the Bolshevik artillery had destroyed the Saint Basil Church of Moscow, he resigned in protest from the Commissariat of Public Instruction, a resignation withdrawn when the rumor was proved false. He was supported by Lenin in his cultural policy of fostering the new without destroying what was new in the old. He denounced the falseness of wanting to reject all the wealth that had gradually been accumulated in the long history of humanity. At the same time Lunacharski stimulated the work of the young people, the workers' theatrical clubs that performed revolutionary episodes like the trial and assassination of Rosa Luxemburg, *The Blue Blouses*, a kind of dramatized diary that dealt directly with the problem of the revolution, and was acclaimed not only in Russia but by audiences in Germany and China. Its technique inspired some of the works of Brecht.

In a discussion in 1908 with Meyerhold, who would later become one of his closest collaborators on the concept of Aristotle in tragedy, Lunacharski was surprised that Meyerhold did not understand that, if mimicry served to illustrate interior movement, the theater was distinct from a book precisely because it "illustrated" interior movements and illustrated them directly. "Meyerhold," wrote Lunacharski, "would understand this

86

if his decadent and fearful instinct did not prevent him." He took on the defense of the theater of Stanislavski, of Gordon Craig, of Max Reinhardt, and he wrote: "I was privileged to attend the Reinhardt spectaculars in Berlin, in his theater. They approach my ideal. Here are performances filled with life, poetry, and beauty."

Once in the government, Lunacharski turned over to Meyerhold the

Anatol Lunacharski (front left) with
Lady Astor, Bernard Shaw, and eminent
Russian writers, Moscow, 1931

general direction of theatrical activities in the republic. Meyerhold was told to keep alive the old academic theaters and the young auxiliaries, the "studio" theaters, to which was granted a certain freedom of initiative. He was to support the young theaters created by the revolution, in which one could easily organize instant exemplary experimental spectacles, completely adapted to the triumphal currents of socialism.

The two points of view, those of Lunacharski and Meyerhold, once so far apart, gradually merged, although Lunacharski was far from sharing the view of his associate that the theater should not be psychological, not even be a theater of ideas. Its main function was to achieve a combination of the techniques of the stage, the cinema, and the circus, a joyous combination that would amuse people. For Lunacharski the theater outside of Russia had become a more and more capitalistic enterprise. The theater, which according to him should be for the people, especially for the younger generation, an instrument of artistic education, renewed itself much more slowly than painting or literature. In the few years since the Russian Revolution, Lunacharski told me in 1928, the theater had become a people's theater. Ticket prices had been greatly reduced. The laborer and the peasant could afford to buy reserved seats. The public had learned to be critical about the theater, to choose from the best of what already existed. The proletarian theatergoer had no right to reject Hauptmann, in his first period, or Zola, or Ibsen, or Bernard Shaw, even if these were not his kind of authors. At the same time, the proletarian theater had to face up to itself and not become mere phraseology. It had to transform the mentality of the actor to make him a man capable of performing any role with an emotion that would appeal to the masses, a man capable of making himself universally understood. "I have been and I continue to be an energetic defender of the professional theater in its loftiest expression," Lunacharski went on. "Perfection in performance. But at the same time audacity in revitalizing the content. The people will be satisfied only with a theater capable of presenting in a form that is extremely clear, simple, persuasive, and profoundly realistic the great ideas and the great emotions that must be present in a revolution of the proportions and the universal scope of our revolution."

In 1933, years after our meeting, Lunacharski published in *Izvestia* a significant article: "Stanislavski, the Theater, and the Revolution." In it he told how the revolution of the theater in Russia had been achieved. The Art Theater had performed Stchedrin's *The Death of Pazukhim* and the public had enthusiastically applauded Moskvin, Leonidov, and a setting full of innovations. And Lunacharski told how a Communist worker, of above average culture but a confirmed supporter of the "Proletkult," had told him that the Art Theater was a fiasco. "What?" Lunacharski answered him. "Can't you see that it's a great success?" "You're fooling yourself," the man answered. "It's only the bourgeois public applauding its own bourgeois theater."

It is interesting today, fifty-five years after the Russian Revolution, to recall the policy of its principal leaders with regard to literary and artistic freedom during its first years. Lenin, for example, was rather stern in his view of the "Proletkult" and he repeatedly asked Lunacharski to restrain the excesses of an organization in which arbitrariness and innovative caprice won out over objective analysis and balanced judgment about the old Russian culture. Addressing the Third Congress of the Union of Communist Youth, Lenin granted that the bourgeoisie had exploited the old values, but he declared that it was "false to try to reject all the teachings of the past and not to give due appreciation to what is indispensable for the achievement of communism through the use of all the riches accumulated by human knowledge."

It was fascinating to hear Lunacharski talk about Stanislavski. I saw him a few days after his encounter with the intransigent Communist. "As always I view with pleasure this serene, determined, affectionate countenance, illumined by a kind of inner radiance, with a somewhat timid smile, this magnificent old man with the stature of an oak tree. The theater of Stanislavski was a theater of difficult times. All of Stanislavski's research, all his foresight, all his mature understanding are focused on a single truth: art is sacred, the theater is something magnificent and lofty, artistic creation is a noble enterprise."

Tolstoi's library in Yasnaya Polyana is of fundamental importance for anyone studying his literary career. Books in Russian alternate with priceless French editions from the eighteenth and early nineteenth centuries. There are countless books on China and India, a book in English on Mahatma Gandhi, works in Russian of Pushkin, Gogol, Turgenev, Dostoevski, with abundant marginal notes. The two books that Tolstoi was reading just before he died were by Dostoevski and Anatole France. We know that Tolstoi considered Dostoevski a great writer but he rejected Dostoevski's tendency to "mix everything together," religion and politics. Dostoevski's style was too complicated for his taste.

Tolstoi's goal was a language that could be understood by the simplest peasant, a language that could help to "serve the people." This plan, "to serve the people," which was the title of one of the three most widely read books of Mao Tse-tung, helped to explain the homage paid him by the Soviet government in the person of Lunacharski. Lenin, although he admired Tolstoi's writing skill, considered him excessively moderate politically. Tolstoi used to say that his most successful literary work was *The Prisoner of the Caucasus*, because it was written in a popular language that could be understood by the humblest *moujik* that worked on his land, provided that the *moujik* was literate, and few of them were. He greatly admired Semyonov, a rustic writer, identified with the Russian peasantry.

There was no mystery about Tolstoi's repudiation of the wealthy existence that he was expected to lead. At the age of eighty-one he lived in Yasnaya Polyana in the simplest imaginable style. One of the causes of disagreement between him and his wife, Sophia Andreyevna, was the unhappiness that he felt at any show of luxury and his consequent refusal to buy any new clothes. The feeling that he was a privileged being in a society filled with so much poverty caused him almost physical pain. In the letter that he left for his wife when he abandoned Yasnaya Polyana to go to die in Astapovo, he makes clear the asphyxia that he felt at the thought of living to the end of his days in a lordly dwelling.

The simplicity of Tolstoi's life is most clearly shown in his bedroom. It has been preserved untouched, just as it was on the night of 27 October 1910 when, before his tragic departure, he slept there for the last time. There was the famous embroidered red hassock, a gift from his sister Maria Nicolayevna. There was the night table with his favorite objects: a small clock, a pillbox, and a box for his pens, because he would sometimes wake in the night and want to write.

The suffering that Tolstoi felt at the contrast between his life at Yasnaya Polyana and the life he would have liked to lead was softened by three compensations: horseback riding, the school that he founded, and his contacts with the common people. The weather had to be horrible for him to give up his daily ride, enjoying nature and the birds in the spring. Nightingales delighted him, and so did eagles, whose majesty he described superbly. "Frenzy" was his favorite horse. His love for nature stands out in all his novels, in *War and Peace* as in *Anna Karenina*. He adored children and his school is testimony to this love. He taught the children to read and told them stories. He put on plays for them. And he was a stern critic of literature written for children. Knowing that the peasants' children had no toys, he undertook to buy and distribute them. For children who knew how to read he always had books in his pockets and he would have the children read aloud to him and he would correct their mistakes.

Tolstoi's capacity for work was amazing. He found time for everything, even for answers to the thousands of letters that he received from all kinds of people asking him questions about philosophical as well as personal matters and many of them asking him for money. The latter placed him in a most embarrassing position. In 1892 Tolstoi had given up the ownership of the house and the lands of Yasnaya Polyana and of his other properties in Moscow and in the interior of Russia. All his wealth was divided between his wife and his many children. He had given up the royalties from his novels and the only money he received was royalties from performances of his plays. In spite of this, he did whatever he could to answer appeals for financial help.

He felt it his duty to answer all the letters that he received. His correspondence occupies thirty-one volumes in the jubilee edition of his works. In his letters the theme of the revolution was always present. To those who wrote advocating the use of violence to transform Russia, Tolstoi generally answered exalting the virtues of peaceful struggle. But people who report having discussed this in private with him say that he accepted the inevitability of the use of violence.

There are many letters from young people won over to the ideology of Tolstoi, telling him of their resolve to break with society, to abandon their studies, and to go to live among the peasants and to help them to educate themselves so that they could more effectively reclaim their lands. In his answers Tolstoi would praise their good intentions, but he would urge them to continue their studies, because Russia needed lots of well-educated young people.

Tolstoi's creative activity in the last year of his life, at age eighty-two, is impressive. Witnesses to his conversations in those months are solidly in agreement that he was much younger intellectually and quicker in his reactions and comments than visitors who were only half his age.

In some parts of the interior of Russia I could understand how the peasants managed to exist after the emancipation of the serfs, which affected some fifty million. Wood was the principal building material. In most cases the peasants built their houses with their own hands. They also made their crude farming tools while the women wove their clothes. So their lack of money was not felt so keenly. But no matter how poor the house was, there was always a room where one could take refuge from the cold and indulge the love of company that was so deeply a part of the nature of the Russian, who has always been noted for his hospitality. This central room, well heated, served as kitchen, dining room, and bedroom for the whole family.

The greatest danger in these wooden houses was from fire. In addition to this fear, the peasant was overburdened with children. Chekhov, in *The Peasants*, has a heroine who is the mother of thirteen children. Peasants ate very meagerly except on great feast days, when a sheep was slaughtered and drinking was unrestrained. Chekhov describes Kiriak drunk for three days in a row and rounding out his pleasure by beating his wife. But in spite of what has frequently been said about the Russian peasant's fondness for liquor, his normal daily preference was not for alcohol but for tea.

The Russian nobility, though minute in numbers compared with the peasant population, was very influential. The emancipation of the serfs dealt it a hard blow. In Chekhov's *The Cherry Orchard* we see the son of a serf buying the vast estate of a ruined family of the nobility. Dostoevski describes Prince Myshkin in *The Idiot* almost as a beggar. But in reality things happened otherwise than in novels. At the beginning of the nineteenth century Count Cheremetiev owned three hundred thousand serfs. The nobles did not treat their serfs benevolently. And that was one of the reasons why Tolstoi could not put up with his wife's airs of rural gentility and why he left Yasnaya Polyana.

Because industrialization came late to Russia, the laborer, who was to be the chief actor in the great October Revolution, appears very little in the Russian novel of the nineteenth century. It was Maxim Gorki who introduced him to literature. The factory worker is a major figure in *The Mother*. Among all the Russians, Gorki is the proletarian novelist. Although at the beginning he was opposed to the revolution, he later became a supporter and he helped stage scenes that evoked the advance of socialism through struggle and defeat to victory. In Petrograd, with Stockmart Square as a setting and the floodlights lighting it all from the Neva, he staged the solemn opening session of the International Communist Congress. But in addition to the factory worker, in *The Artamonovs* Gorki gave us the unforgettable likeness of the Russian merchants, while Gogol in *The Inspector General* with his mordant irony focused on the civil servants. All Russian society is portrayed in the great works, poetry, plays, novels, of its writers of the nineteenth century.

The social position of the writers themselves is quite varied. Next to aristocrats and landowners like Pushkin, Turgenev, and Tolstoi there are writers of humble origin: Chekhov, the son of a shopkeeper, Gorki, from a poor family and in his youth a dishwasher on a Volga boat. In between the two extremes was Dostoevski.

Writers did not in general become wealthy through their writings. The greatest of them were too much interested in the social problems of their time or in the spiritual currents that stirred their intense lives to pay much attention to their fees. Dostoevski, notoriously addicted to gambling, was always in debt, always making the rounds of pawnshops. When he could, he would get an advance against royalties and gamble it all away before he wrote the first page of the promised book. Then the necessity for producing something for the publisher made him work intensely. The custom of publishing a work serially before it appeared in book form was widespread. This is what happened with *War and Peace*. Authors were paid by the page or the line, and some malicious critics have said that this system of payment was responsible for the excessive length of Russian novels.

In 1924 and in several succeeding trips I alternated my interest in the special problems of the Russian Revolution with conversations with writers, painters, and people in the theater and the ballet. In Russia intellectual activity continued with undiminished liveliness for years after the revolution. Whenever I can I go to the Bolshoi Theater and one night in 1924 a beautiful woman suddenly came up to me during an intermission and asked me if I was del Vayo. She was the wife of a friend of mine, a painter who knew me from my Paris days, when I had come to know Diego Rivera and many other artists. Her husband had spoken to her about me; she had heard that I was in Moscow and had identified me through a group photograph in her house.

Two days later the three of us had dinner together and from that time on I have visited them whenever I have been in Moscow. In view of

Author as Spanish representative to the USSR

what has happened since, the spontaneity of those discussions with my friends and their friends on every imaginable subject has led me to set down some of them in detail.

Lenin had died not long before, and there had not yet occurred within the political leadership of the country the ideological struggles, or at least they were not evident outside the Kremlin walls. Among the intellectuals there was great admiration for Trotsky. They were fascinated by his brilliance. And he was admired not only among the intellectuals. In 1924 I attended a huge meeting at which he was to speak and five minutes before he mounted the platform we could hear from the street the applause that accompanied his entrance into the hall, applause that was merely the prelude for the ovation that he received inside. The audience was electrified by the powerful words that emphasized the feeling of strength that came from the speaker.

At the house of some friends I once asked about the best young Russian poets, and Pasternak was mentioned as being in fact better as poet than as novelist, even though thirty years later it was his novel *Doctor Zhivago* that won him the Nobel Prize and the reverence of multitudes of people in Europe and the United States who had never before heard his name. The virtues of this great novel are its poetic passages, the descriptions of the gentle Russian countryside, the lyricism of the doctor's love for Lara. Its weakest side is its theorizing about the revolution. It's not that he criticizes or condemns a certain period of the Russian Revolution, the era of Stalin, for example. It's that his whole concept of the revolution is false. There has not been, nor will there ever be, a revolution in history that will be acceptable to the sensibilities of a Doctor Zhivago, that is to say, of Boris Pasternak. He wants a social transformation without convulsions, as a proof of man's capacity for perfection and because convulsions offend his sense of beauty. If the old Czarist State is not quite deified, the State that followed it is viewed almost with repulsion. The dream of Doctor Zhivago is an idyllic and idealized Russia: "The dream of living on your own land thanks to the toil of your own hands, in complete independence and with no obligation to anyone. But in fact he found that there had merely been a switch from the oppression of the old State to the oppression of the new State, the much harsher yoke of the revolutionary superstate." Even Pasternak's poem *1905*, which has for its theme the first Russian Revolution, a prologue to the great Russian Revolution of October 1917 with the mutiny of the fleet in the Black Sea, is a lyric homage to the valor of man but not a profession of revolutionary faith.

The question of Soviet censorship of Soviet writers was a theme much discussed in my presence and one that continues to keep all its current importance, as in the case of Solzhenitsyn, for example. On one of my trips to Russia the question was discussed at a meeting that I attended at the home of Maxim Gorki. One of the guests was Romain Rolland.

Boris Pasternak, 1929

The sympathy of the author of *Jean Christophe* for the Russian Revolution had surprised some of his admirers. But his novel was dedicated to "free souls in all countries who suffer, who struggle, and who will triumph." The Russian people had suffered, had struggled, and had triumphed. That Romain Rolland should pay tribute to this revolution was natural. Some years after I met him in Moscow came the Fascist aggression against the Spanish Republic. In some superb letters sent to Luis Araquistain, the Spanish ambassador in Paris, Rolland took a vehement stand on the side of the Spanish people in their struggle for their independence and freedom. Romain Rolland was opposed to any official pressure on any writer or artist.

Maxim Gorki had been equally opposed. But on that occasion he defended the priority of socialism over aesthetics. The working-class writer, said the author of *The Lower Depths*, must recognize clearly that the antagonisms between the working class and the bourgeoisie cannot be overcome and that there is no alternative but to conquer or be conquered. The writer must write nothing that could harm the Socialist State.

I found Gorki physically strong in contrast to Rolland's fragility. I told him so. He answered: "I am saved by my Russian peasant stock." His militancy did not prevent him from praising the best of Russian literature in the past — Tolstoi, Gogol, Chekhov — and one of his favorite foreign authors, Balzac. Balzac, said Gorki, is a realist who wrote novels that were far from realism. In his time there was no problem of defending a socialist revolution that had triumphed but was threatened on all sides.

Boris Pasternak had grown up in an atmosphere of devotion to pure art. His father, the painter Leonid Pasternak, and his mother, the pianist Rosa Kaufman-Pasternak, were friends of Tolstoi, one of whose editions of *War and Peace* had been illustrated by Leonid. The painter has left us portraits of Rachmaninov, Scriabin, and Rubinstein; the best composers and artists of his time were among his friends. He painted Tolstoi after he died because at the death of the novelist, Leonid was summoned to Yasnaya Polyana, where he found a final message addressed to him, one that deeply impressed his son Boris. "Remember always, Leonid Ossipovich, that everything will pass," wrote Tolstoi. "Money, position, the very empires are condemned to disappear. The only thing that will live forever is the tiny garden of authentic art that we have planted in our work."

This evocation of the tiny garden of art inspired all the literary activity of Boris Pasternak. When, at the height of the fervor of the October Revolution, he heard action on behalf of the masses exalted above everything else, Pasternak praised, in opposition to it, the value of meditation. It was inevitable that, years later, Pasternak would reject Stalin's definition of writers as "engineers of the human soul," and when in 1935 he was sent to Paris to attend the Congress of Anti-Fascist Writers, which I also attended, he kept his distance from Malraux and Cocteau.

The uproar about *Doctor Zhivago* began in 1956. Pasternak had finished it the year before. The Soviet writers who make the decisions about whether a novel can be published in Russia voted against it. Among these writers was Constantine Fedin, Pasternak's friend and neighbor in Peredielkino, where Pasternak had his *dacha*. The journal *Novy Mir*, even though it risked Khrushchev's condemnation for having published Dudintzev's novel *Not by Bread Alone*, rejected *Doctor Zhivago*, as did also the novelist consecrated by the Soviet leaders, Michael Sholokhov, author of *And Silent Flows the Don* and one of the most implacable critics of Pasternak.

Pasternak had agreed that his novel should be published in the Soviet Union, with the prescribed omissions but with no change in the essentials of his original manuscript. Meanwhile Feltrinelli, the Milan publisher, defied the warning that he might be excluded from the Italian Communist party and, with the publication of *Doctor Zhivago*, created a worldwide sensation. In order to ensure the popularity of the novel, all that was necessary was Khrushchev's disastrous decision to refuse Pasternak permission to go to Stockholm to receive the Nobel Prize for literature, which folly made the author of the novel the most famous Russian literary personality among an enormous number of people who had known nothing about him up to then.

In contrast to Pasternak, two great poets much admired during my first trips to Russia, Sergei Essenin and Vladimir Mayakovski, sing the revolution with all their hearts. If they find themselves in opposition to some of its current moods, it is because of the exaltation of their own revolutionary fervor. Mayakovski is unquestionably a genius. Lunacharski said of him: "He was an essentially lyric artist who produced light and heat. His initial formalism is transformed into a kind of martyrdom. Mayakovski, with a tormented and quite characteristic enthusiasm, stamped upon the throat of his own song. He sought to stifle his own lyricism, individualistic and petit bourgeois, so that his individual song would not be an obstacle to his social song and would not prevent him from being a giant organ whose echoes would give resonance to the revolutionary storm."

The poetry of Sergei Essenin is devoted principally to proclaiming the profound transformation of the Russian peasant in a vehement and violent style. He was a futurist poet with a vehement and driving style much greater than that of the usual futurists. Impatient with the present, disillusioned with its slowness, after a romantic escapade, an affair with Isadora Duncan at the height of her beauty, he committed suicide in

Poet Vladimir Mayakovski

1925. At the time of my third trip to Russia, Essenin was dead. In both Mayakovski and Essenin there was a break with the purely aesthetic poetry of the past.

There was a very emotional reunion in Moscow in 1961 between those who, at the end of the Spanish War, were the Spanish children welcomed by the Russians as a proof of solidarity and those Russians who had given them the opportunity to study for a career, something that they could not have done in Spain. Some adults whom we had known in Spain had gone with them, like Doctor Planelles, who in the interim had become a member of the Soviet Academy of Sciences and, as a young woman of thirty-three, an associate professor of history at the University of Moscow. When one of the Spanish children, now grown up, returned to Spain, and was asked what her professional occupation was, she said that she was a railroad engineer. Her questioners burst into laughter because they could not conceive that, having left Spain as a small girl, she could now be running a train. Each one of these Spaniards had a story to tell. They had lived in the Soviet Union during the worst years of World War Two. And the Russians provided milk and food for these refugee children. It was no wonder that they were so loyal to a country that had welcomed them so generously.

The contribution of the Spanish refugees to the Allied cause in World War Two is well-known, and many reports and books have been written on it. Less familiar is their struggle within the Soviet Union, about which we heard several impressive accounts during our many visits to Moscow after the war.

The story is filled with heroism and Spanish daring. Most of the refugees enlisted in the Red Army. The German military command soon realized this and in the Kuban region controlled by Hitler's troops an order was circulated that said: "Citizens who give aid to Spanish groups traveling through Kuban will be severely punished." This was Germany's recognition of the importance of the Spanish contribution to the war on Russian soil.

There were legendary events. One concerned the seventy-four natives of the north of Spain, mainly Bilbao, who took part in the siege of Leningrad. By September of 1944, out of these seventy-four only seven survived. One of them, Francisco Gullón, promoted to captain, fought on every front. He finally fell in November of 1944. His journey in search of his battalion, the Voroschilov, in 1942 recalls the travels of the Spanish *conquistadores* four centuries earlier as they wandered across an unknown and unfriendly land. Gullón crossed through the German lines in quest of his comrades. After two months he finally found the remnants of his battalion. There were Spaniards in the battle of Stalingrad. In that battle died Rubén Ruiz Ibarruri, the son of Dolores Ibarruri, the "Pasionaria."

Among the fighters worthy of the battle of Stalingrad, which altered

Poet Sergei Yesenin

the course of the war in Russia and on the whole Allied front, was Manuel Alberdi. He began his action in Kirov, at the foot of the Ural Mountains. In fact, there was no front there, but he regrouped volunteers against an imminent German attack. And meanwhile he worked day and night in the local factory to supply the Leningrad front. The strenuous effort broke his health. He recovered slightly but he did not return to the factory. Instead he begged for and was granted permission to join the Red Army in the company of other Spaniards. Most were killed by German fire, but he continued in the vanguard of the Russian advance until it reached the gates of Berlin. He reminds one of the Spanish member of the *maquis* who entered Paris at the right hand of General Leclerc — a Spanish fighter on one side, a French fighter on the other.

Manuel had fought on the Oder River in the spring of 1945. The German attack had been one of the fiercest of the war. He shouted to the Spaniards who had survived: "To the tanks!" In Spain in 1937 the Asturian miners had attacked the German tanks with dynamite. Alberdi was always at the most dangerous point. He had complete confidence in victory. He worked enthusiastically to build a bridge over the Spree River. He said to his men: "To the water!" as he had said: "To the tanks!" From the opposite shore the Germans fired constantly but Alberdi and his forces crossed the river. They regrouped in a section of liberated Germany. Manuel found a street that had not been destroyed by artillery fire, took down its street sign and put up a new sign; "José Díaz Street," to honor the secretary general of the Spanish Communist party during the Spanish War.

Another of the Spanish fighters who won distinction on the Soviet Front was Manuel Martínez. He was not lucky enough to get to Berlin. He was much honored by the Russians. He heard old Russian women of the liberated territories call him "son" and the men call him "brother." He died in Poznan, when a street had to be mined. There was no time to lose, and without any assistance he tried to mine the street against enemy fire. Many other Spanish heroes helped carry on the great battle against fascism in Russia. One of them was Lieutenant Nelkin, son of a deputy, Margarita Nelkin, who emigrated to Mexico, where she worked for many years as an art critic for the press.

But when the war ended, despite a short interval of boycotting the Franco regime in the United Nations, the western democracies ended up by helping to keep Franco in power.

In squares and gardens throughout the interior of Russia I saw tombs and little monuments that bore witness to the bravery of my compatriots. They had fought for the Soviet Union, their unquestioned fatherland in those socialist times, but they had also fought for Spain. They volunteered for the most dangerous missions. Antonio Arizona, who was not demobilized until 1948, had taken part in a hundred and fifty air battles.

The Spanish girls served as nurses. Everyone thought that, when the war was won, the resulting glory and the freedom would be extended to the Spanish people, who had fought one of the greatest proletarian wars in history. In July 1966, in Saint George's Hall in the Kremlin, several of the Spanish survivors were decorated. On that occasion the feats of arms of the Spanish exiles who mobilized against fascism on Russian territory were retold and exalted by the Soviet orators. Moscow's *Izvestia* wrote: "Today the rails beneath the trains must have sung a song beyond their steely songs because there had been guerrilla dynamite to thwart the trains of the invaders. Today the waters of the Azov must have become as clear as a mirror so that in them the Spaniards could see one another, Spaniards who stained these waters with their blood when they fought in a bloody barren plain. And today the roses of Bulgaria must have become Spanish carnations and the sun must have cast its golden light upon the Spanish names on the ruins of the Reichstag in Berlin."

Spanish songs mixed with Russian songs were heard during the evening rests on the many Soviet war fronts. Spanish songs that the survivors of that epic fight still hope to sing again one day in a Madrid that will be the capital of a free Spain.

SEVEN

Memories of a Journalist

In my long career as a journalist I have had four chiefs who contributed greatly to increase my love for the profession: Jorge Mitre of *La Nación* of Buenos Aires, Freda Kirchwey of *The Nation*, J. W. Gitt of the *Gazette and Daily* of York, Pennsylvania, and C. P. Scott of the *Manchester Guardian*.

Jorge Mitre was a member of an Argentine family that was, all by itself, a national institution. One of his ancestors was General Bartolomé Mitre, once President of the Republic and a national hero. Jorge had journalism in his blood. When World War I broke out in 1914, he, as editor of *La Nación*, had a problem of concordance with *La Prensa*, the other great Buenos Aires daily, which was richer in funds than in imagination. Mitre understood at once that the course of the First World War was going to develop in his readers a growing interest in foreign news and he began to form a team of correspondents of which I had the good fortune to become a member in 1920.

I met with good fortune, and I also had a good journalistic sense. I was in Berlin, reporting for Spanish papers, when the Kapp *Putsch*, the reactionary uprising against the young German Republic, caused surprise and alarm throughout the world. That morning I won the battle against the clock with great swiftness. I had to do two things to be able to send the secret information on the uprising that I had gathered, thanks to my contacts with parliamentarians and politicians. Before the order was issued that would close the banks I had to draw out the marks that I needed to be able to wire several thousand words to the office of *La Nación* in Paris, for I didn't have the funds to send that many words by cable directly to Buenos Aires. And I had to get to the central post office to send my story before the censorship was initiated. Both tasks were accomplished, and a half hour later both would have been impossible. A great coup for *La Nación*. Jorge Mitre was appreciative and he appointed me correspondent for *La Nación* in Central Europe.

Two years later luck again gave me a resounding success. It was at the Genoa Conference, the first world meeting which Communist Russia attended. It was the diplomatic setting for a *coup de théâtre* that overnight changed the international policy of the great powers, the Treaty of Rapallo. This treaty reconciled Russians and Germans, and its shadow is still felt today each time that the bonds are strengthened between Moscow and Bonn.

Through my good friend Walther Rathenau, the German minister of foreign affairs (later to be assassinated by the precursors of Hitler), I obtained before any other correspondent the details of the famous treaty, and *La Nación* was the first newspaper to publish these in the entire world. It was quoted by the great newspapers everywhere. That earned me the confidence of Jorge Mitre and it sustained me, despite the pressure from conservative directors of the paper and rightist elements in Buenos Aires, until the proclamation of the Spanish Republic, when I was named Spanish ambassador to Mexico.

It was the beginning of the Nazi movement and I had covered for *La Nación* the Munich trial, where the chief persons accused were General Ludendorff, the most famous military leader of the war, then bent on preparing a political comeback, and Adolf Hitler. I don't know what kind of intuition led me to concentrate my attention on Hitler, while the imposing general and his statements got the attention of all the other reporters. I made an attack on Hitler, calling his agitation the prolongation of the Kapp *Putsch*. Ten years before he rose to power I announced that his demagoguery would sweep to death millions of Germans, although at the time there were very few who had even heard his name. Without any vanity for having foreseen it all, I do want to have it on record that already in the early twenties I was informing my newspaper, *La Nación de Buenos Aires*, about the importance of the Nazi movement, and about the revival of German militarism. I had frequent discussions about Hitler with my colleagues, other foreign correspondents in Berlin. Most of them couldn't understand why I should devote so much space to him in my articles. They found Hitler absurd, ludicrous, and without any political future.

Nazi agents in Buenos Aires made known to the services of the movement in Germany that my cablegrams were attracting much attention in Argentina and other Latin American countries and that I was an enemy who ought to be taught a lesson. German nationalists were also extraordinarily irritated that I should be aware of the violations of the Treaty of Versailles and of much of what was being plotted around General Hans von Seeckt, whose silhouette, with his monocle and his slenderness, which was rare among soldiers of his country, attracted attention in diplomatic

Author as an editor of *The Nation*

gatherings. Quite secretly he was laying the foundations for the new German army.

For these reasons the Nazis decided to give me a warning. My *Nación* office was in a basement room and therefore easy of access. I had had the room furnished nicely under the supervision of the painter Klossovski. It was near Potsdam Square. One morning I found it in complete disorder. There were papers and books on the floor, the typewriter was broken and a chair smashed. On top of my desk was a copy of a speech by Hitler.

The series of cables about the newborn Nationalist Socialist movement were the object of a violent attack by a German newspaper published in Buenos Aires and in this way the cabled stories came to the notice of Hitler's followers, who assaulted my office and who, if I had been there, might have smashed me as thoroughly as they smashed my files.

Another kind of pressure was put on Jorge Mitre to dismiss me from my post when, after four years of service in Berlin, I was assigned to Madrid. Because of the size and the economic influence of the Spanish colony in Buenos Aires, the Madrid desk was one of the most important. In 1924, when I got the assignment, Spain was governed by General Primo de Rivera. His dictatorship was benevolent in comparison with that of Franco. But there was strict censorship of the press. To get around this censorship I set up a border service. Someone in San Sebastián with whom I was in touch by code would cross over into France and telephone the news to our Paris office. In this way *La Nación* was kept very well informed.

The government of Primo de Rivera was very resentful of my actions and was waiting for me to make some open move in order to arrest me and close my office. A correspondent of *La Nación* in jail was not an attractive prospect for the directors of the newspaper, and, in addition, they were afraid that the big Spanish firms in Buenos Aires would cut or stop their advertising. Jorge Mitre firmly resisted these pressures, and he kept me in Madrid despite many demands that I be transferred to Moscow.

In other circumstances the post of Moscow correspondent would have attracted me. But in Madrid I was in an exceptionally good position to follow the course of the dictatorship, and I continued to do so until the fall of Primo de Rivera. Two years later, Alfonso XIII himself fell. He had committed the fatal error of entrusting the governing of Spain to Primo de Rivera and then of not knowing how to get rid of him.

If I was always grateful to Jorge Mitre for keeping me in my various posts, I was even more grateful that he never suppressed a single line of what I sent to the paper.

From Freda Kirchwey I learned a lot about American journalism and the liberal movement in the United States. Years of work with her made one appreciate her talents and her strength of character. To begin with, she wrote extraordinarily well. She could have been a novelist or any other kind of writer; she loved journalism. Fortunately Freda Kirchwey is still living and if I speak of her in the past tense it is because I knew her most closely when she was publisher and editor of *The Nation*.

Freda had a fluent and graceful style but, when she wanted to, she could be devastating to a malicious opponent. She wrote brilliantly and edited copy with great ease. A plodding report, written by someone who had something to say but didn't know how to say it, would emerge from her hands entirely transfigured but without any change whatever in the author's essential thoughts.

When World War II broke out, Freda gave to *The Nation*, which had a tradition of neutrality, a tone of belligerent anti-fascism. She thereby lost some of her subscribers, but she never let herself be intimidated by the journal's financial difficulties. She was used to coping with them. For her, *The Nation* was a political journal and she thought it absurd for it to try to follow the major newspapers in their obsession over circulation and profits. *The Nation* was not a business but a cause. And she was a true fighter.

Some of the foreign correspondents who saw her for the first time could not imagine that within a person so beautiful and so feminine there could be such strength of character. Freda Kirchwey was occasionally mistaken on a point, but no position she took was ever influenced by any kind of opportunism. She was a woman of principles, conscious, despite her modesty, that destiny had assigned her a lofty mission to fulfill.

In the second year of the war she entrusted to me the editing of a new department, "The Political War," which soon came to be very controversial and which provoked a certain undeniable interest. It answered the need to make it clear that the war was fundamentally a war against fascism, or at least that it ought to be such a war if we were to avoid the danger that the defeat of Hitler would be followed by some form of reactionary totalitarianism under another name. Churchill, despite his vigorous leadership, his brilliant insight into the character of Hitler, and the promptness with which he held out his hand to Stalin on the very day that German troops invaded Russia, was basically conservative and anti-Communist. There was therefore danger, at the end of hostilities, of a shift in alliances, the allies of yesterday becoming the enemies of tomorrow. And that is exactly what happened.

Some of the articles that appeared in "The Political War," already by the early forties, had anticipated the change that was to come. The turnabout was in some cases brutal and total. Once the spectacular Nuremberg trials were over, Nazi survivors who had been Hitler's diplomats and judges reoccupied high posts. It took Japan longer to recapture the smiles of her former enemies. But she ended by becoming one of the keys to American policy in Asia. After a few sessions in the

Assembly of the United Nations in which Franco Spain, because of its Nazi origins and its fascist conduct, was declared unworthy of membership in the international organization, the sentence was gradually softened to prepare the way so that Franco could be jubilantly admitted to the family of the "free world."

I fought hard against all that in *The Nation*. Freda Kirchwey had in Lillie Shultz an exceptionally capable and efficient associate who tried to make of *The Nation* associates a gathering together of the liberal forces in the country. We three, Freda Kirchwey, Lillie Shultz, and I, were in San Francisco, with Izzy Stone, when the United Nations was created, and we worked through *The Nation* to prevent the United Nations from going down the same road which had led to the undoing of the League of Nations.

With materials gathered by Lillie Shultz that were a devastating exposure of the Franco dictatorship, the Polish Ambassador Oscar Lange, seconded by Gromyko and Manuilski and by Australia's Foreign Affairs Minister Evatt, easily persuaded the majority of the United Nations delegates, including the United States delegation, that Franco Spain should be declared "outside the law" by the international organization. During one of the debates, Léon Jouhaux, the famous French Syndicalist leader, delivered a denunciation of Franco that shook the entire auditorium.

Through *The Nation*, I came to know well what a liberal American stood for. There were formidable liberals like Harold Ickes, Roosevelt's secretary of the interior, on whom I called each time I went to Washington, while Freda Kirchwey had meetings with Archibald MacLeish, the poet and Librarian of Congress. *The Nation*, under Freda Kirchwey, returned blow for blow and kept its reactionary critics at bay. While she was in charge, *The Nation* was an instrument of militant liberalism. It enjoyed the support of that small group of labor leaders who were not content to limit themselves to working for better salaries and greater comforts for the workers but instead fought for civil rights and against any form of McCarthyism.

One of the campaigns of *The Nation* that won it a good deal of sympathy was in defense of United Nations officials who were victims of the Cold War and who had not been sufficiently supported by Dag Hammarskjöld, then Secretary General of the United Nations, so greatly glorified after his tragic death.

Lillie Shultz and I were together in Switzerland on the day when Freda Kirchwey, because of financial difficulties and after years of struggle, finally lost the fight for *The Nation*. It was a sad day for Lillie and for me. We knew that, no matter how competently it might be managed in the future, it would never be the same *Nation*. I am moved by the loyalty with which its former readers remember it. Each time they meet me they speak fondly of a journal that symbolized the best progressive spirit in the American people.

For J. W. Gitt of the *Gazette and Daily* of York, Pennsylvania, I had the highest personal esteem. I was flattered to be a kind of roving correspondent for an independent and progressive newspaper for which Mr. Gitt, already in his eighties, continued for many years to write editorials of notable importance and aggressiveness. Joseph Barnes, who had been an excellent journalist before becoming one of the senior editors of Simon and Schuster, once told me that he considered the *Gazette and Daily* one of the best newspapers in the United States.

As his main assistant in the York office Gitt had James Higgins, who came to him from the labor movement and who later distinguished himself in the campaign against the War in Vietnam and in defense of the Cuban Revolution. As Jim had gone to Havana to write a book about Cuba, the crisis that led to the sale of the paper found Mr. Gitt without Jim's help.

The *Gazette and Daily* was losing money. The union asked for an increase in wages. To the union it was of slight importance that a progressive newspaper defending the cause of the workers should disappear. When I was with *The Nation*, which was also going through difficult economic times, I had a private discussion with the union representative, whom Freda Kirchwey was trying to convince that if the union forced its demands the paper might fail. I advanced as an argument the progressive character of *The Nation*. "Don't talk politics, mister," he cut in. "As far as I'm concerned *The Nation* is just like the *Daily News*. What I want is more money for the staff. Nothing else matters."

I can well understand that, in a moment of irritation, Mr. Gitt should sell the paper. He told someone that he had received only one letter of sympathy. That is hard to believe. I myself thought at once of going to York to reassure him of all my friendship. I couldn't go. But the memory of the *Gazette and Daily* and of its uncompromising editor remains vivid and warm within me.

Another great editor to whom I feel deeply obliged for having increased even more my passion for journalism is Charles Prestwick Scott of the *Manchester Guardian*. When I went from Madrid to Manchester to see him, he was already advanced in years but he bicycled every day from his home to his office. C. P. Scott told me all the difficulties that he had had to overcome to maintain the independence of the *Guardian*. Like Freda Kirchwey, he insisted that one cannot be half independent. He had resisted the assaults of the English chauvinists during the Boer War when he supported the struggle for freedom in South Africa against British domination. But he would have preferred to see the failure of the newspaper, which was his life, rather than yield on a matter of principle.

With Kingsley Martin, who worked on the *Guardian* before becoming the editor of the *New Statesman and Nation*, I talked many times about C. P. Scott. He maintained that it was absurd for a journal of ideas to try to compete with a journal based on wide circulation, but that if it could keep itself going its influence was much greater.

For five years I was the Madrid correspondent for the *Manchester Guardian*. And I had the great satisfaction of sending them on 14 April, 1931, a really inside story on the proclamation of the Spanish Republic, the very day it was announced. It really couldn't have been more inside, because (although unofficially, to be able to preserve my freedom of movement) I was very close to the Revolutionary Committee that became the first government of the republic.

Speaking of journalism, I want to pay homage to a great American journalist, the late Edgar Snow, with whom I shared a friendship for and an interest in China; and to Izzy Stone, an excellent reporter, with whom I worked on *The Nation*; and to journalists of courage like Joseph Kraft, Tom Wicker, and Anthony Lewis, who in the *New York Times* have written about the War in Vietnam with a frankness and independence that are a great service toward the formation of an American conscience.

EIGHT

Geneva

When this book appears, if Joseph Paul-Boncour is still alive he may have achieved the distinction of being a centenarian. He was premier of France between the two wars. I am bound to him by an old friendship forged during the Spanish War. I last saw him at the home of Geneviève Tabouis, that tireless journalist, another of those faithful to the cause of the Spanish people. At her house, in addition to admirable food, one always finds interesting people, ambassadors, writers, politicians. In defiance of all his doctor's orders, Paul-Boncour presided lengthily and heartily at a well-decorated and well-served table. Madame Tabouis devises very ingenious table settings: she has a variety of statuettes with which she can make many settings, sometimes a classic Parisian scene, sometimes an important international event.

Paul-Boncour was extraordinarily alert for a man of his age. He would ask me how things were going in Spain and he would explain the reasons why he, a Socialist, had been on the side of General de Gaulle. His vision of the future of the world was exceptionally just and lucid. And that is why Paul-Boncour, as opposed to other French Socialist leaders, supported de Gaulle and his policy of assuring the national independence of France, of placing her apart from the maneuvers of the two superstates, the United States and the Soviet Union. De Gaulle's objective was a strong France within a strong Europe.

With Paul-Boncour I had lived through an especially interesting time related to World War II. It was in 1938. He was with the French delegation to Geneva and I was representing Spain on the Security Council of the League of Nations. The Czech crisis was going through its most crucial stage. One night, walking along the shore of Lake Geneva, we talked at length about what could be done to stem the tide of capitulation in the Western governments, a tide that would lead a few days later to the catastrophic Munich Pact, which was Hitler's greatest diplomatic victory

115

and which made World War II inevitable. We agreed that there was still a possibility of stopping the policy of successive concessions to the Axis Powers if Prague could be helped to hold firm. That could happen only if the Czechs felt themselves firmly supported by the Russians.

We returned to the Hotel des Berges, where there was a diplomatic reception and where I knew I would find Litvinov, the Soviet foreign minister, with whom I could talk with a frankness rare in the case of a high-ranking Russian official. I asked Litvinov whether, in case Prague resisted the double pressure of Hitler and Chamberlain, even at the risk of taking up arms, the Czechs could count on Russian military assistance. "Unquestionably," was his reply. "Even if France wavers?" I asked. "We would act independently of what the French do, although it is to be hoped that France will fulfill her obligations to Czechoslovakia," Litvinov repeated, and there our conversation ended. Before we separated I asked his permission to tell Paul-Boncour what he had just told me and he gave me permission. It was very important that the French should know the feeling of the Russians, not only through the official Kremlin announcements but by means of an explanation as personal and intimate as this one.

Paul-Boncour and I left the diplomatic reception and we went to his room, where I told him what Litvinov had just told me. For him this constituted a very valid argument for pressure on the French government, although with Edouard Daladier as prime minister, intelligent but no longer the fighter that he was years before, and with Georges Bonnet as minister of foreign affairs, for whom Munich would be not a disastrous but a desired capitulation, the possibilities of success in any recommendation of firmness were very limited.

At any rate, and although it was a fleeting hope that lasted only a few days, the horizon was not entirely closed to our eyes at that moment. Paul-Boncour was very skillful in military matters. In case the Czechs resisted and France finally entered the war on their side, he saw a great opportunity for the Spaniards to cooperate with the French in Africa, thereby creating an impossible situation for Hitler and Franco. We spent a couple of hours talking it all over, and the next day I tried to persuade him that the only course to follow in the face of fascism was the course that we had chosen in Spain: to fight.

The responsibility of the French government for making Munich possible instead of opposing firmly the absurd improvisations of Chamberlain on "Peace in our time" is enormous. From Georges Bonnet there was nothing else to be expected. But Daladier knew perfectly well that Munich was a fraud.

From then on the fate of peace and the fate of Litvinov were also sealed. The most brilliant diplomat produced by the Russian Government would stay on at his post a few months more, but his policy of creating a vast international front to block fascism would be replaced by an accept-

Del Vayo addressing the League of Nations
assembly, Geneva, 1936

ance of the fact that the Western democracies were incorrigible in their fear and in their toadying to Hitler. This acceptance led to the signing of the German-Soviet Pact.

Of the personalities of my days in the League of Nations in Geneva, personalities whom I interviewed and of whose activities and conversations I have a very fresh memory, I shall mention, apart from Litvinov, and Paul-Boncour, Herriot, Politis, Titulescu, Ramsay MacDonald, and Aristide Briand.

On his first visit to Geneva, Briand, who later became a great defender of the League, found it lacking in interest and vigor. To begin with, he didn't like the city, which was too Calvinist for his tastes. Then, he was irritated by the fact that the atmosphere of the League and its favorite language were both English. Briand was a fabulous orator and he had the feeling that his French was not going to be sufficiently appreciated by that Anglo-Saxon audience.

His only diversion was to take evening walks along the shore of the lake. He soon became a familiar figure to the Geneva public. Dressed like a Bohemian, with a cigarette unfailingly dangling in French style from a corner of his lip, he would stop his walk to launch a lengthy oration at anyone lucky enough to be with him, for he was a delightful conversationalist. The famous definition of Philippe Berthelot: "The difference between Poincaré and Briand? Poincaré knows everything and understands nothing; Briand knows nothing and understands everything," defined very aptly the apostle of peace.

When Briand, in 1925, succeeded Herriot as the chief of the French diplomatic corps, he held a higher opinion of the League of Nations, as I learned from Alexis Léger, later known in the world of letters as St. John Perse but at that time a high official in the Quai d'Orsay. In those days, differing in this from Poincaré, Briand was deeply interested in reaching an understanding with Germany that would strengthen an accord that originated with the Rapallo Pact. It was the prologue to the signing of the Locarno Treaty.

This treaty, the first of its kind signed by the Germans since the Versailles Conference, seemed to guarantee for a long time that France would have a frontier on the Rhine. Later, Hitler undertook to destroy that illusion. The treaty was celebrated by a great night parade in Locarno. Briand did not attend it, not because he did not share in the general rejoicing but because he always went to bed early and preferred to hear the fireworks from his bed.

I was in Geneva in 1926 when Briand received Germany into the League of Nations with one of his most brilliant speeches. It was followed by another good speech by Stresemann. The German spokesman told Briand confidentially that, if he had not sounded as enthusiastically pacifistic as Briand would have liked, it was because he had to keep in

Aristide Briand

mind his nationalistic compatriots, especially Hindenburg. Briand soon became convinced that the understanding between France and Germany was more a theme for oratory than a fact with any real basis.

I was in Madrid in the spring of 1929 when the League of Nations, wishing to give special welcome to the return of Spain to the League, which it had left out of wounded pride over its loss of a seat on the Security Council, decided to hold its meeting in Madrid. In honor of the League, the Spanish dictator, General Primo de Rivera, always a good Andalusian, organized a great bullfight. Briand, one of the guests of honor, who knew nothing whatever about bullfighting, found the whole spectacle senseless. He said: "If they would take all the bullfighters out of the ring and let me go in alone, I would make peace with the bull." Briand's last effort to give new life to the League of Nations was his proposal for a European Federation. It was the first call for a constitution of the United States of Europe.

Briand got only some promises and a shrewd warning from Beneš not to trust the Germans too much. Stresemann, one of the few Germans who might have understood him, died a few weeks later. Meanwhile, Briand's health got worse. Already in weakened health, he made the unfortunate decision, in the spring of 1931, to declare himself a candidate for the presidency of the Republic, though at first he had sensibly resisted invitations to do so. The election was in Versailles. But his enemies in Paris, with Tardieu at their head, intrigued against him, as they had intrigued years before against Clemenceau, the man who had won the war. Briand was defeated. All he had left was Geneva. There he presided over the commission that was working on his proposal for a European Federation.

In March 1932 Briand died, and one of the noblest figures of the League of Nations disappeared from the international scene. It was the end of the period of ambitious attempts to place the cause of peace on a firm base and the beginning of the massive attacks against the League by the dictators.

Yet Titulescu and Politis were still there and they had a clear vision of what was being planned. But they were isolated among a legion of capitulators and even though they received the backing of Litvinov when Russia was at last admitted to the League of Nations, it was too late. In the French camp there were only Briand's worthy successor, Barthou, and naturally Paul-Boncour. In the English camp, Ramsay MacDonald, sabotaged with all his power the Disarmament Conference, which in his eyes was inconceivable without Germany. MacDonald was a pro-German Socialist who set the example of compromise for Chamberlain.

In 1971, almost forty years later, the day after Chancellor Willy Brandt returned from his meeting with Brezhnev in the Crimea, I was dining in

Paris with some French officials who must be nameless because they are still officials. There was general consternation around the table. "Abominable!" one of them said. "With this coup of Brandt," said another of the diners, "Germany, Western Germany, has just become the leader of the Common Market." Another said: "Of the Common Market and of all Europe." And a little later, closing a discussion on the problem of Germany, one of the most famous of those present said jokingly: "If tomorrow our French Communists tried to rebel they would be squashed by the Germans on orders from Moscow."

A few days before the announced visit of the top Soviet official to France, the cordiality of the German-Soviet encounter had fallen on Paris like a bomb. Brandt had stolen a march on the French and had brilliantly and swiftly taken advantage of the new desire of the Russians to foster peaceful coexistence, Moscow style, throughout Europe. It would be Germany that would benefit most from the European federation that the Soviets were finally "resigned" to see form in 1973.

The German chancellor was in high spirits as he gave all kinds of details about his welcome in the Crimea. "Mr. Brezhnev's cordiality surprised me. I did not expect the first secretary of the Soviet party to come out to the airport to welcome me. And he invited me to have dinner with him." And Brandt described the meal with obvious pleasure: "Melon, roast suckling pig, blinis of meat and preserves, all Russian specialties. There was vodka and my glass was never empty. At home I scarcely touch alcohol, but there I had to keep up with the others." Brandt really kept up. Brezhnev had begun by saying to him: "Call me 'Godospin' Brezhnev and this will allow me to call you 'Herr' Brandt." The German reporters who were with the chancellor couldn't believe their eyes when they saw a Brezhnev who was all smiles. Brezhnev and Brandt swam together and walked together, and in two days of intimate comradeship they wove the tapestry of a Europe in which the two main figures were going to be the Soviet Union and Germany.

"Germany, period," clarified one of our dinner companions. "Because one of these days the two Germanies will unite and we, the French and the other Europeans will be left facing a strong, united Germany, as in 1914, as in 1939, but with the difference that this time the Germans will have the Russians not as enemies but as allies. This is one result of the Russian obsession about China, which they see constantly increasing in importance as a world power."

I exaggerate nothing in describing the atmosphere of that dinner, dominated by fear of a Germany that, having once been defeated largely by Russian power, was emerging again, now thanks to Russian support, as the first power of Western Europe. The panic of those Frenchmen faced with a Germany in control of Europe left a deep impression on me.

121

In the days just before Munich I conferred with many statesmen who gave me much confidential information on the reasons that moved this or that diplomat to yield one position after another in the face of Hitler's blackmail. As a person I was of secondary importance. But the cause that I represented was the cause of the Spanish people, the only people to stand up and fight almost alone against the combined forces of international fascism. This cause placed me in a privileged position to receive the confidences of those who were trying to inject some vitality into the resistance of the democracies.

Munich was not only a betrayal to the peoples who wanted to see fascism forced to retreat. It was at the same time an incalculable stupidity. Those who worked for Hitler in Geneva occasionally dropped a word or a phrase that let us conclude that, if the Western democracies had shown any firmness, Hitler would have quickly yielded ground.

To say "Peace for a generation" was either to ignore the nature of fascism or to resign oneself to a world dominated by the Nazis. I predicted that war would soon come. And within a year the Second World War exploded. For us Spaniards, already at war with fascism, there was nothing to do but wait to see our front become part of an extensive anti-Nazi front that finally included the Soviet Union and the United States. We, the legitimate government of Spain, had not intrigued to bring about this worldwide conflagration in order to escape from our difficulties. On the contrary, we had done everything in our power to avoid the war. We had encouraged the other countries to withstand the Fascist maneuver of advancing by means of threats: "You either yield to our demands or there will be war!"

Once Munich made a Second World War inevitable, the Spanish line of conduct was clear: to continue resisting until war broke out. It was the basis of our policy, "To resist is to win," and it led us to continue the fight in the central zone even after Catalonia was lost. The fight ended in Spain through the treason of General Casado, who was in command of the Madrid front. This was the second military coup against the legitimate Republican Government; it occurred in March 1939. Madrid fell six months before the start of the Second World War.

After the Munich Agreement had been signed, I returned to Spain to talk with a different kind of people. Instead of the Geneva diplomats, they were the soldiers of the Republican Army. They had already been fighting for over two years and they had amazed the world with feats like the battle of the Ebro and the defense of Madrid. I explained to the soldiers how, in the future, we would have to go on fighting despite the cowardice and the lack of vision of the Western governments, and with more determination than ever. Those magnificent Spaniards had a sense of history that was far superior to that of the governments of Paris and London. Their determination to fight, if it had been matched in other countries equally threatened by Hitler, would have spared the world the millions and millions of dead in World War II.

In the months that preceded the outbreak of the war, Geneva was for me a school of political education. I learned to recognize all the empty arrogance that was hidden behind the air of superiority of men who considered themselves great statesmen and diplomats but who were incapable of seeing that we were striding toward disaster. I could exchange impressions with Edouard Herriot, with whom it was always a pleasure to talk, and with Anthony Eden, who understood the war in Spain, even though in his character there was more finesse than belligerence. But I clashed with Colonel Beck of Poland and with Lord Halifax. Halifax was very pretentious and he hated me from the day that I told him that in Spain we would die fighting and that it was useless for him to advise us to follow the example of Beneš. I told him: "I am very fond of Beneš. But he is weak and you take advantage of him." Halifax was returning to Geneva that day after a meeting with Mussolini and he tried to convince me that our policy of resistance in Spain was madness. I answered him: "Madness, perhaps, but not betrayal. On the day that England sees herself involved in the war as a result of Chamberlain's policy, and your policy, you will possibly begin to understand a little about our fight in Spain against the advance of international fascism."

Edouard Herriot told me one day in Geneva: "What you Spaniards must do is demand respect for international law, which is on the side of the Spanish people." It was well-intentioned advice. But I answered: "An appeal to international law is not enough. Hitler and Mussolini laugh at international law. What we must all say to Hitler is: 'Not one more step, or it's war!' Fascism is the product of a policy of force. Hitler understands only a language of force."

In view of the enormity of the Spanish tragedy, no personal vanity is permissible. But when, thirty-four years after my Geneva activities, I hear friends from those times comment generously upon what I then did, I have to admit that not I but the heroic Spain of the Spanish War does deserve such recognition even now when the Spanish people continue to fight for their freedom. "The Spanish War opened a cycle that will have to be closed one day with the victory of what you represent." This was said to me by Nehru in New Delhi in 1957.

NINE

The Gypsies of Spain

In Geneva today one hears more Spanish spoken than French. Although the Swiss authorities, responding to nationalist pressure, are trying to protect the country from the invasion of foreign labor, the hotels and the construction and other industries need workers, and the Spanish are welcome. It's the same all over Switzerland. Between Saanen and Gstaad, two neighboring towns, the second one famous for its winter sports, with a combined population of hardly more than two thousand, there were about two hundred Spaniards, men and women, working last summer. They earn more than they do in Spain, and some of them realize that, in contrast to Spain, Switzerland is a free country, with no Burgos trials. Let the reader note the plural. Because in addition to the first, sensational trial late in 1970, which shook the conscience of the world, in the summer of 1971 there were three trials in a row, also in Burgos, also with Basques being persecuted and condemned, one of whom was a young girl, sentenced to twenty-one years in jail. On July 25 of that year, in Santiago de Compostela, General Franco declared: "It is easier to wage war with God as an ally." This was Franco's answer to Paul VI, whom Franco's intimates called the anti-God Pope.

I had seen all kinds of Spaniards attracted to Geneva by the strength of the Swiss franc. But it was only on my last trip that I saw three gypsy women who had come from Andalusia to read the palms of the people who sat on the terrace of Paquis Street. One of them was very young and very beautiful. The veteran of the group was eagerly collecting the coins of a public entertained by the group's appearance. The Swiss girls would stop in the street and hold out their hands, laughing but clearly interested in what the gypsies were telling them.

For me they predicted three things. First, a long life. Well, that I already had. But a still longer life. Second, success in my work, an encouragement very much needed when one is in the midst of writing a new book. And, third, apparently contradicting the second, no money. Of the three, this last was a fairly safe prediction.

The gypsies are an inseparable part of the charm of the South of Spain, and they have contributed enormously to the arts of dancing and bull-fighting. They are the enchanting protagonists of some of the best works in Spanish literature, from *La Gitanilla* [*The Gypsy Girl*] of Cervantes to the poems of Federico García Lorca. About the origin of the gypsies there have been various theories through the centuries, but the dominant one is that they came from India. Their presence was especially marked in the Middle Ages and the Renaissance. But as far back as Byzantine

Spanish gypsy women

times we have chronicles attesting to their unrivaled skill in divination. The classic fortune telling, the art of reading the calendar of death and the secrets of love, has deep roots in antiquity.

Gypsies or Bohemians, the latter term introduced into England by Thackeray in *Vanity Fair*, are the source of many legends, some of them of Russian origin, and Russian literature is filled with gypsies and with gypsy music enlivening the night clubs and cabarets that weathered the changes in regime.

The gypsy vocabulary is proof of the universality of their presence. The French expert François de Vaux de Foletier maintains that it was in Greece that the gypsies enriched their means of expression most abundantly. They have taken from the Greeks the words for the numbers seven, eight and nine, thirty, and forty, and they have used them to mean "week," "Sunday," "Friday," and "sky."

In their fondness for the wandering life, they travel through all the lands that separate the East from the West. They adopt the customs of these countries but without ever losing their own identity. At the height of the ascendancy of the Roman aristocracy and the lords of Venice, the gypsy chiefs, not to be outdone, gave themselves the titles of princes and dukes. In the middle of the fifteenth century, "Duke" André invaded Italy at the head of a numerous contingent of gypsies and installed himself in a royal residence. The gypsies made contact with the pope and they believe even to this day that they enjoy his special blessing.

In Andalusia, in the same period, they were received with all honors. They ate at the lord's table and showed their gratitude by entertaining their hosts with dances and by introducing an exotic and original note into their fifteenth-century austerity. Their customs were not appreciated by everyone. "Unstable vagabonds, with an excessively broad sense of the concept of private property" can be read in some chronicles of the time that make their contribution to the treasury of the historical gypsy. In 1499 the Pragmatic Sanction at Medina del Campo, promulgated by Ferdinand and Isabella, gave the gypsies two choices, to abandon their wandering ways or to leave Spain within sixty days.

Other countries followed the Spanish determination to defend law and order against a people who gave the impression of being the anarchists of all epochs. But Russia was exceptionally tolerant. The imperial authorities never interfered with gypsy customs. Elsewhere, however, these precursors of the hippies, who flaunted their long hair and beards in the face of a society very careful of its manners, when they were judged intolerable, were punished by jail sentences or, more frequently, by being shaved and shorn.

The music and the dances of the gypsies changed according to the countries where they settled. And settling with them was always a relative concept. Travelers in the sixteenth century who visited Hungary spoke of gypsy dances as showing an oriental influence which they got from the Moslem invaders whom the Hungarians were so tenaciously opposing.

In Russia, under Catherine the Great, gypsy musicians and dancers were a feature of the gay parties organized by the Orlovs and other lovers of the empress. The gypsy women were given sumptuous dresses and the men got the best obtainable musical instruments. One of the classic travelers to Russia in the first half of the nineteenth century, the Marquis de Custine, still quoted to this day, enjoyed describing the "wild and passionate song" of the gypsies that enlivened Moscow nights spent among the artists and beauties of his time.

Cervantes' Preciosa, and the dancers that Molière, in *Le Malade imaginaire*, parades across the stage to counteract the hypochondria of his hero, had in real life a model whose attractiveness was extolled by the chroniclers of the seventeenth century. She was the renowned Léance, sung by poets and often painted, who conquered Paris when she was sixteen, and who refused to be imprisoned either in the Palace of the Condés or in the convent where the mother abbess tried to confine her under the pretext of protecting her virtue.

Dancers, singers, quack healers, and soothsayers — they all go together. Fortune-telling, — the gypsy women were saying nice things that afternoon in Geneva to the Swiss girls, who were still capable of blushing (a rare thing these days) — is a very old custom. It inspired some of the famous vignettes of the Renaissance. A gypsy foretold good luck to the future King George IV. Fortune-telling prospered in imperial Spain until it reached its apogee, when the priests who clustered around the Emperor Charles V condemned it as one more manifestation of heresy.

Among the gypsies there have been educated men who have defended fortune-telling as a genuine science and not just a device to get money out of people. I gave five Swiss francs recently to a gypsy in Geneva and asked her to sit down at my table. This is an invitation that they generally reject, for they are very superstitious and they reduce any interchange of words with a stranger strictly to fortune-telling business. But she did sit down and argued with me in defense of her art. She knew enough French to be able to describe what was in store for her Swiss consultants. And she told how in Paris a Belline or a Madame Frédérika made fortunes as experts in handwriting analysis, readers of ink spots, practitioners of palmistry, astrology, tarot- and Egyptian-card reading. There are specialists in advice about the *tiercé*, on which the humblest Frenchman spends all his pocket money every Sunday and Thursday, trying to guess three horses that enter in "order" or "disorder," that is to say in a row or alternating. *Tiercé* is the current passion in France. "Well, all that," my gypsy told me, "the professional French fortune-tellers have learned from us. Only *they* charge a hundred and fifty new francs for a consultation and *we* charge only a couple of francs."

From time immemorial the gypsies have claimed to possess the power of healing. In their travels about the world they have sold amulets capable of restoring health, or the "good stone," or simply salves that would as surely restore happiness to the lovelorn as limberness to a limb stiffened by arthritis.

Many gypsies had a certain measure of knowledge of ancient medicine based on the use of miraculous herbs. They used them to cure people as well as horses. Gypsies have always been drawn to horses and to horse trading. They bought the horses, or got hold of them in some more direct way, and then they resold them. They had the reputation of being able, through the use of certain herbs, to transform an old nag that could scarcely move into a horse impressive to look at, and to watch as it galloped by. Donkeys they made incredibly resistant to fatigue by putting mercury in their ears.

François de Vaux de Foletier has brought to the history of the gypsies a very detailed documentation about their customs. Their originality has always attracted artists. They are central figures in the Tapestry of Tournai, in pictures of Hieronymus Bosch, and very frequently in Spanish painting. Since for a long time they were called Egyptians, they appear in scenes that have Biblical Egypt as a background. Later on, in the eighteenth century, they change their costumes, adapting them to those of the countries that make up their interminable itinerary. But the taste for lively colors, especially red and green, never leaves them. Until the eighteenth century the women wore their hair confined in a turban and spent all the money they earned buying bracelets and necklaces. Sobriety is not their most distinctive trait.

The gypsies, especially the women, have had the distinction of seeing themselves for many years imitated by the upper classes. It was very fashionable for the ladies of the British Court in the middle of the sixteenth century to adopt for masquerades the "Egyptian" style of dress. The theater of that time and of the following centuries found in gypsy motifs a constant source of inspiration for choirs and masquerades.

Gypsy cuisine is based on chicken, goose, and turkey. The hedgehog was for a long time the favorite food of the wandering gypsies. Among the vegetables, onions and green beans were preferred. They drink anything they can get their hands on. And they want lots of chewing tobacco. The women smoke it and chew it.

Their life is a group life. They like to recruit followers. And to accomplish this, wherever they pass by they leave a sign: a bough bent in a way known to them all, scattered leaves, inscriptions on walls, every conceivable form of recruiting. And gypsies were by no means always rejected. In the South of France, under Louis XIII, local authorities were instructed to give shelter to gypsies.

A characteristic trait of the gypsies is the strength of the family tie. The family is never separated. Women and children follow the husband or the father, follow them sometimes to jail and join ranks with them in the face of any and all accusations that they have broken the law. It is a loyalty that has been praised in some of the masterworks of Spanish literature, in "The Sand Pit of Segovia" of Lope de Vega among others. Preciosa, Cervantes' heroine, says of virginity: "It is a flower that must never be sullied, even in the imagination." Many foreign travelers to Spain observe that, despite their indigence (and this was written at the beginning of the nineteenth century), despite their extreme poverty, it was impossible to seduce their women or their daughters, who were frequently "of a beauty that would have brought a high price." Prostitution is almost unknown among gypsy women. "There is no sacrifice or privation or danger," wrote Mérimée, the great Hispanophile, "that a gypsy woman will avoid in an effort to help her men." Mothers will go to any extreme to help their children. In Hungary, at the time of Maria Theresa, they fought like lionesses to protect their young from being taken off to places where they could, in fact, have a much better life than the one they were leading and could get a good Hungarian education.

The gypsies of Hungary and Andalusia are different, but they have many characteristics in common. No regime, however strict it is, has been able to make them change completely, either in the past or in the present. They celebrate their great feasts several times a year. The feast of Santo Cretchuno corresponds to our Christmas. Men and women exchange a single embrace and there is drinking and singing. But if a person's heart is not at peace, he withdraws voluntarily from the festivities. New Year's Eve is the moment of pardon. The whole group kneel and bow before the oldest member and beg his pardon for sins committed and, once they have heard the rite of clemency recited, they kiss his hand and hug.

In Russia the feast of Santo Cretchuno is frequently celebrated under the direction of the Orthodox Pope. In his company the Cross is carried to the river or to the lake, the ice is broken, and the Cross is dipped into the water. If anyone has the courage, he gets into the water behind the Cross. Certain feasts are preceded by a fast decreed by the father of the family.

As we have said, the gypsy family is very united. There is strict observation of the regulations about birth, baptism, marriage, and death. The mother must breast-feed her infant and not stop until the child has lost the taste for the mother's milk. She never leaves her children. She will not even let them be sent to a vacation camp for a few days. The same devotion is given to the sick and the aged. If it is absolutely necessary to send someone in the family to the hospital, it will be done, but only for the absolute minimum length of stay.

The father and the mother are in charge of the selection of the spouse in a marriage. They propose a candidate. If he or she does not find favor with the future bride or groom, the parents propose a second choice, and a third, and so on until the preference of the young person and the authority of the parents have been reconciled. Once the choice has been made, the parents give the newlyweds bread and salt, saying to them: "Neither bread or salt is distasteful to anyone. When people lose their taste for bread and salt, you may separate, but not before." The spouses reply: "Since you make the invocation in the name of bread and salt, if we do not heed your words, may God condemn us for all our lives."

As soon as the bride is married she puts on the woman's veil, which she will wear always as a symbol of her dependence on her husband. The husband is free; he can go anywhere, but he will continue to revere the authority of the head of the family. In the great family of gypsies, each member's possessions are the common wealth of all. If on a given day a gypsy has nothing to eat he sits down at the table of another member of the family. In this way the demons of egotism and avarice are driven away. And the unity of the family is maintained. Gypsies reject the term "tribe." Their ties are voluntarily established, laws of the family to which all must conform. The treatment of illnesses is another example of family solidarity. As we have said, only in extreme cases is a sick person sent to the hospital. The old women know ancient healing practices handed down from parents to children.

Since the gypsies have no country they have no special places of pilgrimage. But in all countries through which they pass they venerate the holy places because they are fundamentally very religious. Since they are good credulous people believing in the supernatural, the miraculous tradition of Lourdes attracts them. In 1957 there was a mass gypsy pilgrimage to Lourdes which was of great publicity value to the promoters of the "city of cures." Gypsies like to go on pilgrimages to Rome and they consider that they have a special privilege to be received in the Vatican, if not by the Pope himself at least by some high dignitary of the Church. Cardinal Tedeschini, whom I knew when he was nuncio in Madrid under Alfonso XIII and who had the reputation of being a gallant Renaissance cardinal, still had happy memories of the gypsies from his visits to Andalusia and he received them very warmly in Rome. They consider that the Holy Father is their own father, but since they are a dispersed people, they do not dare to write to him directly.

Gypsies are proud of their Christian origin. Some claim that the first gypsies were Christianized earlier and more sincerely than the Christians of the West. Among them are a good number of Orthodox and many Roman Catholics. The Spanish gypsies have been saying for generations that they are the favorites of Mary. They have visited many churches dedicated to Mary all the way from Poland to Spain. A medal of Mary and the new moon brought them luck.

In the past the hierarchical insignia was the staff with a silver head (which belonged to the chief of the group) and the silver chain worn around the neck. Their tales and fables are of great variety and of a great poetic richness when they are dealing with the cycles, for example, the cycle of the poor man transformed into a king. Or tales with the theme "He has dethroned the powerful and elevated the humble." There is the tale of the twelve good thieves who have stripped the rich of their ill-gotten money and have distributed it among the neediest. This is perhaps the origin of the legend of the good bandit so popular in Andalusia.

In some cases he became a reality and acquired a certain egalitarian nobility.

Zanko, one of the most famous of gypsy chiefs, bases the fate of the gypsies on the initial curse. "They have abandoned us to our fate. If the leaders of the countries that put on such fancy advanced airs had held out a hand to us, if they had given us a place in which to establish ourselves, our lives would be different. But instead they have set the gendarmes to hunting us down." In Andalusia "gendarmes" means the Civil Guard, that Civil Guard attacked so bitterly by García Lorca, who understood well the gypsy soul. Zanko continues: "Our only leaders are those of the countries through which we travel. We are used to being dispersed. We can bow our heads before misfortune and raise them later. If people will only love us a little all will be well."

Gypsies like to be near the water, for fishing. And near the woods, for hunting. They look back with nostalgia to the time when Princess Victoria, the future Queen of England, showed them special sympathy. In her diary, written when she was a young princess, Victoria speaks of her visits, with her mother, to a family of poor gypsies. One of the gypsies kissed her hand, turned it over, looked at her palm, and predicted that she would win the eternal love of a handsome prince. It was the anticipation of the royal romance of Victoria and Albert.

Even though cursed and dispersed, as Zanko complains, the gypsy women have kept through the centuries their elegant and dignified carriage. In Geneva, when the gypsy girl, grateful because I had acted as an interpreter for her with the Swiss girls who stopped to have their hands read and who gave her only a franc, thanked me, got up, and resumed her walk toward Zurich Street, an admiring Swiss who was seated near my table said: "Look how she walks, like a queen!"

TEN

Litvinov

In the two and a half years that I worked with Maxim Litvinov in the Council of the League of Nations, the equivalent of the Security Council of the United Nations, the great Soviet diplomat was, even at a distance, the most impressive personality in Geneva. He was aware of this but he never took advantage of his intellectual superiority. He was too deeply interested in maintaining a front against Hitler to play the star. Although he was firm in maintaining his positions, he tried not to wound anyone unnecessarily.

This was in public. Lunching alone with me in his hotel room, he exercised his sense of humor on the behavior of our colleagues. He was stocky but not stout. Behind his glasses were wonderfully intelligent and lively eyes. This militant Bolshevik of the heroic years astonished me by the serenity of his opinions.

He knew the British well. He was married to a brilliant Englishwoman whom I never had the pleasure of meeting but about whom he talked to me more than once. He liked Anthony Eden. He considered him weak but well-intentioned. Our French colleague Yvon Delbos he thought an old-fashioned political hack, and the Polish delegate, Colonel Beck, he considered more presumptuous than capable, already won over to the stream of those who supported Hitler rather than a leftish regime.

Litvinov knew that the era of his diplomacy was coming to an end. It would end at the moment when that pro-Hitler stream prevailed over the national interest. "They, the Western members of the Council, cannot be so stupid as not to realize that you are right when you define the war in Spain as the first battle in the Second World War," said Litvinov one day. "But the idea that an army like yours, composed of workers and peasants, could win a war fills them with terror. They know that if the Spanish Republic is crushed by the Fascists no one can avoid a widespread war, but they prefer the reign of Hitler to socialism."

137

Neither Litvinov, the master, nor I on a more modest level, had any illusion in 1938 about the ability of the League of Nations to stop the wave of defeatism that had crashed down on Western politics. For three years the League had been in constant retreat. At the beginning of the Ethiopian crisis in 1935, there was a moment, when the Italian troops began to march, when it seemed as though the League might remember that its principal mission was to oppose aggression and defend peace. But it was only a moment. Sanctions against Italy were decreed. Pierre Laval, predestined for treason, as was clear later in Vichy, was rendering a service to Mussolini by sabotaging the sanctions.

France was entering the era of capitulation. When on March 7, 1936, Hitler occupied the Rhineland, in flagrant violation of the Versailles Treaty and the Locarno Pact, Litvinov pointed out to the French diplomats that, given France's strong legal position as the victim of an unquestionable aggression, if Paris reacted with severe measures she would find strong international support.

Albert Sarraut, the French prime minister, limited himself to making a tough speech and did nothing. Hitler and Mussolini knew that now they could get away with anything.

"If Hitler and Mussolini," said Litvinov to me one day, with his biting smile, "should decide to send their delegates back to the League, Avenol would run to meet them with open arms. Welcome to the aggressors!" Joseph Avenol, a Frenchman, was the secretary general of the League. But even when we realized perfectly well that the League suffered from an incurable anemia that corresponded to the weakness of the Western governments, Litvinov and I took advantage of the Council's rostrum to warn against the danger of a Second World War. As a rostrum the League was useful. Even today, thirty-five years afterwards, I meet people who remember my speeches in Geneva.

Munich, the surrender of England and France before Hitler, placed Litvinov in an almost impossible position to try to prevent the Second World War. Defeatism was coupled with the crudest cynicism. It has frequently been told how Edouard Daladier, the French prime minister, when he was greeted with applause on his return from Munich, turned to his neighbor and said: "Do these imbeciles realize what they are applauding?" But he had been one of those who made Munich possible. Chamberlain, without any sense of reality and at bottom closer in feeling to Hitler and Mussolini than to Beneš of Czechoslovakia and to the Russians who were supporting Beneš, was capable of the stupidity of believing that he had assured peace for a generation. But Daladier didn't believe this and yet he had behaved just like Chamberlain.

Although Litvinov's efforts to persuade the West that Hitler could be stopped received a crushing blow at Munich, the great Soviet diplomat tried in the succeeding months and right up to the end to correct a situation from which the Fascist powers would be the sole beneficiaries.

After Munich the capitulators had set about completing their work. For example: the declaration of friendship signed by Bonnet and Ribbentrop, the French and German ministers of foreign affairs on December 6, 1938; the deterioration in Franco-Soviet relations; Poland's lack of cooperation when the Russians, "logically demanding" — in the words of General Gamelin, the top French military authority — the right to cross

Maxim Litvinov, Anastas Mikoyan, and associates at
the League of Nations, Geneva, 1936

Polish territory if they should have to come to the aid of France or Czechoslovakia.

Against all this Litvinov counterattacked as well as he could. It was all useless: peace for a generation became peace for a few months. Litvinov terminated his brilliant career as a great ambassador. In a gesture of deference to Roosevelt, Stalin sent him to Washington as ambassador. There I saw him again. Not having been able to avoid the war, he was working with his usual determination to assure an Allied victory.

In Geneva, Litvinov had a great reputation. He was a lifelong Communist with deep convictions, but at the same time not at all dogmatic when it was a question of seeking the road to disarmament and peace. As a debater he had no equal around the Council table of the League. When we had lunch together, I found him a fascinating conversationalist, cultivated and understanding. As I listened to him I realized how he naturally equated peace with socialism. In his eyes the basic characteristic of the capitalist state, and especially the imperialist state, was that in international affairs it was seeking objectives almost impossible to achieve without recourse to war. But he conceded that not all capitalist states behaved alike in their expansionist drives. Their grasp of a situation could vary according to the circumstances. And any state, no matter how imperialistic, could become, at a given moment, a pacifist state.

This was the reasoning behind his strategy within the League of Nations and outside the League, as head of the Soviet Delegation. He was a diplomat who gave me the impression that he was acting, even under Stalin, with his own authority and personality. Stalin respected him. When the whole panorama of the international scene changed, as the result of the Munich-style diplomacy of Great Britain and France, and when Litvinov, who represented the East-West collaboration against Hitler, therefore had to resign as minister of foreign affairs, his resignation at the Kremlin occurred not in an atmosphere of persecution but one of esteem and respect. I remember, on one of my trips to Russia after the war, that I expressed a desire to call on him at his home near Moscow and there was no opposition to the planned visit. But he was ill at the time and I had to be content with sending him wishes for his recovery.

I well remember Litvinov's appearance at the side of Nicolae Titulescu, in the great hall of the League of Nations, when Russia was finally admitted to membership. He had followed carefully the course of an international policy which talked constantly in public about peace and conspired behind the scenes against peace. He recalled to me how, while the ministers of foreign affairs proclaimed their devotion to peace, the war (or "defense") ministers worked in the shadows to ruin any policy of reconciliation. He was well acquainted with every delegate to the League of Nations and I enjoyed hearing him describe each one. The struggle against world communism became, in his eyes, a hidden struggle for the acquisition of new zones of influence. Even so, with all its imperfections, he saw in the League of Nations a usable instrument to spread Soviet ideas on possible ways of maintaining the peace and promoting disarmament.

Today, forty-five years after Litvinov's activity in Geneva, in the Disarmament Conference that is now struggling with the same problem, one hears, from time to time, allusions to the clairvoyance and the realism of the eminent head of the Soviet diplomacy of that time. Litvinov did not confine himself to establishing the bases for true disarmament. He introduced a definition of "aggressor" and, going from theory to practice, he incorporated the definition into a series of treaties with the countries of the Petite Entente (Czechoslovakia, Yugoslavia, Rumania) and Afghanistan. That was another action with current consequences, because it is still being discussed in the Commissions of the United Nations. Litvinov's definition of the aggressor was at the time judged by the leading authorities in international law to be a powerful contribution to the prevention of war. It was a practical way of establishing, in a specific case, whether or not there were "aggressive tendencies" in the foreign policy of a given nation.

Litvinov's language, whether he was speaking in Geneva or in Russia, left no doubt as to his eagerness to bring about peace. I was privileged to read the text of a report presented by Litvinov to the Central Executive Committee of the Soviet Party. In the report he said: "The core of our foreign policy was given to us by this brief but expressive formula of Stalin: 'We do not desire an inch of foreign territory, but we will not yield an inch of our own territory.'" And later on: "We have never rejected and we will never reject an international collaboration designed to organize the strengthening of peace. Not being doctrinaire, we shall cooperate with any international group or organization among those that exist or that may come into existence if we have enough information about it to be convinced that it is going to serve the cause of peace."

I witnessed all this and I am probably one of the few surviving witnesses. Another one is Lord Avon, then Anthony Eden. But Eden in his *Memoirs* does not give the complete version of what took place in Geneva in those decisive years that preceded the Second World War. And it is of great historical importance to reestablish the truth, because none of the fundamental problems of that period so abounding in cowardice and hocus-pocus, neither the problem of disarmament nor that of using an international organization (now the United Nations) to cope effectively with aggression, has been solved. Let the reader note that these are not old diplomat's tales but very lively and contemporary tales.

When Litvinov first appeared in Geneva in 1927, the Preparatory Disarmament Commission had spent two years listening to admirals, generals, experts and lawyers, in an interminable tournament of conflicting theses and opinions. The commission was accustomed to all the tones, from the elegant and cynical tone of the one who goes to and returns from Geneva at each announced meeting with the pious smile of one who is in on the secret of the futility of struggling against war to the tormented and tragic tone of Lord Robert Cecil. Litvinov's first speech shook the Chamber. It was a model of irony assessing the work that had been accomplished. He had the authority of being the spokesman of a country that, although described by enemy propaganda as impatient to invade all Europe, had given repeated proofs of moderation in international affairs. In Brest-Litovsk, Lenin had imposed his policy of prudence in the face of the exorbitant demands of the German General Staff, against the advice of Bukharin and Trotsky. In 1922 Russia, despite her suspicion of maneuvers on the part of Germany, signed the Treaty of Rapallo, with a consequent decrease in international tension. Although Chicherin, the Russian foreign minister, had little faith in the League of Nations, as he told me in Genoa, he arranged for his country to be represented at the Naval Conference in Rome in 1924, and it was on this occasion that Russia began to make contacts with the League.

The first part of Litvinov's 1927 speech in Geneva consisted of a shattering criticism of how little had been accomplished up to then and how little was still being accomplished in disarmament. Everyone talked of disarmament and went on arming. But his criticism was immediately followed by a general disarmament plan. His program included "the complete abolition of all armed forces on land, on sea, and in the air."

Whether out of courtesy or conviction, Litvinov's speech earned him these words of acknowledgment from the phlegmatic Dutch president of the commission, Dr. Loudon: "Among the very valuable services that we expect from our new collaborators [the Russians], we can already count on one, which is the very effective service of a sharp criticism that will prevent us from resting on our laurels." Litvinov lived up to the expectation. He became an alarm clock with a dependable sonorousness. In the fifth session of the Preparatory Commission, in March 1928, he presented a Convention Project, on the basis of his original plan, worked out in every detail, in sixty-three articles. He defended his Project with precise words and a tone of passion that at times succeeded in impressing the Assembly.

The various delegates replied, all with approximately the same tone, a defensive one. After a lengthy debate, the committee resolved that it be stated that the majority of the members of the commission judged the Soviet Project to be unacceptable. There was a moment of respite. The delegates welcomed the prospect of returning to the comfort of their academic discussions. But it was only a brief moment of respite. The secretary had scarcely finished reading the resolution and the president putting it to a vote when Litvinov rose and, to general stupefaction, drew from his pocket another disarmament project, just as perfectly elaborated as the first one, but a little more modest in its proposals, looking toward a partial and gradual disarmament. If my memory is correct, it roused no greater enthusiasm among the delegates than had the first project. But Litvinov's patience and ability were repaid when, during the sixth session of the Preparatory Commission, it was noticeable that, probably under pressure of public opinion in some countries, there was a certain hesitation about rejecting out of hand the second Soviet proposal.

At the Disarmament Conference, in February 1932, Litvinov returned with his authority considerably strengthened. In the years that had gone by since his previous contributions, the League of Nations had been faced with the most serious conflict since it was created. In 1931 the Japanese occupied the port of Mukden, provoking a crisis whose epilogue was the withdrawal of Japan from the League. In the light of events Litvinov could express himself as follows: "In the Preparatory Commission the Soviet point of view encountered an almost unanimous opposition. But recent events have justified our point of view. It is a useless and dangerous obsession to subordinate everything to security. There are no treaties or pacts or protocols that will guarantee a real security for all countries. The Disarmament Conference is gathered here at a moment when two countries that are united by the Pact of the League of Nations and by the Treaty of Paris have been for five months in a de facto state of war."

Later Litvinov proposed to convert the Disarmament Conference into a permanent Peace Conference. He justified his proposal with an irrefutable statement: "There is only one kind of peace, peace without arms." When Russia was admitted to the League of Nations, Litvinov could bring the influence of his great intelligence and his sense of reality to bear on matters beyond disarmament. He spoke on all the activities of the League. His voice remains in my memory like that of a herald of the Second World War, which he tried heroically to prevent.

Litvinov was very amusing talking of his pre-diplomatic period, in the years when, having escaped from the Kiev Prison in 1902, he went to meet Lenin, who was already in exile, and to help him in publishing the illegal newspaper *Iskra*. His life abroad from 1905 to 1917 was divided between conspiracy and diplomatic training. In 1917 he was appointed by the Bolshevik Government as its representative in London, but he was arrested as a hostage to be exchanged for R. H. Bruce Lockhart, the aggressive British representative in Moscow. From his conversations with me, supplemented by the notes dictated by him to my friend Ivan Maiski, the U.S.S.R. ambassador to London during the Spanish War, there emerges a clear picture of one who personified Soviet diplomacy at its best.

Lenin appears as a complete realist in matters of foreign policy, an aspect of his record less well-known to the public at large. Litvinov tells how Lenin was involved at the very beginning of the policy of peaceful coexistence, which was later distorted. Lenin was much interested in the Genoa Conference, the first overture of Russian communism to the West. He was anxious to meet Lloyd George, for whom he felt a certain interest, but his illness prevented their meeting. Litvinov relates how no one wanted to accept the responsibility of negotiating with the Western bourgeois powers, except Lenin, who had unparalleled political courage. Lenin never hesitated to make any agreement or temporary alliance with anyone as long as it served the cause of the revolution. He would do this even though certain sectors of the left did not approve. That position of Lenin, as presented by Litvinov, today ought to help toward the adoption of a more sympathetic attitude with respect to revolutionary governments that on occasion make opportunistic decisions.

Until Litvinov became minister of foreign affairs in Narkomindel, a building that became familiar to me, he was Chicherin's deputy minister. When he was minister, I used to visit Chicherin in the evening, for he was a night worker. He was also a person of great intelligence and he and Litvinov complemented each other.

From 1926 on, when Chicherin's health began to fail, Litvinov practically took over the running of Narkomindel. He referred at times to the Jewish question. When Lenin tried to persuade Trotsky to be Chairman of the Council of Peoples Commissars, Trotsky argued that counter-revolutionary propaganda would exploit the fact of his Jewish origin: "The Soviet Government is in the hands of the Jews!" Lenin laughed and replied: "They say that we are all Yids anyway. And those of us who aren't Jews must be Lithuanians or Chinese."

There was a conversation between Stalin and Litvinov in which the Jewish question reappeared. Stalin said that, for reasons of expediency at home and abroad, it would be necessary to cut drastically the number of Soviet Jewish diplomats. Stalin made a malicious allusion to Litvinov's accent: "The trouble is that one Jew makes more noise than ten Gentiles, that's why they are so conspicuous." In fact Litvinov had a very shrill voice. But Stalin soon corrected himself: "Of course I speak Russian with a Georgian accent." That conversation ended with Stalin saying: "I have already told you and I am repeating: 'Whatever may happen, I shall not let you down.'"

This seems to put an end to the stories that circulated about Litvinov in danger of being purged after he resigned as foreign minister. One of the stories was that Litvinov always had a briefcase ready with a toothbrush and a few other necessities for the moment when the police would knock at his door, and that when Stalin heard of this, he sent him a message to say that nothing would happen to him, that he never forgot that it had been Litvinov who had saved him from being expelled from the Party in London. I have written of this before. In my opinion Litvinov was never in danger.

Litvinov was loyal to Stalin, as he had been to Lenin. But he evidently suffered a great deal because of the persecution and execution of some of his best friends and associates. The death of Alliluyeva, Stalin's wife, plunged him into deep sorrow. He must have suspected its cause, as many others did. He wrote: "November. Shocking news. Alliluyeva is dead. I went to the Hall of the Columns, where the body is lying in state. Koba [Stalin] was also there. He looked tired, his shoulders were bent, and he was pacing slowly. Even his walk was changed. I had never seen him in such a state."

Later Litvinov wrote: "At the People's Commissariat everybody is talking about Alliluyeva's death and noticing the strange fact that the funeral did not take place in the Kremlin but at the Novodievich Monastery, where she was buried next to the graves of the suicides Joffe and Lutovinov. Some say that this is an admission on Koba's part that she committed suicide. Others say that, on the contrary, this was her last wish, expressed in a letter to Koba. There are many rumors about the content of that letter. Koba is said to have been seen in his office reading that letter again and again. He always keeps it in his pocket, and he is said to have shown it to several members of the Instansia, including Klim [Voroshilov] T. Molotov, and Seryozha [Kirov]."

The opinion of Litvinov is quite important in the historic and even current debate about which of the two, Stalin or Trotsky, would have been more effective in the effort to set up the Soviet Union and to put it, industrially and organically, in a position to contribute decisively to the Allied victory over Hitler. Several casual observations by Litvinov allow one to conclude that in spite of all Stalin's faults, the purges, his obsessions, Litvinov considered him superior to Trotsky as a statesman.

In 1926 Litvinov ran into Trotsky at the house of a common friend: "I couldn't help reflecting on the degree to which a political struggle could blind even such brilliant men as Davidovich [Trotsky]. He seemed to me to be out of his mind. I was very upset to see him in such a state, him, Trotsky, one of the most brilliant of our revolutionaries, the man whom Ilyich [Lenin] wanted to see at the head of the government. The conversation left a bad taste in my mouth, a feeling of helplessness in the face of destiny. It seemed obvious that an alliance between Stalin and Trotsky would have given our country a brilliant government, a strong and united leadership. The quarrel between these two leaders did not involve political principles. It arose simply out of incompatibility of temperament. It is the human tragedy of two persons, one of whom has to go."

It is clear that Litvinov felt himself attracted by the intellectual brilliance of Trotsky, which attracted and still attracts so many people, especially intellectuals, as we realized when we attended a Trotskyite memorial in 1972. Trotsky was spiritually superior to Stalin, but Stalin was more reliable as a ruler. This is the opinion of two authorities on Soviet affairs, of Georg Lukács and Isaac Deutscher, neither of whom can be accused of being Stalinists. Despite his many weaknesses they recognize his great capacity as a statesman. This was also the opinion of Churchill, with whom Stalin frequently clashed in the great war conferences, but who found him strong, direct, and shrewd. This is the opinion that I heard frequently in Peking. The Chinese had no reason to be grateful to Stalin, who supported Chiang Kai-shek, but they recognized his importance as a revolutionary leader. And that is the reason why one of the four portraits displayed in Tien An Men is that of Stalin. The other three are Marx, Engels, and Lenin.

Litvinov naturally gave tribute to the sharp instinct of Stalin in foreign policy: his suspicion of Germany. When Beneš was president of Czechoslovakia, he told me once that Stalin, who was then on good relations with him, had confided to him: "I do not believe in a new Germany. Germany is always the same, militaristic and aggressive." This observation is very timely now that Brezhnev is basing part of his foreign policy on an approximation to Bonn, a position that, according to reliable sources in Moscow, meets a certain opposition in some members of the Politburo and in the Red Army.

Stalin trusted Roosevelt. Litvinov quoted him: "Roosevelt is a man who takes a broad view in international affairs. He looks far ahead. He is not a Chamberlain, with Birmingham ties and petty bargaining instead of a really broad policy." I talked with Litvinov at length about Roosevelt. He agreed with Stalin that the President understood the nature of fascism better than most Americans and that he would eventually be the one to put an end to Hitler's designs to rule the world. One must admit that Stalin had vision.

Litvinov praised Stalin's discernment in his distrust of the American labor movement. Stalin did not expect a revolution in the United States. Not for a long time at least, not as long as the unions were in the hands of the present leaders. He said to me: "They have not even been able to create a Labor Party like the British, even though that has plenty of weaknesses."

Roosevelt deserved all the faith that people had in him, Litvinov felt. He was a genius in his patient task of gradually rousing the American people to a feeling of international solidarity in opposition to its traditional isolationism. At the Democratic Convention in Philadelphia in June 1936, when he accepted the nomination for the second time as a candidate for the November election, Roosevelt declared: "There is a mysterious cycle in human events. To certain generations everything is given. Of others, on the contrary, much is asked. This generation of Americans has a rendezvous with destiny."

I had occasion years later to learn that the Russian esteem for Roosevelt was not limited to Stalin and Litvinov. In 1946, soon after my arrival in Moscow, Molotov invited me to a diplomatic reception. The reception was for chiefs of mission only and my presence did not pass unnoticed by the French ambassador, General Georges Catroux, afterward grand chancellor of the *Légion d'Honneur*. He invited me to dine at the embassy and that night, aside from telling me many interesting things about Russia, he told me two especially interesting things: one, that if at the end of the war elections had been held in Russia, secret ballot and absolutely honest, American style, Stalin would have won by an overwhelming majority; the other, that Russians wept in the street when they got the news of Roosevelt's death.

At that Molotov reception I saw Ivan Maiski, whom I had not seen since London. He talked to me a lot about Negrín. I got the impression that Maiski's position was fairly secure. This impression was strengthened when a couple of days later he telephoned me at my hotel to tell me that he felt that my request for an interview with Stalin was quite justified. To telephone a foreigner in a private conversation was a rare and risky thing for a Russian to do at that time. Yet soon afterwards I learned that Maiski was in jail. And there he did something fantastic. As he was forbidden to have paper, pen, or pencil, he composed an entire book in his mind. And when he got out of jail he dictated the whole book. Maiski is still alive, although very old. He is doing research in diplomatic history.

Litvinov supported me in the League whenever I expounded the cause of Spain. In his remarks to the Council on 28 May 1937, following my plea that the League put an end to the scandalous violations of the non-intervention agreement, the Soviet commissar of foreign affairs said: "I venture to remind you of these simple, indisputable facts because some people are beginning to forget them. They are beginning to forget that in the present case there can be no talk of sides having equal rights. Foreign governments have the right to enter into relations with the Spanish Government, to conclude with them any commercial transactions, including the sale of munitions, without violating any international principles and obligations. But relations with mutinous generals and supplying them with war materials constitute a classic example of intervention in the internal affairs of another state."

This was a very clear presentation of the difference between the support that Russia gave to a legitimate government, which I represented, and the supplying of arms and men by Hitler and Mussolini to Franco, a mutinous general, with the hypocritical complicity of the Western democracies sheltered behind the farce of nonintervention. Litvinov tried in every way to give life to a League of Nations overcome by the panic of the Western governments facing Hitler, and some of them not with panic but with secret sympathy. In that same speech, Litvinov said: "There are some people who consider themselves supporters of the League of Nations and who think that the League can be kept alive only on the condition that nothing will be asked of the League and nothing expected of it, and that any appeal to the League in any serious international affair is an attempt upon the existence of the League. Such people would like to change the League into a universal mummy and admire its imperturbable calm."

On the eve of Munich, when I was having lunch with Litvinov alone in his hotel room one day, he expressed to me his conviction that Hitler could be stopped. He spoke of a series of reports by his government about Hitler's hesitations over going to war, waverings that ceased when he saw in Munich Chamberlain's naïveté and Daladier's skepticism as easy prey for his policy of blackmail.

Litvinov was the precursor of a revolutionary policy for which there is still a place, and a large place, today. We have an example in Rumanian diplomacy which under Ceausescu is capable of such delicacy as to get along well with Israelis and Arabs, which is in itself a certificate of skill. And Rumania remains independent within the Socialist camp, without letting herself be intimidated by what happened in Czechoslovakia, which is a proof of courage.

I first heard Ceausescu speak in Bucharest at the Rumanian national celebration. I had just made my second trip through Rumania, the one Latin country in the European Socialist world. I have reported elsewhere on all its progress. I was impressed by the sobriety and clarity of thinking of the Rumanian president.

As for Chinese diplomacy under Chou En-lai, there is Vice-Minister Chiao, who presided over the Chinese delegation at the session of the United Nations that immediately followed the admission of China, there is Huang Hua, China's permanent representative on the Security Council; there are her ambassadors in Berne, Tchen Tche-pang, in Rome, Shen Ping, and in Paris my good friend Huang Chen, Mao Tse-tung's companion on the Long March, a member of the Central Committee of the Party, and today in charge of negotiations with the United States. When a China encircled and boycotted everywhere has been able to break through the fence and place herself at the very center of international activity, there is much to be said for the value of diplomacy.

Even though for years summit conferences between heads of state and foreign secretaries seem to have diminished the importance of a good ambassador, his role has not been abolished. A good ambassador, like Manac'h, France's ambassador to Peking, whom I know well, has fulfilled a successful mission. Among the United States ambassadors, and in connection with the most important international problem that the country has had, the Vietnam War, Averell Harriman was the best, and William Porter the worst, that we have seen in Paris.

I heard from the Vietnamese in Paris that one could negotiate with Harriman but not with Porter. They found Harriman an experienced and imaginative diplomat. Harriman realized that the North Vietnamese, after so many years of war and sacrifice, were not about to yield to Washington's demand that they accept President Thieu as an irreplaceable member of any agreement. All the more so since Thieu was hated by many non-Communist South Vietnamese and since his Saigon regime was becoming more and more repressive and authoritarian.

Porter, on the other hand, seemed to the North Vietnamese in Paris to be arrogant and the spokesman more of a diplomacy of war than a diplomacy of peace, a speaker for the Pentagon rather than for Secretary of State Rogers.

From my conversations with Litvinov I have enough material to write a biography. As a journalist, as a diplomat, and finally as foreign minister, I have known diplomats from every country. In my early youth I knew Paul Cambon, a great ambassador of France. Then in Berlin, after the First World War, Britain's Lord D'Abernon, very quick-witted in a difficult situation, during the time when I was presiding over the League of Nations Commission to establish peace in the Chaco War between Bolivia and Paraguay. I knew Cordell Hull, the United States secretary of state. Of all the diplomats of my acquaintance, two men that I have had the privilege of knowing well have raised diplomacy to the level of genius: Chou En-lai and Maxim Litvinov.

ELEVEN

The Spanish War: Léon Blum

At the time when I was closest to Léon Blum, during the Spanish War, the Socialist leader was over sixty-five, but he looked young, tall, and slender. This youthful impression was due in part to his proverbial elegance, his animated conversation, and his lively eyes. Lively but short-sighted, for myopia prevented him from serving in the front lines in the First World War.

In Blum were joined a vast intellectual training and a control of style that had put him, as literary critic, essayist, and creative writer, on the level of the best writers of his youth — together with a legal training that was of constant help to him during his political career. He had held high office in the *Conseil d'État* before he became a member of the Chamber of Deputies at the age of forty-seven.

Despite the claims of some of his enemies, Blum was not a millionaire, either by inheritance or through his legal practice. He came from a well-to-do Alsatian Jewish family, and his father owned a silk factory. He had been an *enfant prodige*. One of his old friends claims that Blum could read at the age of three. One day as we were having dinner in his beautiful home on the Île St.-Louis, he said to me, smiling: "Let's say at the age of four."

At the age of thirteen he had read all the works of Victor Hugo who, with Jean Jaurès, would be his lifelong hero. Blum had a fantastic memory, and I had many opportunities to note this. His life as a young man corresponded to the multiplicity of his character. He was a serious student in the École Normale, one of the most exclusive schools in France. Yet he was also worldly, a good dancer and an organizer of night parties in the Latin Quarter.

One of his earliest political acts was his passionate intervention in the Dreyfus Affair, which split France at the end of the century. Alfred Dreyfus was a captain in the French Army. He was Jewish and was

Premier Léon Blum in his study

unjustly accused of treason and he became the target of French anti-Semitism. With two other Socialists, Juarès and Lucien Herr, the librarian of the École Normale, who did much to make Léon Blum the leader of French socialism, he was one of the defenders of Dreyfus.

It was a deep sense of morality and justice that shifted Blum from literature to politics just when his literary reputation was taking shape. François Mauriac, a severe man in his judgments, said that Blum had been the most lucid critic of his time.

Blum was more revolutionary in thought than in action. This was true not only when dealing with the Spanish question. I heard him discourse on Marxism, on the assumption of power by the working class, with a conviction contradicted by his own vacillation. On several occasions he preferred the role of conciliator to that of proletarian leader. The great movement of general strikes throughout France in the summer of 1936 held out a promise of revolution. The day after Blum assumed office as premier, his reaction to the threat was to avoid at all cost any shedding of blood. To save France from civil war and from foreign war was his unbreakable determination. Instead of offering the workers a revolution, Blum offered them a series of sizable material gains which, he was convinced, had transformed their lives.

In theory, in his writings, he defended himself against being classified as a reformist and maintained that he had never lost sight of the revolutionary goal of the party. He went so far as to admit that a revolutionary situation would probably make a short period of dictatorship necessary. In practice, he refused to follow "those who want to implant Russian methods in France."

From the Bourassol Prison, during the war, Léon Blum supported General de Gaulle, the leader of the Free French, and at the same time tried to convince him of the usefulness of "purified" political parties in future French democracy. Blum miraculously escaped death in the last phase of the war. He never lost his courage, which was tested on several occasions, among them one in which he was wounded and almost lynched in a street fight with extreme rightists.

Two years later after the war, Doctor Juan Negrín and I went to see Léon Blum. He was leaving for the United States, as ambassador extraordinary, to outline the needs of the French economy. He was accompanied by Jean Monnet, commissaire general of the plan that aimed to modernize the instruments and the methods of production — the application of which required financial aid.

We did not say anything about the Spanish War, but I did speak of the unquestioned awakening of the Spanish people. Negrín had great admiration for General de Gaulle, whom he had known in London, and I know that the admiration was mutual. In 1946 de Gaulle worried Blum because of his preference for a presidentially dominated regime. "Besides," observed Blum, "he doesn't understand anything about the working class." This is just what André Malraux said in a by-now famous interview in the *New York Times* in August 1972. Malraux had already regretted that "this great man never sat at a workingman's table." Talking with John Hess of the *Times*, Malraux made it clear that "he had a profound relationship with the woodcutters of Colombey, but the woodcutters, you see, are the Middle Ages." For the general, "the people" were people of the twelfth century.

I had to smile when I read this, for a few years earlier, in the United States, in the question period following one of my lectures, I had defined de Gaulle as having one of his long legs in the fourteenth century and the other in the twenty-first. Léon Blum, on the contrary, coming from another class, did feel identified with the working class and he tried to pay it service in his fashion.

In the course of my trips to Paris in the twenties and thirties I witnessed the political decay of France, which led first to an attempted Fascist coup, then to the ephemeral experiment of the Popular Front, and finally to Vichy under the pathetic twilight of Marshal Pétain.

Especially after 1934 the destinies of the masses of the French and Spanish peoples are parallel. In Spain we tried to anticipate the assault of fascism by taking the offensive ourselves. We were defeated in 1934 but the heroic uprising of the Asturian miners, who fought not only to defend republican legitimacy but to implant socialism under the cry of UHP — *Unidad de los Hermanos Proletarios*, Unity of Proletarian Brothers — created a revolutionary climate that would make possible in 1936 the great, epic, anti-Fascist war in Spain. In hiding, so that I would not fall into the hands of the police, I listened from my refuge to the broadcast news of the assassination of the king of Yugoslavia and of the admirable Louis Barthou, the French foreign minister, an outrage that was part of the same diabolical Hitlerian plan to suppress the adversary everywhere.*

In Paris about 1935 there was an irresistible advance of the base of the workers movement toward unity of action. I was a witness of the great street demonstrations in the French capital. In previous years as a journalist I had interviewed the leaders of the left. I later took part as a militant in the belated effort to cut off reaction.

Faith in French republican institutions had been crumbling in the postwar period. The discrediting of the parliamentary system was aggravated by the economic crisis that crashed on the United States in 1929 and then swept through Europe, to be exploited by the enemies of the people's

---

* And there I received a telegram from General Lázaro Cárdenas, sent to my home because he knew that his invitation to me to go to Mexico to be present at his presidential inauguration would protect me against the designs of the pre-Fascist government of Lerroux and Gil Robles.

Blum greeting supporters

liberties. Governments in France were born and quickly died. There were governments like that of Chautemps that were defeated on the very first day that they were presented to Parliament. Paul-Boncour's government lasted a month. Between the victory won by Clemenceau, rejected soon afterward by a confused and insecure electorate, and the time that the Popular Front came into power with Léon Blum, there were thirty-six governments in France. It was a most useful situation for French Fascists like Colonel La Rocque and for opportunist politicians like Pierre Laval, who became a promoter of the politics of Mussolini, whom he greatly admired.

During those perilous years for the future of democracy I interviewed the main political leaders and unionists in France, including vacillating politicians like Edouard Herriot who, although very consistent in his loyalty to the League of Nations and fundamentally anti-Fascist, was the leader of a leftist government in 1924 and a rightist government in 1926.

But in both France and Spain there were the masses of the people, more faithful to democracy than the professional politicians. Called upon to defend democratic liberties by demonstrating on July 14, 1935, it was the Socialist and Communist masses that went together to join the others and from their meeting and mingling was born the famous "July Oath."

The memories of those years in which both the French and the Spanish peoples were perfectly conscious of the Fascist peril have unquestionable importance for the present. As this book is being written we can witness in Europe the preparation of a new clash between neo-Fascist currents and the forces of the left. Spain has entered the final phase, with a clear intent by the supporters of the Franco regime to make it survive the disappearance of Franco by means of a fatally reactionary monarchy.

In France, whatever they say, the flame of May 1968 is not entirely extinguished. Pierre Mendès-France, a politician kept in isolation but who has more analytic power than other fashionable politicians like François Mitterand who try to shape a divided left into a force capable of taking power, keeps saying that May 1968 can be reborn some day, even though in another form. The present stability of the situation in France is more apparent than real. That's what Mendès-France thinks. That's why it is so necessary to study the French Popular Front. One of its surviving figures, Jules Moch, has just published a book: *Le Front Populaire, Grande Espérance*, which has the virtues of its author, a graduate of the École Politechnique, a naval engineer, which is to say a man of scientific scrupulousness in his statements. I had dinner in the summer of 1971 with Jules Moch and I found him rather skeptical about the new Socialist Party and with no desire to play a leading part in it. He refused to run for the National Assembly in the last elections. He thinks it a waste of time to be a member of Parliament. He has decided to devote himself to his books, to his lectures, mostly scientific, and to international affairs. The day after I saw him he was leaving for Helsinki, where there was a meeting of the Socialist International, attended by Mrs. Golda Meir, German Chancellor Willy Brandt, and other outstanding figures in the Socialist movement.

Jules Moch is a well-informed speaker with great experience in disarmament matters. From 1951 to 1960 he was the permanent French delegate to the Disarmament Conference, and the Russians and the neutral nations listened to him with great attention. On this occasion I did not find him sharing the opinions, especially the Washington opinions, on the importance of the results obtained in SALT, from the Soviet-American consultations on the reduction of nuclear arms. Jules Moch feared that, even though a limited agreement were reached in SALT, the two superpowers would continue to arm more and more. And that is what seems to be happening today.

One need only see the French film *Le Grand Tournant*, which was a sensation in Paris in 1970 and which tells, in a documentary way, the pathetic story of the Popular Front and the Blum government from its formation until its fall, to realize the great opportunity that was lost. One need only look at the faces of the demonstrators who went into the streets to stop the advance of fascism, the passionate attitude of the working masses, one need only hear the clamor of thousands of voices shouting "Planes for Spain!" to realize how the fate of the Popular Front in France was tied to the fate of Spain.

My whole quarrel with Léon Blum revolved around this same subject, that the future of the Popular Front of which he was the leader and our victory over fascism in Spain were as closely united, to quote Chinese leaders of today, as teeth and lips. He admitted this, for he was too intelligent not to see it, but he did not act with the required energy. In Geneva, where from the platform of the League of Nations I denounced the scandalous violations of the Non-Intervention Treaty, I had to deal directly with the French foreign minister, Yvon Delbos, who belonged to the Radical Socialist party. Delbos was even softer than Blum and less friendly to the Spanish Republicans. I had tried to put pressure on him through Edouard Herriot, the leader of the Radical party, but without success. Delbos alternated courtesy with excuses, while within the Cabinet, another man belonging to the same party as the foreign secretary, the secretary of aviation, Pierre Cot, struggled valiantly to help us, ignoring the attacks of the French rightists. Knowing that it was useless to try to move Delbos, I kept turning to Léon Blum insistently, harshly, even knowing how much my arguing disturbed him and tortured him, doubtless because he knew that I was right.

Blum kept telling me that the crux of the matter was in London, that what we had to do was to persuade the English that in practice non-intervention was favoring Hitler and Mussolini. I answered that probably, in the eyes of the Conservatives in the Government, this was all to the good. Even a Conservative politician like Winston Churchill, who was not then a member of the Government but whom I heard, in the House of Commons some months before the Spanish War broke out, furiously denouncing the Nazi peril, never really understood the true international significance of the Spanish War. His sympathies, at least in the first two years of our war, were rather with Franco than with the Spanish Republicans.

In Geneva I was aware of the weakness of my British colleague Anthony Eden, who never failed to show me a certain personal sympathy, but who as foreign secretary of his country followed unwillingly the Conservative line until his clash with Chamberlain. It was therefore not in London but in Paris, I said to Blum, in Paris where there was a Popular Front government led by a Socialist, that an end should be put to the enormous error, even crime, that the Western democracies were committing by retreating more and more in the face of the blackmail of Hitler. By so doing they were making a second World War inevitable.

An important moment in that desperate struggle came early in 1937 when I published the White Paper with all the documents seized by the Republican Army from Mussolini's troops when they were defeated at Guadalajara. Here was the irrefutable proof demanded by Eden and Delbos, showing that the Non-Intervention Agreements were being constantly violated by Germany and Italy. The White Paper had given me a chance to present a public case before the League of Nations that many journalists described as absolutely conclusive and unanswerable.

This was the moment when France, with a Popular Front government, should have spoken frankly and forcefully to London. I tried to convince Léon Blum that if the French needed the English, the English needed the French just as much, and that the best service the French could perform for the British was to persuade them to resist Hitler. Later, with Chamberlain as leader of the British government and Daladier as leader of the French government, there was no longer any hope of doing anything. As I lunched in London in 1937 with Lloyd George, who was always on our side, he said to me: "I am sorry for you. Baldwin was bad enough. But his successor, Chamberlain, is much worse."

Since I have spoken of the Non-Intervention Agreement, I should correct an error that appeared in several books on the Spanish War, in which it was stated that I, as Spanish minister of foreign affairs, had given my approval to the signing of the Non-Aggression Treaty. This is not true. And Blum himself never claimed that it was so. The treaty was signed before I became minister of foreign affairs, early in September, when a government was formed led by Francisco Largo Caballero. A few days after I took over the Foreign Ministry I drew up two identical notes addressed to the governments of France and the United Kingdom. They were couched in terms so severely critical of the nonintervention policy that President Azaña was distressed. In the Cabinet, the secretary of the navy and the air forces, Indalecio Prieto, spoke of the concern expressed by the president of the republic that the tone of my notes might have an unfavorable effect on our relations with the two governments. Largo Caballero, who was presiding at the meeting and who did not want to see another worry added to all those that Azaña was trying to cope with, suggested that I soften the tone of the notes, and I yielded to his request. But even after they were toned down, the notes were a repudiation of the policy of nonintervention. I returned to the attack in Geneva on several occasions, while in London the Soviet ambassador, Ivan Maiski, kept an intelligent surveillance over the violations that continued to occur.

Several contradictory versions have appeared about my relations with Léon Blum when he, the leading French Socialist, was French premier during the Spanish Civil War. Recently, in his *Rencontres avec Léon Blum*, Jules Moch pictures me as unjust toward his chief and comrade. I therefore judge it fitting to give my own account of my relations with Blum, as a contribution moreover to clarifying a many-faceted character. Blum was above all a deep Socialist thinker. At the height of his power, in 1936, he was one of the few Socialists worthy of being ranked with the great theorists of the movement in the first quarter of the century: Kautsky, Rudolf Hilferding in Germany, Gramsci, later a Communist, Turati in Italy, and Sidney and Beatrice Webb in England.

I had followed Blum through the Socialist Congresses and through his column in *Le Populaire*, the organ of the French party. His oratory was filled with great ideas expressed in simple words. His journalistic style bore the trace of someone who dreamed of writing novels, someone who in fact had been in his youth a perceptive drama critic. In conversation with him, one was fascinated by his vast culture and by the subtlety of his exposition and analysis. There were not many Socialist intellectuals of his stature. But my experience with him at a dramatic moment for my country and a very difficult moment for his country forces me to rank him higher as a thinker than as a man of action.

I remember one day when he came late to lunch from a session in the Senate that had left him angry. He felt that his eagerness to transform French society gradually into a Socialist state was being fatally endangered. It was being thwarted by the egoism of the privileged, the rich who in the Senate had their ideal place of resistance to any noble effort. A man of his sensitivity felt outraged in the face of such a gross display of lawless interests. The rich lacked the vision to realize that even the national security of France, threatened by the rise of Hitler, would be strengthened by the support of a working class that had acclaimed the first actions of the Popular Front. In similar circumstances a Clemenceau would have attacked without any hesitation and would have pulverized the opposition. The sensitiveness of Blum led him to withdraw into an attitude of disappointment and defeat. He was, he implied, a great and unappreciated humanitarian. That day I saw him he had already lost.

This has nothing to do with Blum's personal valor. He was a man of great personal and moral courage, as he proved during the war. But when he came down to the low level at which politics and fighting are often waged, it was against his nature, and he found himself in an inferior position with respect to his adversary.

I knew quite well all the difficulties that Blum encountered in trying to help us and his own country at the same time. I knew them from his own lips in very intimate conversations of which I have scarcely spoken up to now. In order to face these difficulties the only policy that he should have followed was to rely on the masses. That was the advice that I gave him, relying on the friendship that he showed for me. Our discussions were not always clashes about the non-intervention policy. I spent delightful hours at his home on the Quai Bourbon talking about socialism, literature, and the theater.

To rely on the masses it was necessary to believe in them. And Léon Blum, while he was premier, did not believe in them. That is the truth. In her interesting biography of Blum, Colette Audry, author of *Soledad*, a play about the Spanish resistance, insists on the significance and consequences of a phrase used by him: "the profound and inorganic masses." They were to him unpredictable. In his vision of the mechanics of government, the masses ought never to replace the regular functioning of the Executive Branch. Léon Blum as party chief and Léon Blum as chief of the government were two distinct persons, even though he used to say that there were no Socialist ministers, just ministers who were Socialists.

On this question of the difference between a Socialist in the Opposition and a Socialist in power, the case of Harold Wilson in Great Britain has a very current importance. When I knew Wilson his reputation was that of a Leftist Socialist. After he became prime minister he had some opposition from the leftists in his party. But his party had a majority of less than a half dozen members in the Commons. And since the leftists did not want to be responsible for making his Cabinet fall, they did not dare to vote against him. One day I met Michael Foot in the House. He could not bear it that Harold Wilson, whom he had loyally supported in the Opposition, should now be supporting United States action in Vietnam. But, he told me, he could not assume the responsibility of rounding up the leftist votes and making the Laborist Government fall.

The same thing happened with Léon Blum within his party and even within the government that he led. Other Socialists would have liked to see him adopt a more vigorous policy in support of the Spanish Republic.

But they did not dare to bring up formally the need for a more energetic policy for fear that such action would cause the fall of the Popular Front Government.

It would be unfair, however, to speak of Blum as of an ordinary Social Democrat opportunist. For one thing, he was more intelligent than the sad series of Socialists who were Socialists in name only and who could have functioned equally well in any other party that offered them the same opportunity for a career. A few days before the outbreak of the Spanish War, Largo Caballero and I, on our way back from a syndicalist conference in London, met Paul Faure, secretary of the French Socialist party. Largo Caballero, who was a real Socialist, emerged from the interview stunned that a man like Faure could be the arbiter of the Party in France. But he was. And within the Popular Front Party he was one of the opponents of Blum. He added his vote to those of the Radical ministers who were without vigor or fighting spirit.

Léon Blum had a Marxist training much superior to that of his successors, and his association with Jean Jaurès, the great debater, had led him to share his rebellion against social injustice and his passion in the defense of simple people. Following his actions through Party Congresses during the various political crises of the twenties and thirties, I felt that he sounded like a true Marxist Socialist. In his speech before the special Congress of Bellevilloise, on January 10, 1926, he declared that he was deeply convinced of the necessity for a revolutionary seizure of power: "Whereas radicalism foresees only a series of slow and continuous reforms, we think that Socialistic transformations cannot be the result of minor reforms. Some day, we shall have to attack by a categorical and decisive act, going straight to the principles that constitute the heart and substance. In other words we do not think that one can go from the present capitalistic regime to a new regime through a series of transitions of almost imperceptible size. We are revolutionaries because we are determined to make the great leap."

Ten years later, premier, in his year-end address on December 31, 1936, Léon Blum said: "We do not seek either directly or insidiously to apply, while in power, the Socialist program." It was not that he lacked courage. In the Riom Trial, under the German occupation, with all his enemies, the French collaborators and the usual reactionaries, waiting to see when his spirit would break, Blum showed great self-assurance. He was firm and brilliant. "In the age in which we live," he said to the judges, "each man must accept his responsibilities. I give the example. I accept mine." He was a quite different man in and out of power.

In Parliament, before becoming head of the Popular Front government, Blum blithely ignored the shouts of "Back to Jerusalem!" that came from the benches of the far-right racists. He had no inferiority complex

163

about being Jewish. On the contrary, he was a Jewish patriot and a French patriot. He was saturated with French culture, delighted that he was writing in the language of his favorite authors, Stendhal, Anatole France, Marcel Proust.

I repeat: it was not lack of courage that caused Blum's failures as premier of France. It was his obsession to be the just man. He had a compulsion to be correct in dealing with his political associates, the ministers of the Radical Party, radical in name only, who were in the coalition Cabinet. The Communists had rejected his invitation to join the government, with the result that the leftist element in the government lost influence. With the exception of Pierre Cot, who identified fully with the cause of the Spanish people, the Radicals were opportunists and maneuverers.

In the case of Spain, the first error of Blum was to yield to Daladier. I got to know Daladier fairly well. I dined with him at the Spanish embassy in Paris during our war and I saw him a few times afterwards. When he capitulated in Munich his weakness did not surprise me at all. He had the reputation of being energetic and terrifying. It was pure fiction, the result of his awesome physical appearance.

At the beginning of the Spanish War, France had a large supply of reserve weapons, antiquated, not of very good quality, but which would have been at that moment of great help to us. In order to sell them to us, the Blum Government needed only to use the French-Spanish treaty of commerce, which included the supplying of arms to Spain. Blum, seconded by Vincent Auriol, his minister of state, and by Cot, tried to do this, but Daladier opposed their action in the Cabinet. Instead of facing up to him, Blum yielded. The way was open for future retreats. More than two years later, when Blum was out of the government, at the most critical moment of the battle of Catalonia, I went to Paris to try to talk to Daladier. At that time what we wanted from him was an advance shipment of machine guns and anti-aircraft weapons to tide us over until we received a shipment of purchased arms. It turned out later that this shipment was stopped in France by those same Frenchmen who were waiting eagerly for our final defeat. The shipment reached Barcelona after Franco took the city, so it became a present for him.

In *Freedom's Battle**I told about my fight in the League of Nations against the false and perverted policy of nonintervention, the initiative for which unfortunately came, as we have seen, from the Popular Front Government, in part because Léon Blum was timid about a possible clash with the British. But Colette Audry in her biography of Blum mentions a fact that does not appear in my book. She writes: "The official speech

* *Freedom's Battle* (1940; second edition, New York: Hill and Wang, 1971).

164

made by del Vayo, with its direct appeal from the platform of the League of Nations to the democratic governments, was not published in *Le Populaire*." This was the Socialist newspaper, the newspaper of Léon Blum.

All this, the weakness of the Popular Front Government's attitude toward Spain, the Munich Pact, France's trailing behind England, which was sabotaging military cooperation with Russia, led to the catastrophe of 1940. The news of the fall of Paris reached me in New York and it shook all my American friends. We happened to be at the home of Jay Allen in Washington Square. Jay was one of the most brilliant American journalists that I have ever known, and during the Spanish War he was a most enthusiastic supporter of our cause. One of his assistants was Barbara Wertheim, later Barbara Tuchman, author of the best-selling *The Guns of August* and *Stilwell and the American Experience in China*, published very opportunely in 1971, when China was much in the public eye.

Jay Allen had gathered during the Spanish War a tremendous amount of material and he was well equipped to write a book much superior to Hugh Thomas's *The Spanish Civil War*, accepted in many countries as the masterwork on the defense of Madrid. But the book had many errors and it neglected other momentous actions in that heroic war. In spite of his frivolous manner and his fondness for jokes, Jay Allen was a perfectionist. He never could push himself to the point of finishing a project. He kept rewriting his books and so never got them written. That evening at his home, on the day that Paris fell, someone recalled my warning in the Council of the League of Nations: "I speak not only as a Spaniard. I speak as a free man, thinking of all free peoples, and especially of France. If Spain is allowed to be destroyed by the forces of aggression of Adolf Hitler, those same forces will be in Paris within two years." That was what I said in November of 1938. The defeat of France was not just a military setback. It was the collapse of the whole French nation. Jean Chauvel, a brilliant diplomat and later a great French ambassador, wrote: "The misfortune was incalculable. Not the misfortune of the Army. The misfortune of France and the French. It was not merely the collapse of an army or of armed resistance. It was the collapse of a country and a people. They had both melted like snow in the sun, the sun of that 1940 summer. The men just stood there. They believed in nothing. They no longer had tastes or preferences. They were alive. That was all they asked for."

The question of military competence was really of secondary importance. The generals of the great French Revolution, as soldiers, were not superior to their German counterparts. But behind them there was a revolutionary people, there was a flame, there was Saint-Just. This was

165

what Goethe discovered. At first he couldn't understand how the well-equipped soldiers of Friedrich could be crushed by the ragged rabble of Valmy.

Some years later, when Léon Blum was still alive and when I was back in France, I spoke to people to find out what the Vichy regime was like. As everyone knows, the regime was personified in Pétain. Some of those who were in contact with him during the time when he embodied France in defeat and who opposed his actions have in recent studies tried to be fair to him, stressing his advanced age. They were no doubt hesitant to contribute to the destruction of a legend, the hero of Verdun. At the beginning of the Second World War, on the basis of Pétain's enormous prestige, Daladier offered him the vice-presidency. Pétain rejected the offer, probably because from the very first day of war he was without any hope of victory.

It is true that when Pétain assumed the supreme power he was eighty-five. He was, however, firm and erect, with no sign of physical decay, his blue eyes still shining with the brilliance of past years, and with such a desire to extend his knowledge that when he was interned in the fortress of Portalet, he decided at age ninety to begin the study of English. No, it was not his age that was responsible. A study of his past forces one to conclude that at any other moment of his life and under similar circumstances he would have acted as he acted in Vichy.

In a certain sense defeat for Pétain in 1940 was welcomed. His acceptance of it with realism and humility was for him the start of the purification of the French people, the people who had dared to become part of the Popular Front. The Marshal promised France "the national revolution, the return to the state of virtue in which authority is respected with no flighty dissidence." It was a return to a primitive economy, more agrarian than industrial, the spurning of swift fortunes won through the help of Jews, and a consequent anti-Semitism and a hatred of England and Anglo-Saxon utilitarianism.

Vichy under Pétain was a mixture of all the current reactionary ideas: the ideas of Charles Maurras, who appeared in Vichy as soon as the marshal was installed in power; Mussolini's scorn for parliamentary democracy; Hitler's concept of the state as expressed in *Mein Kampf*; and the ideas of Franco (Pétain had been ambassador to Madrid). Fortunately for France there was a Charles de Gaulle. Pétain did not heed his call from London. But when he learned of its content his comment was: "How can any soldier who has served under me talk like that?"

Some people may say that all these accounts of the Spanish War are old stuff and that too many important things are happening today to keep harping on the old stories. Wrong, because as Nehru told me in his office in New Delhi, a historic cycle began in Spain in 1936 that has to be closed. And until Spain is once again free that cycle is unclosed.

In France there was May of 1968, and some of its flame is still with us. The next years in France are going to be tough from the point of view of social agitation. But a battle such as the one that is being prepared in Spain is not visible. Italy has a very belligerent working class and its political life in 1973 is more intense than in France. But a victorious revolution in the next few years is not probable in Italy either.

But it *is* probable in Spain. And when the Franco dictatorship is destroyed in its original form or under the masquerade of Prince Juan Carlos, Franco's creature, what happens in Spain will have great repercussions in the rest of Europe and in Latin America.

In the years of the Spanish War France behaved badly to Spain. And its policy toward Spain has not really changed. Two things affect it. There is the Mediterranean. Because of France's interest and involvement in it, she pays court to Franco. And there is business. France sells airplanes to Franco and forgets that he was always an enemy of hers and continues to be one. The French Government chooses to forget that Spanish Republican refugees fought and died in the ranks of the French resistance. And they made this sacrifice while Franco was sending his Blue Division to fight on the Russian Front against the Allies and to win the Iron Crosses with which Hitler decorated Franco's generals.

TWELVE

The Spanish War: Don Manuel Azaña

Of all my trips abroad during the Spanish Civil War, the most painful was the one to Paris early in 1939, to try to persuade Don Manuel Azaña, president of the republic, that he should return to the central zone, where the war was still continuing. The government of Doctor Juan Negrín, of which I was foreign minister, was facing a difficult political situation, the result of the defeatism of many leaders in the Loyalist ranks who considered the cause a lost one. The situation was aggravated by the absence of the chief of state, and it was said that he was about to resign his office.

Some of my other trips abroad during the war had not been particularly agreeable. In fulfilling my duty to defend outside Spain the interests of the Spanish people, I had been obliged more than once to use harsh language. But I was dealing with colleagues in the Security Council in Geneva who were yielding to Fascist pressure not only on the Spanish question but on others that affected them even more directly, such as the increase in the political and diplomatic offensive of Hitler against all the rest of Europe. No one could witness the abandonment of moral positions that led France and England to the disaster of Munich without saying what he thought directly and brutally. A diplomacy in the service of peoples who were the victims of Fascist aggression could not be a velvet-gloved diplomacy.

But these clashes were at least with foreign politicians and diplomats. In the case of Don Manuel Azaña, my compatriot and superior in rank, the controversy became much more embarrassing. My relations with President Azaña had been relatively good during the year that followed the proclamation of the Republic and during the first period of the war. But they began to deteriorate rapidly when he realized that I was one of the main obstacles to a negotiated peace, which basically would have amounted to a capitulation.

Del Vayo with Manuel Azaña (left)
and Juan Negrín

Juan Negrín and del Vayo

Even today, more than thirty years later, it is hard for Spanish Republicans to criticize Manuel Azaña. Many of them continue to be hypnotized by the originality of his intelligence and by his extraordinary oratorical skill. I probably would not have written what I am going to write here (as I have not in previous books) had there not recently appeared in Spain some *Memoirs* of his, filled with venom directed towards his former companions. I speak up not because of references to me, for long ago, in exile, I made a decision never to answer personal attacks, however grave and vicious they might be.

However, Azaña's *Memoirs* are being used by the Franco elements to attack not only Azaña's wartime colleagues but the admirable effort carried out by the Spanish people during the war. To me, the defense of the Spanish people is more important than anything else, even worth risking the animus of Azaña's supporters who are still busily sustaining the legend of an exemplary Republican leader. At the beginning of the Spanish Republic, his conduct as prime minister in the years 1931–1933 undoubtedly had a certain merit. But during the war (1936–1939), his influence was extremely harmful, and at the time of my visit to Paris he was about to cause the greatest possible disservice by resigning as president of the republic, just when the government was trying to continue the resistance in the Central Zone.

I regret that Azaña is not alive and that he cannot read this correction that I make to his interpretation of the Spanish War so that he might in turn answer it if he should think it worthy of consideration. Azaña's case has often made me doubt whether an intellectual is the most adequate leader to direct a country engaged in a bitter, harsh struggle.

President Azaña never really believed that we could be victorious over fascism. Perhaps he did, for a moment, at the time of the battle of the Ebro in 1938; but only for a moment. From the beginning, his attitude was skeptical. I went to take leave of him in September 1936, only two months after the beginning of the war. I was going to Geneva with the hope that I would be defending from the forum of the League of Nations a cause that by that time was enthusiastically supported by a great majority of world opinion precisely because of the bravery with which our people were fighting against the forces of Franco, Mussolini, and Hitler. On that day, Azaña was very cordial, paying tribute to my proposal to fight the policy of non-intervention,* which was already being revealed as a scandalous fraud.

But when Azaña said goodbye to me he could not help remarking,

---

* *Non-intervention*: A program subscribed to by the Great Powers at a conference held in Nyon that, as the name implies, would proscribe the Powers from assisting the belligerents in the Spanish conflict. It was observed by the Western democracies and made a mockery of by the Axis powers. (See White Paper presented by the Spanish Government to the League of Nations, 1938.)

"When you get back, all this will be lost." This was in September of 1936. The war lasted until March of 1939; it could have continued and it could have finally been won if we had held on six months longer, waiting for the Spanish War to become part of World War II. I stood looking at him, and then, smiling, he said: "Don't worry. I won't talk that way to the one who's coming in to see me after you." The one who was waiting was Leon Jouhaux, at that time a very important French syndicalist leader, whom I had earlier briefed with an emphasis totally the opposite of the president's.

Another example of Azaña's defeatism, and this a more serious one, occurred in the last phase of the battle of Catalonia. After Barcelona fell, the government was trying to hold back the advance of the enemy toward the Franco-Spanish frontier. One of the reasons for this effort was to allow the government time to negotiate with France for the admission of a half million Republicans, some of them very much involved in the war and in danger of the gravest reprisals.

I was in charge of these negotiations, which forced me to move back and forth across the frontier. In order not to demoralize our people with my frequent departures, instead of using the main road I would travel late at night and take a secondary route. On these night excursions, going alone, without escort, on foot, I had crossed paths with deserting officials who, when they recognized me, tried to get off the road to avoid being identified. The road was already known as "Desertion Road." Fortunately, the number of deserters was small.

One day, the prime minister, Doctor Negrín, telephoned me very excitedly and indignantly to tell me that rumor was rife that Azaña was intending to use this road to pass into France. The prime minister said that if Azaña tried to do this, he would have him arrested. Negrín said: "He may consider that the war is lost, but he is the president of the republic and he must be able to lose with dignity and stand by his country up to the end. The president of the republic sneaking out of Spain like a common deserter? Never!"

I tried to calm Negrín and he finally authorized me to negotiate with the French government for Azaña's official exit to France with the personal excuse that he needed to consult a doctor. It was thus that Manuel Azaña left Spain for the French capital, and it was to the Spanish embassy in the Avenue Georges V that I went from Alicante to see him, with the mission of trying to persuade him that his place was at the head of the government and the Loyalist Army, which was continuing to fight.

In *Freedom's Battle* I have explained in detail the basis of our "To resist is to conquer" policy, defended by Negrín and myself, supported by the Communists and some other elements of the governmental coalition. The policy declared that after Catalonia was lost the government

174

should move to the central zone and continue the fight. This aspect of our war policy was later much criticized, but I continue to insist to this day that, in the light of what occurred with liberation movements in Yugoslavia and other areas where whole German divisions were pinned down by partisan fighters, that our resistance policy was completely justified.

In view of what I knew of the state of mind of President Azaña, I undertook the mission that the government had entrusted to me almost convinced of the futility of my trip. But in the desperate circumstances in which we found ourselves, we had to try everything. We had agreed in the central zone that if Azaña returned to Spain, he would of course be entitled to name a government that would be more acceptable to him than ours.*

The discussion in the Paris embassy was a dialogue of the deaf. Instead of letting himself be persuaded that he ought to return to Spain, Azaña tried to persuade me to remain in Paris. From Paris, according to him, it would be easier for me to develop a diplomatic campaign aimed at saving from Franco's repression the greatest possible number of Loyalist lives. I answered that the Western democracies would do nothing to help, as they had done nothing to stop the abuses of non-intervention, and that Franco would kill as many as he pleased, an unhappy prophecy that continues even now to be valid. As for any diplomatic program of mine in the direction that he suggested, I did not see it as very viable now that he was preparing, as he had told me, to resign as president of the republic. This would surely give the western chancelleries in London, Paris, and Washington the hoped-for excuse to recognize Franco. In short, I said that I wanted nothing more to do with ambassadors and that my place was at the side of the soldiers of the republic. And so, on the last Loyalist plane that was left in France, I flew over enemy territory and returned to Alicante.

Now, thirty-two years later, it seems fantastic that during a struggle as ferocious as was that of the Spanish people from 1936 to 1939, President Azaña could amuse himself by spending time noting in his diary the incidents and anecdotes that would be the basis for his *Memoirs*. In these, few escape his scorn and irony. Not even those whom we then supposed to be his favorites find favor in his eyes. He feels for them the same contempt as for all others. Few are the ministers and political friends who are not ridiculed or accused of stupidity or ineptitude.

Less surprising is Azaña's position, already mentioned, with regard to the war itself. He did not accept, nor did he try to understand, that a civil war like that in Spain brought with it, as revolution will, violence

---

* When Negrín, to strengthen the Cabinet's will to resist, in 1938 reappointed me foreign minister, President Azaña, on seeing my name on the list, said to Negrín: "This is a personal insult."

and actions that wounded his aesthetic sensitivity and his inclination toward moderation. In this he is not alone; we have seen intellectuals from all countries draw apart from a revolution whose cause they had originally praised or supported as soon as news about violence to which it had given rise exceeded the limit that they could tolerate intellectually and emotionally. Few, indeed, are the intellectuals who would subscribe to Robespierre's revolutionary concept of "to virtue through terror." A vast desert separates an "engagé" intellectual such as Sartre from fastidious figures such as Azaña.

Looking back, it seems to me that Azaña never appeared more at ease during the entire Civil War than he did in those last fateful days in the Spanish embassy. The war, it was true, in his eyes had been lost; he was no longer surrounded by comrades-in-arms (the very term must have been distasteful to him — "associates," if he was in a particularly expansive or generous mood, would have been more apt), instead Gobelin tapestries surrounded him; an honest, discreet, loyal ambassador Don Marcelino Pascua was his courteous, if pained, host.

Blood had not touched his hands — he had been on the side of reason, a lost cause in Spain, an "impossible loyalty." He had been with the people and the liberal tradition; indeed, he had been their symbolic head, but he had always been "far from the madding crowd." He could say with St. Paul, "I am with you, but not of you." Now he would no longer even have to be with them. The author of *El Jardin de los Frailes* [The Garden of the Friars], that remarkably sensitive portrait of a young man in clerical Spain; the successful playwright of *La Corona* [The Crown] could return to his books and to the cold life of cultivation where he was most happy and finally at home.

A far different point of view at the time from that of the president was that of Pablo Neruda, South America's greatest poet, now Chilean ambassador to Paris, and Nobel Prize Laureate, who in an interview given to *Le Monde* on April 30, 1971, said: "I was saved from despair by the Spanish War, which made me a kind of warrior protesting injustice, a warrior fighting for peace, or, if you prefer, a pacifist who fights so that humanity may be left at last in peace."

THIRTEEN

The Spanish War: Largo Caballero and Juan Negrín

I think that I am the only living member of both the Spanish Republican War Governments. There are people living who were members of one or the other, but not of the two. This circumstance imposed on me, until quite recently, a special caution about any public mention of inside stories of the war. In the present work I feel freer to speak because I have the feeling that when the book appears the Franco regime will be close to its end and that there will be little danger that the indiscretions of an unusual witness (unusual not because of his qualifications but because of the circumstances) could be used by Franco's propaganda.

It was this danger, the desire not to give the enemy a weapon, that kept me silent for many years. To keep silent was difficult. It was easy to ignore the attacks of the Franquists. But not to react to the attacks of one's own fighting comrades took a great deal of patience and self-control.

Of those attacks the most painful one pictured me as having betrayed Largo Caballero. I had loved Don Francisco like no other of my chiefs. I was unquestionably one of the Socialists in whom he confided most at the start of the war. I was already his foreign minister and when the time came to create a War Commissariat he insisted that I become the general commissar in spite of my arguing that with the foreign ministry I had all that I could manage. My opposition to the appointment was well reasoned, because the War Commissariat became the cause of my conflicts with him.

Largo Caballero filled me with immense respect. He was an exemplary Socialist, completely at harmony with the working class, from which he had come. He had served ably as secretary of labor when the republic was proclaimed in 1931, and at that time I had acted as a kind of liaison between him and the Revolutionary Committee.

With a noble face and youthful blue eyes, Largo Caballero easily won the affection of the masses, among whom, at the start of the war, he

was much more popular and beloved than any other leader. I was co
pletely devoted to him. But at times I was worried by his stubbornne
In this regard I remember his attitude during the crisis of May 19
which led to his resignation as head of the government. He summon
me to his office before he went to see President Azaña in order to subn
to him the names of the members of the new government. The gover
ment had fallen a few days before as the result of the resignation
the Communist ministers, who disagreed with Largo Caballero's policy
the War Ministry. He read to me the list of names that he was going
submit for Azaña's approval. My name was listed as secretary of sta
which in itself destroys the slander that "from the month of March Lar
Caballero knew that Alvarez del Vayo was betraying him." But the poi
that I want to emphasize here has to do with him. On that list he ga
himself the posts of prime minister and secretary of defense. He was n
content to keep the ministry of war, which was almost impossibly dif
cult. He demanded the complete direction of defense, arguing that
defense should be in the hands of a single person, himself.

To begin with, this meant removing Indalecio Prieto from the minist
of navy and air, and he enjoyed the support of an important part of t
Socialist party, including its Executive Committee. He was also support
by the Republican parties and by the president of the republic. Durir
those days of crisis I had been working behind the scenes to bring abo
general acceptance of the idea that Largo Caballero was the best possib
head of the government. It was essential to assure his continuity in offic
for he still enjoyed great popularity throughout all the Loyalist territor
But from the moment when he insisted on being not only prime minist
but also secretary of defense, there was nothing that could save him. I
had to resign as head of the government, to be succeeded by Jua
Negrín. Largo Caballero never forgave me for giving my support
Negrín when he became premier. But I was giving my support not
Negrín but to the Spanish people in the midst of a war.

This was my only disagreement with Largo Caballero. I believed th
in wartime any personal feeling (and my admiration for Don Francisc
was and continues to be enormous) should be sacrificed to the necessi
for supporting the war effort. This feeling was also the cause of my fir
differences with him. It had to do with my activities as general commi
sar of war. When Madrid was attacked at the end of 1936 by Franco
forces with such pressure that the Loyalist Government had to move
Valencia, I increased the number of political commissars. The morale
the volunteers, both men and women, was very high as they rushed in
the front lines to dig trenches. But the commissars could help them
organize themselves better and could prevent friction between those
different political persuasions. And they could write the propagano
messages that would be broadcast to those in the opposing camp. At

180

Largo Caballero and family

Guernica, by Pablo Picasso,
symbol of Loyalist cause

point in the war was the use of commissars more justified than in the defense of Madrid. This defense became, in the next two years, a magnificent epic struggle that aroused the admiration of anti-Fascists all over the world. Those were days when the Loyalist people, moved by a fantastic fighting spirit, made up by their bravery for the technical superiority of the armies of General Mola, who was, in addition, counting on the help of Fascist elements hidden in the city. It was then that the expression "Fifth Column" was coined. "Four columns," announced General Mola, "are marching on Madrid. And within Madrid itself there is another column, a fifth column, waiting for our arrival."

To combat the poisonous efforts of that fifth column, composed of Fascists in hiding who spread the lie that Madrid could not be defended, was one of the tasks assigned to the political commissars. I appointed them without paying any attention to their political affiliation, after studying their dossiers and in many cases talking with them. Their party or political affiliation made no difference to me. In the end it turned out that the Communists were greater in number than the commissars who belonged to other parties.

Largo Caballero was immediately informed by the Socialists who surrounded him (and some of them owed their posts to me) that I "had delivered the War Commissariat to the Communists." The prime minister and I had a heated discussion, but with no serious consequences, and I continued in my post of general commissar of war for quite a while until the hostility of the new minister of defense, Indalecio Prieto, toward the existence of the Commissariat of War made me submit my resignation.

After Largo Caballero left the government, he broke off relations with me, and this was extremely painful for me. But shortly before he died I had the great satisfaction of seeing our friendship resumed. I had read in New York that he had been freed from the concentration camp in Germany where he had been sent as the result of the shameful alliance between Marshal Pétain and the Nazis. I sent him a telegram at the address that seemed safest to me, *Le Populaire* of Paris, the journal of the French Socialist party. In a few days I received his answer at 180 Sullivan Street. He had taken the trouble to look up my address in Greenwich Village.

When I saw Largo Caballero in the hospital in Paris, he was already very ill. They had had to amputate his leg. All that was alive in him was concentrated in his unforgettable blue eyes. If he had lived a few years longer many of the disasters of the Spanish Socialist party in exile would have been avoided. In the free Spain that will come, it will be around his name and that of his great predecessor Pablo Iglesias that a strong Socialist party will be rebuilt.

Other labor leaders may have had more power than Iglesias but few have inspired more affection. Today, almost fifty years after his death in

1925, there is no Socialist worthy of the name in or outside of Spain who is not filled with emotion on hearing the name of Grandfather Iglesias. He was everybody's grandfather and the founder of a party with a great history, a party that will still play a great part in the future of Spain.

Iglesias came from a very poor family. His mother, Juana, a widow, who adored Pablo and was in turn adored by him, had to give up her two sons because she couldn't feed them or bring them up. She had to send them to an orphanage, urging Pablo, the eldest, to study and work hard.

In the orphanage Pablo chose the trade by which he proposed to support his mother, typesetting. It was a trade that would contribute greatly to the growth of socialism in Spain. Ramón Lamoneda, the last secretary of the Socialist party in Spain at the end of the war, extraordinarily intelligent and honorable, was also a typesetter.

All of us keep as a kind of relic the name of a printshop in Limón Street where Pablo Iglesias worked as a boy. "What a joy it would be to go and see it, if it were still in existence" wrote the author of the best biography of Pablo Iglesias, Julian Zugazagoitia, who was himself the editor of the *Socialista*, the newspaper founded by Iglesias.

Iglesias left to work for a more important printshop but with little increase in wages. At six *reales* for a hundred lines — a little more than an American quarter — he helped to put together a Latin grammar. He took part in the first labor conflict. He was sent to a Madrid jail called the Saladero (Salting House) in 1882. All the members of the board of directors of the Printing Arts wound up in the Saladero under orders of a liberal prime minister, Don Práxedes Mateo Sagasta.

For Iglesias socialism was humanism — but also struggle. He had read the texts of the founders, he had familiarized himself with the essence of Marxist doctrine. He was working class to the bone and he devoted the rest of his life to it. In Spain, before Iglesias founded the Socialist party in the 1880's, laborers tended to be anarchists. Bakunin and Prince Kropotkin, both Russian aristocrats, had found in Spain and in Italy, but especially in Spain, enthusiastic followers, the laborer who preferred direct action to the remote language of Marx and Engels.

Iglesias was a candidate for deputy from Bilbao on several occasions, always defeated but each time winning more votes. In the 1910 elections he won in Madrid. And he won every time that he ran afterwards. The fact that he was the only Socialist deputy in Parliament did not inhibit him from making his presence forcibly felt. One day attacking the leader of the Conservative party, Antonio Maura, eloquent, theatrical, and scornful, Pablo Iglesias said to him: "We have reached the extreme of considering that, before we allow your lordship to assume power, we should go so far as personal assault."

It created the wildest uproar that the Chamber of Deputies had seen in many years. Curses, insults, attempts from the Conservative benches to attack the speaker. Iglesias witnessed the tempest with crossed arms. To the request of the president of the Chamber that he withdraw his words, he answered: "I do not withdraw them." He finally consented to "explain them." "No explanations," answered the president. "Withdraw them." "Well, I won't withdraw them."

The uproar spread to the street. Surrounded by police, Iglesias left the Chamber. He was accompanied by a few of us young people who had just had a stone-throwing scuffle with the police. Paving stones, the weapons of yesterday and today.

Another instance of my supposed yielding to the Russians is an event of greater repercussions than my differences with Largo Caballero: the shipment of gold to Russia. Even after the war was over and I was in New York, I was practically assaulted on a radio interview over the shipment to Russia of the gold from the Bank of Spain "on del Vayo's initiative."

I was attacked by James Farley, the postmaster general of the Roosevelt administration, and by a very insolent Washington lawyer whose connection, certainly not very disinterested, with Franco's propaganda service, was a secret to nobody. But instead of letting myself be put on the defensive, I returned the attack. This was easy for me because ever since I arrived in the United States, after the fall of France, I had used all my journalistic experience to find out what had been the real cause of President Roosevelt's change of heart with regard to the embargo which contributed to the defeat of the Spanish Republic. During the Spanish War the United States had an excellent ambassador there, a true friend of the Spanish people and an avowed enemy of Franco, Claude Bowers. He did everything in his power to counteract the evil influence of Farley on the President.

When I was in Geneva fighting in the League of Nations against the violations of the non-intervention policy, whose parallel was the American embargo on the sale of arms to Spain, one day I received a startling and confidential bit of news: President Roosevelt was about to lift the embargo. It was a matter of only a week. Later, in the United States, I learned the details of the miserable intervention of Farley and Joseph Kennedy, which led Roosevelt to retreat. I do not wish even today, although my informant is now dead, to say who gave me the details of the pro-Franco maneuvers of Farley, who told Roosevelt that if he lifted the embargo he would lose the Catholic vote and consequently the next election.

The Spanish Loyalists had another very powerful enemy in the United States, Cardinal Spellman. Proofs of this enmity were an article that he wrote for *Look* Magazine and his efforts to prevent Picasso's magnificent *Guernica* from being exhibited in New York.

All this gave me abundant material to change the occasion of the telecast into a denunciation of Franco and the dark maneuvers of his advocates in the United States. I was not lacking in weapons for the counterattack. I had the good fortune to be a friend of Eleanor Roosevelt. She had told me confidentially one day that "the President is not happy about our policy with respect to Spain." And the under secretary of state, Sumner Welles, who was no leftist but was an expert on international affairs, gave as his opinion that "our greatest error had been made in the Spanish question."

In my counterattack I insisted on the fact that Franco had wished for the defeat of the United States and the victory of Hitler and Mussolini. I also destroyed the myth that Franco deserved any credit for tipping the balance of Spanish neutrality in favor of the Allies, as Franco's American lawyer in Washington claimed. Armed with information from the best diplomatic sources, including the testimony of representatives of Latin American countries in Madrid, I was able to show that if, in the first three months of the Second World War, Hitler had been willing to pay the price that Franco demanded to fight on his side, Franco would have done so without question. Afterwards it was too late. Hitler's victory was no longer certain and Franco was afraid to take the risk. But even so, Franco sent his Blue Division to fight in Russia.

Apart from the broadcast I was often confronted with questions about the gold that I was supposed to have presented to the Russians, and even in exile the matter continued to be a burning issue. Only recently, the most important witness, Doctor Marcelino Pascua, Spanish ambassador to Moscow at the start of the war, decided to publish the whole truth about a matter that had been so erroneously presented. Doctor Pascua, after the war, taught in Baltimore and held important positions in the World Health Organization. I have heard mathematicians say of him that if he had specialized in that subject he would have been one of the great mathematicians of our time. His style of writing corresponded to that rigorous scientific training. No witness could have had a greater concern for exactness. In his article, "Spanish Gold in Moscow," which appeared in the June-July issue of *Cuadernos para el Diálogo*, Doctor Pascua said: "On the other hand, I am not sure that Mr. Alvarez del Vayo, Secretary of State at the time, had any knowledge of the special operation to which we refer. Soon afterwards he did know about it, since I took care to inform him."

Doctor Pascua made it clear that the 7,800 cases sent to Moscow contained 510,079,529.3 grams of gold, or approximately 510 million U.S. dollars. And on the basis of the official data of the League of Nations he calculates that what was sent to Russia was the equivalent of 1300 million gold pesetas and that what was not sent was approximately 882 million gold pesetas.

The 7,800 cases were loaded in Cartagena on October 25, 1936, on the four Russian ships that were anchored in the port, and they headed for Odessa. On each ship there was a Spanish custodian. Doctor Pascua rejects "the hoax," these are his words, "that the gold was deposited in the names of several important figures in Republican politics. There is not an atom of truth in this. The deposit was made, of course, in the name of the Spanish Government, as is shown by the document that bears my signature."

About the other much debated question of the choice of the Soviet Republic as the country of deposit, Doctor Pascua recalls, relying on what was said by Largo Caballero and in statements by Doctor Negrín, then minister of finance, that Russia and Mexico were the only countries that, from the start of the war, showed an understanding of and an interest in the cause of the Spanish Government.

Given the weakness of the French Government of Léon Blum toward Spain and the antagonism of the British Government toward the Republican cause (a hostility revealed from the very beginning when London ordered its ambassador to Madrid, who happened to be in Hendaye at the moment of Franco's rebellion, not to return to his post), Russia was the only logical place to which to send the gold. A sea shipment to Mexico would have been long and dangerous. Doctor Pascua dismisses the suggestion that the gold might have been sent to Switzerland. He writes: "Even if the gold managed to arrive safe and sound in Zurich, it would have stayed there, sterilized, in the vaults of the National Bank for the duration of the war without achieving the essential purpose for which it was shipped out of the country." And that purpose was to buy the arms that were being denied to the legitimate Government of Spain by the boycott of the so-called Western democracies."

The operation of moving the gold to Russia was successful in spite of the great risks involved. Doctor Pascua likens it to the risky crossing of the North Atlantic in 1940 of the British cruiser *Emerald*, transporting to Canada the gold and securities of Great Britain as a precaution against the invasion of England by the Germans. It was a similar worry that weighed on the Spanish Government in the face of the advance of the Franco forces on Madrid. The Cabinet decided, on September 13, 1936, to grant the request of the minister of finance, Juan Negrín, that he be allowed to take whatever measures he judged appropriate to achieve security for the monetary reserves of the Bank of Spain. But naturally the Cabinet, beyond this general authorization, did not inquire about what measures were to be taken. In case any of them were captured, this knowledge would have added one more danger to the many that they faced.

On two later occasions the Soviet authorities declared that all the gold sent to Russia was spent on armaments for the Republican Government and that, in fact, there is a deficit in favor of the Soviet Government.

One morning, very early, André Malraux came to my house. I had met him the year before at an international congress of anti-Fascist writers in Paris, but he didn't remember me. At that congress some of the foreign writers had found him too difficult, in contrast to Louis Aragon, who was very simple and cooperative. But I had read *La Condition humaine* and I could understand why Malraux could assume some air of self-sufficiency. He came to see me that morning in the hope that I, as foreign minister, would intervene on his side in a conflict that he had with the bureaucrats in the Spanish Air Force. Malraux was busily organizing the Spanish Squadron, which he led and which saw action in the battle of Medellín. He complained of delays and obstacles. The International Brigade had not yet been organized, and he was the most important international figure to come to our support. It was only natural that I should give to his militant presence among us a greater importance than that given by other Republican officials. Although they were grateful for his gesture, they found him impatient and irritable. But I knew that the best young writer in France was about to risk his life in the skies over Spain.

We already had on our side two of the best established French writers, Georges Bernanos and François Mauriac, but Malraux came to give on the field of battle an example of international solidarity, and that alliance of valor and intelligence did our cause great service. I had to balance giving him satisfaction against the risk of antagonizing our aviators who had remained faithful to the Republican cause. Among these was a very fine fellow, extremely likable and with a lively sense of humor, Ignacio Hidalgo de Cisneros, who soon became the leader of the Loyalist Air Force. His wife was very popular with the Americans who had come to our support. She was Constancia de la Mora, author of an excellent autobiography, *In Place of Splendour*, and my press chief in the last year of the war. She was the granddaughter of the last Conservative prime minister, Antonio Maura. She died in an automobile accident in Guatemala, a great shock to me. Hidalgo de Cisneros supported my efforts to smooth over the difficulties with Malraux and all ended well.

Aside from being a great writer, Malraux was already the outstanding anti-Fascist that he would be all during his life. His struggle against fascism had a solid basis, the defense of human dignity. Hitler was scarcely in power when Malraux joined the *Comité Mondial anti-fasciste* and the *League contre l'anti-sémitisme*. He had taken part in the defense of Dimitrov, the Bulgarian Communist accused of having set the Reichstag on fire. Much later, when he was questioned in Paris about whether he was now so suddenly an anti-Communist, he had answered: "I know what I am, and I shall never be a Fascist."

These were reasons enough for me to welcome Malraux warmly. I was convinced that the Spanish War would have a profound effect on him. In the light of what occurred afterward, my anticipation was clearly correct. The attraction that grandeur has always had for Malraux, the grandeur that led him to work with de Gaulle in the service of France and that, when the general was dead, led Malraux to speak of Mao Tse-tung as the last of the giants of international politics, that led him to come to the United States to brief President Nixon before his visit to China, this sense of grandeur Malraux felt in Spain. Indeed he perceived the grandeur of the war with greater clarity than many of the faction-torn Spanish Republicans.

From the novels to our revolution, from *Les Conquérants* to *L'Espoir*, in the whole course of Malraux's passionate exaltation of death, which obsessed him but never made him retreat, the Spanish War was the greatest event of his life. Many years later, at the University of Paris, I heard him turn violently against Communist students who suggested that to be a minister in de Gaulle's Government was incompatible with his claim of undiminished loyalty to the cause of the Spanish Republic. Spain has always been the subject on which he is most sensitive.

Because Malraux was able to penetrate more deeply into the historic scope of the Spanish War, *L'Espoir* is a better novel than Hemingway's *For Whom the Bell Tolls*. Speaking of *L'Espoir*, Henry de Montherlant said: "This admirable and neglected book, this book which, of all the books that have been written in the last twenty years, is the one that I would have preferred to live and write." For all of Hemingway's great talent, his novel does not really reflect the true spirit with which the Spanish people endured three years of unimaginable hardships.

Many of my fellow exiles were indignant at Hemingway's book. I was indignant, but not surprised. I had talked with him in Madrid and I had realized that the Spanish War was fundamentally alien to him. Hemingway's was the Spain of the running of the bulls at the Fiesta of San Fermín in Pamplona, the Spain of the great bullfights of Antonio Ordóñez, that was understood by the author of *The Sun Also Rises*, a Spain closer to him than was García, a character in *L'Espoir* who, when Hernández asks him: "What good is a revolution except to make men better?" answers: "Action can be thought of only in terms of action. Moral improvement and nobility are individual problems on the fringe of the Revolution." And Malraux concludes: "It is our side or Franco's side. It is not an organization against a desire, a dream, or an Apocalypse."

One of the people most discussed during and after the Spanish War was Doctor Juan Negrín. This is not surprising, for he was the great revelation of the war. A strong leader is bound to create suspicion and antagonism in weaker men. Named minister of finance, representing the Socialist party in the first Coalition Cabinet under Don Francisco Largo Caballero, Doctor Negrín performed the miracle of financing the republic for three years, though other Republican leaders thought that the money would be gone within a year. But it was when he succeeded Largo Caballero as prime minister and afterwards assumed the post of minister of defense, replacing Indalecio Prieto, that Negrín showed the full measure of his exceptional powers of leadership. I had known him for many years. In the Medical School, of which he was secretary, and in the University City, in the creation of which he had had an important role, he had distinguished himself as a bold and effective executive. With him and with Luis Araquistain, my brother-in-law and a writer and polemicist, I founded in the twenties the España Publishing House, which once was about to make us rich thanks to our publication in Spanish of Remarque's *All Quiet on the Western Front*, the first great German anti-war novel.

Negrín and I used to see each other nearly every day in Madrid. In 1935 we were in Moscow together, he attending the International Congress of Physiology, I making one of my numerous newspaper reports on Russia. That meeting in the Soviet Union, when we exchanged our impressions of Russia, helped me years later, when the Spanish War was ended, to understand the change in his attitude toward the Russians. The shift was so great that he became, in the last years of his life, a severe critic of Kremlin policy. Despite this, some people, out of force of habit, continued to call him a Communist.

Negrín was above all a patriot. Born in the Canary Islands, he would certainly not have been a supporter of their present desire for autonomy. During the time that the War Government was in Barcelona, I had to intervene several times to smooth over the friction between him and the local authorities. He would tolerate no action of theirs that he thought would interfere with the authority of the central power. It is possible that in that ultrapatriotic feeling lay the origin of the story of the delivery to the Government of Franco of certain documents related to the shipment of the gold to Russia, a shipment that later caused him to be bitterly attacked by Spanish Republican leaders, who detested him anyway.

It is possible — I am merely supposing — that Doctor Negrín had told some of his intimates that he would rather see the rest of the Spanish gold in Franco's hands than in Russian hands. And, believing that they were interpreting his ideas, or for other reasons, his intimates may have placed in the hands of the Franco Government the documents of Doctor Negrín.

The Franco version is that those documents, after Negrín's death, were delivered to Madrid by one of his sons, who now lives in Mexico, and by one of his former Ministers, Mariano Ansó, who was one of his intimate friends.

Among the reproaches made from the anti-Franquist camp to Negrín for that decision, attributed to him, was the reproach that he had not consulted me. It was an argument that didn't hold water. First, because the Negrín Government of which I was a part had ceased to exist in 1945, and I consequently held no official post. Second, and more decisive, because if Negrín had really intended to turn over those documents to Franco, I was the last person that he would have talked to about it. He knew without question that I would tell him, "Never." I have never identified Spain with the General Franco who rebelled against the legitimate government and that even after the war was over went on persecuting and killing Loyalist Spaniards.

There have been and there still are Spanish Republicans who say: "Spain first of all." Spain, yes. But Franco, no. To me, everything that favors Franco is bad for Spain. That is one reason for my opposition to American aid to the Franco dictatorship. It contributes to the continuation of a regime that is the negation of Spanish patriotism. Franco's bargain with the United States for Spanish bases in return for millions of dollars in aid was made without consulting the Spanish people, a point very correctly stressed by Senator Fulbright in his criticism of American policy toward Franco.

Negrín was also criticized for his alleged arrogance and intolerance of disagreement. In fact, he was quite above any vulgar vanity. He and I disagreed more than once, but this did not affect our reciprocal esteem or our friendship. We disagreed, for example, about the practical value of a proposal that he made to the League of Nations stating the willingness of the Spanish Government to withdraw the International Brigades from Spain. My argument was that the French and British governments were already so accustomed to tolerating all the violations of the Non-Intervention Agreement and so fundamentally resigned to a Franco victory that such a proposal would result only in depriving us of the military assistance of the International Brigade without any compensation at all.

Negrín presented the proposal in person before the Council of the League of Nations, and the International Brigade left Spain soon afterwards amid a fond and mournful farewell, a reflection of the gratitude with which the Spanish people had seen the arrival in Spain of those magnificent human beings who came from all countries to fight and die for the universal principles of human liberty.

Later, Doctor Negrín, talking with me, acknowledged that his action had been an error. In proof of his feeling of solidarity with the International Brigade, he attended the meeting that celebrated the twentieth anniversary of their arrival in Spain, a meeting celebrated in Belgrade. This was his last public appearance.

I was not very enthusiastic about a plan, which he described to me when we were in San Francisco, during the meeting that established the United Nations. Azaña had resigned the presidency of the republic in March of 1939 at the Spanish embassy in Paris, thus leaving the republic without a head of state. It was of paramount importance that a president be elected since foreign governments accredit their ambassadors to the head of state. Dr. Negrín's plan was that a session of the members of the last freely elected *Cortes* (parliament) be held in Mexico in order to chose a new president. Members came from all over the world to attend the meeting of the *Cortes*. Mexico, with its usual generosity, granted the Spaniards the use of a government building, giving it for the duration of the session extraterritorial prerogatives so that technically it was Spanish territory. A necessary quorum of the *Cortes* elected Diego Martínez Barrio (president of the *Cortes* and legally in line of succession) president of the republic. As was customary when a new president is elected, the prime minister resigns to allow the new president to call a man of his choice to form a new government.

There was danger that Negrín's political enemies would take advantage of this procedure to see that the president did not call Negrín to form a new government.

During our meeting in Mexico with the other members of the Negrín Government, Don Antonio Velao, one of the most intelligent and exemplary leaders of the Republican left, the Party of Azaña, told Negrín that his plan allowed his enemies to put a pistol to his heart, and that they would betray him. Negrín replied that he was acting in accordance with his own sense of responsibility and that he expected others to show the same responsibility. I finally supported Negrín's plan.

In addition, our best foreign friends in San Francisco, the French and the Russians, approved of the Negrín plan. They took it for granted that Negrín would be asked to form the new government. Such a government would have been recognized by France and by certain other governments, among them Russia. There was a strong probability that this action would be enough to persuade Franco to relinquish power. The Argentine ambassador to Madrid said that Franco had sounded out Argentina on the possibility of seeking refuge in Buenos Aires. Other sources have confirmed how close Franco was to leaving Spain.

I took advantage of those two weeks of negotiations in Mexico to enjoy again the beauty of a city in which my wife and I had spent two of the best years of our lives and to visit my great friend Lázaro Cárdenas in the lovely countryside of Pátzcuaro.

There is no corner of the Mexican capital that I do not know well: the best flower stands and the stores with the genuine folk arts. I had kept in touch with all my Mexican friends. The list would be a long one. My first Mexican friendship goes back to Madrid where, in the time of the dictatorship of Primo de Rivera, the excellent poet Enrique González Martínez, the Mexican minister to Spain, was a friend and ally. Then the friends of my embassy days in Mexico, Jesús Silva Herzog, who is still editor of *Cuadernos Americanos*, Juan de Dios Bojórquez, general director of statistics, Eduardo Villaseñor, economist and writer, Doctor Ignacio Chávez, Doctor Manuel Martínez Báez, Daniel Cossío Villegas, guiding spirit of the Culture Center, Manuel Sierra of the Ministry of Foreign Relations, and, of course, the man who was foreign minister when I presented my credentials, Genaro Estrada, poet and author of the Estrada Doctrine, widely accepted in Latin America.

In Mexico everything turned out as badly as some had predicted. Thanks to Negrín's plan, the Parliament named Martínez Barrio as provisional president. But he, instead of entrusting to Negrín the formation of a new government, gave the responsibility to José Giral. This action was a betrayal of Negrín. It was also a betrayal of the republic. After the destruction of the Negrín Government, numerous governments have succeeded one another from 1945 to 1971, each weaker than and less representative than the one before it. These governments in exile were more and more out of touch with the people who, inside Spain, were really fighting against Franco. These governments were content to be symbols, to maintain the formality of the continuity of the republic. It was not enough and it is not enough.

I have spoken of Negrín's differences with the Russians. In 1945 they still held him in great esteem. Some months earlier I talked with Oumansky, the very intelligent and charming Soviet ambassador to Mexico who was killed soon after that in a plane crash. He made it clear that in Moscow no one thought that anyone could replace Negrín. I got the same impression in San Francisco when I had dinner with Manuilski, also very keen and with a great sense of humor. His opinion on Spanish affairs was carefully heeded in Moscow. Manuilski expressed himself in the most laudatory terms about Negrín.

Manuilski was at one time secretary of the Third International and was always a link between the Soviet Communist Party and foreign Communists. He was a member of the Soviet delegation to the San Francisco Conference which saw the birth of the United Nations. Molotov, the foreign minister, had in him a very effective assistant. He was quite a contrast to Molotov, who was so serious and dry to most of his interlocutors, though toward me he was always very friendly and open. But

Molotov lacked Manuilski's sense of humor,* which I could sample on the occasions when he invited me to lunch with him.

The coldness between Negrín and the Russians began two years later and became sharper at the time of the death of Jan Masaryk in Prague. Negrín and Masaryk were united by a warm friendship that went back to the time of their exile in London during the Second World War. But in spite of this coldness, when I asked him (and he was in a unique position to know the truth) whether Russia's aid to Spain during the war had been great or not (a subject much discussed in exile), Negrín answered: "Great and with no conditions, as far as I was concerned. The Russians knew that I would not have accepted any conditions." On several occasions I was a witness of Negrín's independence. When they were planning the Ebro River campaign (which was a great success), the Russian military advisers were at first opposed to it. But when Negrín expressed his determination to go ahead with it and gave reasons for his urgency, the Russians bowed respectfully and gave him full support.

Negrín left unfinished a series of monographs that were a kind of war memoir. One of them, which he read to me in sections as he was writing it, was entitled: "My Relations with the Spanish Communist party and with the Soviet Union." It was full of interest, and it would have been very difficult for his enemies, after what he wrote became known, to continue saying that he was a tool of the Russians.

Once he ceased to preside over the government in exile, Negrín did not act with the forcefulness that one would have expected from his past and his prestige. This was in part for reasons of health, which were not widely known. I was in Paris, in his hotel room, the morning after he suffered a heart attack. They had telephoned in the night to Jules Moch, who sent for Léon Blum's doctor. Negrín showed me a report from this doctor, which prescribed rest and calm. But more than considerations of health, it was the prospect of a deeply divided exile that kept him rather distant. Nevertheless I hoped that, following his appearance in Belgrade at the tribute to the International Brigade, he might be preparing to return to active politics. In Belgrade were two of the Spanish Communist generals, Lister and Modesto, who served under his orders during the war. Lister is today the leader of a faction, a second Communist party, opposed to the one still led by Dolores Ibarruri, "La Pasionaria." He talked to me at length on a return flight from Brioni,

* One day at the Assembly of the United Nations a South American delegate known for his servility to Washington made a mortifying remark after a speech by Manuilski on the Spanish question. Manuilski replied: "It is dinnertime and the distinguished delegate has presented us with a bit of mustard. I am quite fond of mustard, but it has to be authentic, for example, like French mustard. What we have been served here has the taste of American cooking. Though the United States is great in many things, its cooking is not its strongest side."

where we had visited Tito. Negrín was on the same flight, and Lister told me confidentially that Negrín was still the man who could best unite the exiles.

The death of Negrín was a great loss to Spain. Just as Konrad Adenauer at the age of ninety was a much more effective chancellor than his much younger successors, so Negrín, if he had returned to power in Spain at any age, could have brought to the arduous task of restoring democracy there the strengths of his talents, his experience, and his nobility.

FOURTEEN

Mussolini:
The Beginnings of Fascism

When, during World War II, I met Angelica Balabanoff again in New York, she was no longer playing the leading part in the Communist movement that she had played in the years following the October Revolution. She had been the first secretary of the Communist International until she was replaced by Radek in 1920. But she had known intimately all the great Communist leaders of that time, including Lenin and Trotsky, and she was an inexhaustible source of information on important events in which she had taken part. She had a typically Russian gift for conversation.

"La Balabanova," as the Italians called her, was above all an authority on the reconstruction of the personality of Mussolini. She had been his inseparable companion in the days when young Mussolini, already filled with ambition and eagerness, was creating for himself a revolutionary platform by accusing all the other Socialists of being vacillating and reactionary.

Van der Velde, the Belgian Socialist leader, had evolved during the Spanish War from right to left, because he was so impressed with the heroism of the Spanish people. We had several interviews intended to promote the movement of international solidarity toward fighting Spain. In one of them he told me about the behavior of Mussolini during a conference on religion. Mussolini put on anticlerical airs. Arguing with some Italian priests, Mussolini had defied Christ in his invariable theatrical style. Not only Christ but God. Putting his watch on the table, he said: "God, you have five minutes to prove that you exist. I insult you. I attack you. If you exist, you have five minutes to strike me down with a thunderbolt." When the five minutes passed, Mussolini picked up his watch and emerged triumphant from the encounter. He also argued the same topic with Alcide de Gasperi, who was later Italian prime minister and at whose table I had long conversations about Mussolini.

197

Angelica Balabanoff taught socialist theory to Mussolini. She persuaded him that he should go to the University and study languages. Much of the intellectual background that the future dictator acquired in his youth he owed to la Balabanova. He owed to her also his taste for revolutionary action, although in his case it was carried on in a disorderly and confused way. If one day he joined Serrati, a serious Socialist, to found an international library, another day his favorite friend was Emilio Marinetti, the spokesman for futurism, who infected him with a taste for

Del Vayo greeting Italian Communist chief
Palmira Togliatti, 1958

war. Until 1911 Mussolini represented the most violent, most intransigently antimilitaristic tendency within Italian socialism. He was at the head of the Socialists who attacked the Forli Station to prevent the departure of the troop trains. And at his side was a young Socialist, Pietro Nenni, who was to become my great friend during the Spanish War and who was to follow a path very different from that of the excitable comrade Benito.

In 1912 Mussolini was named director of *Avanti*, the official organ of the Socialist party. At first la Balabanova was co-editor. But he soon go rid of her; gratitude was never his most distinguished characteristic. It was a time of great agitation in Italy and Mussolini knew how to exploit it. The circulation of *Avanti* quintupled. Mussolini was consistent in his denunciation of militarism right up to the first months of World War I. On September 22 he organized a kind of plebiscite in front of the newspaper office. He asked the crowd gathered there: "What do you want, peace or war?" And advancing toward the center of the crowd, he screamed: "Those men who are pushing you into the war are betraying you!"

Angelica Balabanoff, who had already lost her faith in Mussolini, followed his movements. She surprised him in friendly conversation with known supporters of Italy's entrance into the war. Suddenly, in mid-October, an article of his dismayed the Party leadership. Its title announced the about-face: "From absolute neutrality to active and operative neutrality." Two days later he wrote: "Do you want to be men or socialists, inert spectators of this marvelous drama?" The leadership of the Socialist party disavowed him and he had to resign as editor of *Avanti.*

Mussolini needed another window at which to expose himself. He began the publication of *Popolo d'Italia* and in its very first number he called to youth in language very much like that of Gabriele d'Annunzio, who later would be his partner in crime: "It is to you, youth of Italy, it is to you that I direct my cry of appeal, a cry that I would never have voiced in normal times, a cry that today I launch with full voice. I cry a terrifying and fascinating word: War!" The call to youth, "Giovanezza," was the prelude to the song of fascism.

During all the rest of the war no one could outdo Mussolini in militaristic fervor. At the first decisive Italian victory he wrote: "Here is the hour of divine victory! It is through such a victory, a victory that surpasses that of all other armies, that Italy gives the coup de grâce to the enemies of the human race!" The language of the mighty warrior of Ethiopia was already there. But later, in Spain, the enemies of the human race, the Germans, were to become his allies.

I was at the Genoa Conference in the spring of 1922 when the thud of Mussolini's boots echoed through Italy. My Italian Socialist friends, with a few exceptions, refused to believe in the imminence of the peril. Armed Fascist bands were circulating freely. It was true that the working class constituted an enormous potential force. It was also true that, in 1919 and early in 1920, many members of the Italian bourgeoisie were resigned to the prospect of a Socialist revolution. But after the Fascist coup of October 30, 1922, when Mussolini's bluff of "the march on Rome" had succeeded and the king had summoned him to form a cabinet, Bordiga, speaking before the Congress of the Communist International in Moscow, admitted that "the revolutionary socialist proletarian tendency that had strengthened after the War, in the heat of mass enthusiasm, had not been able to take advantage of the favorable situation."

Radek was right when he argued, in opposition to the more optimistic Zinoviev, that "the victory of fascism was a defeat far greater than the defeat of communist Hungary and of greater and more terrible consequences for the future."

FIFTEEN

Mexico

For us and our children Mexico always meant one of the happiest periods of our lives. It was my introduction to the diplomatic world. We landed in Vera Cruz in 1931, in the spring. The ship on which my family and I traveled entered the port amid the acclamations and shouts of the Mexican workers and the sailors of the *Habana*, one of the two ships of the Spanish line that plied between Vera Cruz and Santander. On landing, we were able to take only a short walk through the city before official ceremonies of welcome began, but we felt that attraction of an atmosphere that was at once familiar and unreal. It was like returning to one's home by a new road of unsuspected beauty.

In my first speech in Mexico, at Vera Cruz, as the first ambassador of the Spanish Republic, I did not believe that it was enough to follow the advice of Talleyrand, an exceptionally able guide to classical diplomacy, and one whose activities and writings I knew well. He said that an ambassador should "improve what he says and prepare what he is not to say." From the first moment I discovered why I was there: it was to try to put an end to a period of misunderstanding between two peoples equally sensitive about personal bravery and equally jealous of their independence.

The journey from Vera Cruz to the capital was made by day so that we could enjoy the scenery. At the railroad stations where we stopped, Spaniards came from the nearby villages and filled our compartments with flowers for Luisa, admiring the youth and beauty of their ambassador's wife, for she was only a little over thirty. She was of enormous help to me.

I owed to the German Government my appointment to represent Spain in Mexico. It is my only reason for being grateful to that government. The provisional Spanish Republican Government, on naming me ambassador to Berlin, had believed that I knew Germany well. The German

Government must have decided that I knew it far too well. I had written copiously on a subject that had absorbed my attention during my frequent visits to Germany: the constant German disposition to change each military defeat into the point of departure for the next revenge, and the imperishable ability of German militarism to revive and to leap from one war to another, and always to be the force that starts the next war.

In 1931 National Socialism was practically victorious in Germany. Its influence on the *Wilhelmstrasse*, the Ministry of Foreign Affairs, was already great. The German Government made it known to the Spanish Government that any other ambassador would be an improvement over me. Spain yielded, despite the violent protests of the Socialist chief and secretary of the treasury, Indalecio Prieto, who insisted that I be confirmed in my post. A compromise was found: Spain would raise its Mexican Legation to embassy rank and it would appoint me ambassador.

This was not a mission of mere protocol. The Mexican Revolution, with its agrarian reforms, had been offensive to the interests of Spaniards who had owned vast stretches of land that were expropriated to be distributed among the farmers. Feeling themselves members of the Spanish-speaking family and accustomed to being able to buy the favors of the authorities of the pre-revolutionary era, the Spanish landowners and the Spanish businessmen refused to adjust to the new situation. As a result there were hundreds of incidents, claims, protests, deaths, tension between Madrid and the Mexican capital.

What was ahead of me was a patient effort at clarification and reconciliation. It was necessary to convince the Spaniards that they must adjust themselves to what was established in the Mexican Constitution, whose Article 27, one of its key articles, provided for carrying out the measures adopted on agrarian matters. It was necessary to win the cooperation and support of the Mexicans, revealing to them a republican and progressive Spain entirely different from the feudal and clerical Spain with which revolutionary Mexico could not get along.

In order to bring to the Mexican people the message of the Spanish Republic it was necessary to mingle with the people. I did so beginning with a picturesque and most instructive excursion through the state of Guerrero in the company of Narciso Bassols, the minister of education. I discovered on that occasion that the best way to get to know Mexico is to travel on horseback. I reached Acapulco one evening on horseback and had a midnight moonlit swim in the ocean. On horseback I reached the most hidden places in Mexico, where there were Spaniards who had never seen a representative of their country.

The trip through Guerrero lasted many days. The minister was dedicating new schools. He would make a speech in each town and I would follow him with an address in which I would speak of the changes that were taking place in Spain and would answer the questions of Mexican farmers about the condition of the Spanish farmers.

This direct contact with the Mexican people had for me the double value of showing me the strong impact of the Mexican Revolution on the masses and of establishing a current of true reciprocal sympathy. The well-justified rumor that the new Spanish ambassador was a friend of Mexico spread swiftly throughout the country and everywhere I went the reception was marvelously spontaneous and warm.

To visit as much of Mexico as possible was not a duty but a pleasure.

President Cárdenas hears complaints of Mexican peasants,
December 1936

Mexico now reveals all her attractions to international tourism. But in those days it was not crowded with foreigners. Mexico City, which now has more than five million inhabitants, had not more than half a million when I first went there. Each different part of Mexico had its interest and none was ever a disappointment. The landscape was so varied, at once delicate and strong. The flowers were the most beautiful in the world. The flower market was a place that one could never tire of. Fruits like the mango, the papaya, the tiny *zapote* were a constant temptation; and the *corridos* (ballads), the outstanding national songs, very similar to Spanish folk songs, about which Federico García Lorca had talked to me in Andalusia before I went to Mexico. One of the poems that led to Lorca's murder at the time of Franco's rebellion, because the poem attacked the despised Civil Guard, was composed so that it could be sung to the tune of a Mexican *corrido*.

The *corrido* — and the *mañanitas* (dawn), which to the sound of the guitar came to wish us good morning wherever we appeared. The *corrido* was inseparable from the revolution. It rendered the people's homage to the great figures of the revolution — to Emiliano Zapata, about whom the farmers who had fought under his command spoke to me with deep feelings and great enthusiasm, and to Pancho Villa, who defied the American soldiers, a strategist shaped in combat, the most controversial guerrilla fighter of his time, who was the subject of novels and films and who, years later, received official consecration in a solemn session of the Mexican Parliament.

The revolution was still very much alive when I reached Mexico. The Mexican embassy, which formerly had received and entertained only counterrevolutionaries, opened its doors to the revolutionaries. The embassy of the Spanish Republic became the gathering place for the Mexicans who came straight from the revolution and who continued to serve it. I shall name some of them, but those whom I do not mention have an equal place in my affection and gratitude. They all contributed to my dream of uniting Mexico and Spain in a new and unbreakable friendship. Juan de Dios Bojórquez, politician and journalist; Vicente Lombardo Toledano, still very young and destined to be a distinguished leader in the labor movement in Mexico and in all of Latin America; Daniel Cossío Villegas, the founder of the great publishing house, Fondo de Cultura Económica, who later took part in several United Nations conferences; Manuel Sierra, from a family of historians, on the staff of the minister of foreign affairs; and the minister himself, Genaro Estrada, a great diplomat and a great poet, like Enrique González Martínez, like Alfonso Reyes; Generals Mújica and Jara, indomitable leaders. With one of them I remain in active contact even today, Jesús Silva Herzog, who edits *Cuadernos Americanos*, the most prestigious publication in all of Latin America, to which I have the honor to be a frequent contributor.

I knew Silva Herzog in Moscow, in the late 1920s, when he was the Mexican minister. In his legation, on his country's national holiday, I heard Mexican revolutionary songs sung for the first time. Later he was one of the Mexicans who came to meet me in Vera Cruz in 1931. Our friendship has never been broken. He has told us his own story, with his heart always loyal to the origins of the Great Revolution that was like a clear and strong flame in Latin America. Silva Herzog begins with this observation: "In revolutions, when they are really revolutions, there is a mixture of good and evil, of ideals and crime; they are something like a whirlwind, like a hurricane wind that knocks down whatever is standing and lifts up the lowliest and even the manure of the dungheaps."

Silva Herzog tells, for example, how the Constitutionalists reached his city, San Luis Potosí, in mid-1914 and how, at the end of January of 1915, the Villistas, the followers of Pancho Villa, came demanding forced loans on threat of execution. He recalls a Spanish merchant assassinated on the orders of General Urbina, because he had not collected the amount of money that was demanded of him. There followed other series of unnecessary assassinations and humiliations.

"All that," observed Silva Herzog, "offended and wounded my feelings. I was nevertheless steeped in the spirit of the Revolution and I was impelled by the ideals that justified the tremendous conflict." He was most successful in his portraits of the principal figures of the revolution, their whims and their caprices: Villa appearing at the Aguas Calientes Convention and giving a hug to General Obregón, whom he had been on the verge of executing a few weeks before in Chihuahua.

A year later it was Obregón who dominated the stage. He had defeated Villa in four great battles, and in one of them he lost an arm when a grenade exploded. He was to be, for the rest of his life, the glorious cripple, as great a politician as he was a soldier. Those who formerly had been against the general now could not find praise high enough to proclaim him the greatest Mexican revolutionary. And he was indeed one of the best. To Silva Herzog, at that time poet and journalist and now an economist and historian, although his first sympathies never left him, all that shifting seemed too cynical. At a meeting he was suddenly asked to make some remarks. He said that the people had always been deceived in all revolutions, that if Don Venustiano Carranza, the chief of state, did not fulfill his promises to the people, the people should oppose him, and that if General Obregón, who was present at the meeting, did not fulfill *his* promises to the people, the people should oppose *him*. Silva Herzog tells with a sense of humor how he finished his remarks amid whistles and protests and was led off to jail. But this was no joking matter. He was determined that, if he had to die, he would die like a man. I, who have come to know and to love Mexico, know that few people can surpass the Mexican in his scorn of death. Silva Herzog had read a little book about the private life of Maximilian, which told how the archduke, victim of an absurdity of the imperialism of that time, when he fell before the firing squad murmured a few words, and the young journalist in his cell was thinking over what words he would say when he was executed.

The words were never needed. Silva Herzog was finally freed. Of the whole experience, which did not break in any way his allegiance to the revolution, Silva Herzog remembers most clearly and with amusement the farewell meal in jail, offered by a thief who was called the Spider because he always dressed in black to operate more effectively in the dark. In the name of all the prisoners, the Spider praised the humanitarian and generous conduct of the political prisoner toward the nonpolitical prisoners, with whom he shared the food that his mother sent him. For all that period Silva Herzog has great nostalgia because, even though there were many excesses and injustices, the revolution was at that time triumphant in Mexico.

As the most profound analyst of the Mexican Revolution, Silva Herzog, an enthusiastic admirer of Lázaro Cárdenas, nevertheless paid to General Calles, with whom Cárdenas clashed, the justified tribute of saying that Calles was a patriot. I was lucky enough to win the priceless cooperation of these two great Mexicans, one, Calles, during my ambassadorship, the other, Cárdenas, during the Spanish War.

Even though Obregón was still in everyone's memory, and even though his assassination in 1928 seemed to have occurred only the day before, the man who had most weight in Mexican politics when I took up residence in the embassy was ex-President General Calles, a powerful leader of the revolution. From what I heard about Obregón and from my personal experience with Calles, Obregón was more popular but Calles had an extraordinarily well organized mind and a unique capacity for leadership. No matter who was president, whether it was Ortiz Rubio or Abelardo Rodriguez, Calles was the real power. On weekends spent at his handsome house in Cuernavaca I used to listen to him reminisce about the history of the revolution. He would show me photographs as a token of intimacy and friendship. I shall never forget one of them. It was a snapshot of a young officer seated alone on a hillock in open country, at the end of a battle. It gave an impression of quiet strength, of Calles the planner as well as Calles the revolutionary.

During Calles' presidency there was more construction in Mexico than for many years: highways, bridges, dams, electric-power installations and factories. When I was traveling with him in the state of Morelos, he talked to me at length about a Six-Year Plan, which later was announced spectacularly at the 1933 meeting of the National Revolutionary party in Querétaro. General Calles was much interested in my stories of travel in Russia and the carrying out of its Five-Year Plans, which greatly strengthened the Soviet Union, and which would enable it to resist the force of Hitler's armies in the Second World War. Calles was not only a builder, but a destroyer of counterrevolutionary forces. He knew how to put the Church in its place, although he did not go so far as one of his followers, the fanatic governor of the state of Tabasco, Garrido Canabal, who showed the extent of his anticlericalism by naming his two sons Lenin and Lucifer. He also decreed that no priest could enter his state unless he was married.

In 1926, as part of the United States plan to sabotage the Mexican Revolution with the support of the American Catholic hierarchy, the Mexican bishops were emboldened to take a stand against a Constitution which restricted their privileges. Calles replied by deporting two hundred priests and nuns and by ordering all the rest of them to be registered. Neither the United States nor the American hierarchy had realized what kind of a man Calles was. The Church tried to counterattack. The priests decided to abandon the country. "For a fleeing enemy build a bridge of silver," says an old Spanish proverb. On August 1, 1926, for the first time since the arrival of the *Conquistadores*, there was not a priest or a nun in the country. Calles put the churches under the control of committees of laymen who assumed the responsibility for keeping them open.

My special relations with General Calles went quite a bit beyond the diplomatic corps. They caused a certain surprise in the Spanish colony, which realized what was implied. The sensation among the Spaniards was the day when General Calles came to eat a *cocido* (a Spanish stew) at the embassy. No foreign diplomat had ever been so honored. My wife told our Mexican cook that Calles was going to be seated at our table that evening and the cook, scarcely daring to believe this, took great pains to prepare a *cocido* the like of which had never been seen in Madrid.

I was the only diplomat who was with Calles the night when his young wife died. I spent that whole tragic night at his house with some of his closest friends. From time to time Calles would come down from the bedroom to the living room. He would see me and take a chair by my side. The others would leave us to ourselves. About three in the morning a young general arrived from his post of command to be with his chief in his time of grief. It was General Cárdenas. I was introduced to him and I found him at once, in spite of his modesty and reserve, an extraordinarily impressive person.

It was surely with the memory of this brief meeting and because of his firm ideas of revolutionary solidarity that Lázaro Cárdenas, on his election to the presidency, sent to me in Madrid a cordial cablegram inviting me to be present at his inauguration. I was then being pursued by the police as a result of the general revolutionary strike in Asturias and of our attempt to anticipate the outbreak of fascism in Spain by taking power ourselves, under the leadership of Largo Caballero. The cablegram from Cárdenas never reached me. But it had unquestionably been read by the Spanish authorities, which is what Cárdenas wanted, and it doubtless saved me from arrest by the reactionary government of Lerroux, who had named General Franco to lead the suppression of the rebellion of the Asturian miners.

When I became a political exile, General Cárdenas, who was still in office, offered me a Mexican diplomatic passport. This would have spared me many headaches in the long years that followed, but I declined the offer with thanks, since I wanted to keep the same status as all the other Spanish refugees. Cárdenas also offered me and my family a country house for us to use as long as we wished. This second and very moving offer was also declined since I had decided to continue from New York my struggle against Franco.

From my numerous conversations with Lázaro Cárdenas when he was president of Mexico and afterward I reached the conclusion that a second term of office for him would have been a total success. Unfortunately tradition made this impossible. I remembered from the time of my ambassadorship that each official communiqué ended with the familiar formula: "Real suffrage. No re-election." The "no re-election" slogan was the answer to the eternal presidency of Porfirio Díaz. Cárdenas would have been the last man to allow the rule to be broken.

Nevertheless, if there had ever been a case where an exception would have been justified, his was the case. His presidency had thrust him into the heart of the Mexican people. I never saw any leader in any country, except Mao Tse-tung, attract the enthusiasm of the masses to such an extent. On several occasions, traveling with him in the presidential car, I saw General Cárdenas stop to talk with an old woman or with a group of farmers in the most intimate imaginable manner. He was really a people's president, a part of the people.

One could not expect that, once he left the presidency, though he would continue to exert his enormous influence upon people, and especially simple — he would continue to govern. He had given an example of not tolerating a shadow power to continue after a presidential regime ended. In 1935 General Calles, "the greatest leader of the Revolution," expressed in a press interview with Ezequiel Padilla, a former minister, his disagreement with the policy of President Cárdenas in favoring the Mexican workers. President Cárdenas sent General Calles a message asking him to leave the country at once. Jesús Silva Herzog says that in this case Cárdenas did a great service to the nation. "The maximum term became a part of history." From then on each president fulfills his mandate of six years and then practically retires from political life. Nevertheless, and in spite of the correctness observed by Lázaro Cárdenas since he ended his term of office, his moral authority was very great in matters that had concerned his presidency — for example, in the matter of relations with Franco. One day when I was in Mexico, influential Mexican friends informed me of a rumor that, under pressure from Madrid and from powerful commercial interests, Mexico was about to renew diplomatic relations with Spain. To prevent this, I was advised to go to see Cárdenas. I was getting ready to do so when the rumor was proved to be false. But the fact that Cárdenas was thought to be the only one who could squash the supposed diplomatic intrigue was a proof that, even after his retirement, his opinion had weight in Mexican politics.

Spain was the greatest problem in the international policy of the Cárdenas presidency, but it was not the only problem. In Geneva I had witnessed, in the League of Nations, how Mexico, under her consistent and distinguished leadership, gave a lesson of international decorum at a moment in which it was very much needed.

In Geneva, Isidro Fabela, an admirer of Cárdenas and an authority on international affairs, demanded the fulfilling of international justice in the case of Ethiopia, and the nonrecognition of agreements obtained by force. Ethiopia, before the shame of "Non-Intervention" in Spain, was one of the disgraces of the League of Nations, which led to its discredit and to its ruin.

Mussolini knew that he could do anything he wanted and he knew that in the League of Nations Great Britain spoke through the mouths of her foreign secretary, Sir Samuel Hoare, and Sir John Simon, also a notorious collaborator with the Fascists. And France, through her Minister Pierre Laval, was going to join Britain in approving the Italian aggression. On May 5, 1936, Mussolini's troops occupied Addis Ababa, and four days later Italy annexed the invaded country, which was a member of the League of Nations. Nothing happened. On the contrary, the most reactionary members of the League combined with the most "democratic" to carry to its end the strangulation of Ethiopia, whose sovereign, Haile Selassie, took refuge in London. Poland had a leading role in the plot. Months later I had to confront its representative, the odious, shallow Colonel Jozef Beck, consistently aligned on the side of the aggressors against Spain, even though one of the aggressors, Hitler, invaded his country three years later.

Mexico stood firm. Following instructions from President Cárdenas, Isidro Fabela rose to say: "I have just listened with great attention to the statement made by the Honorable Representative of Poland. If I understood him correctly, he did not make any concrete proposal. Nevertheless, as he seems to imply that Ethiopia has ceased to exist and as Mexico's silence might be interpreted as giving consent to this interpretation, in the name of my country I declare most energetically that I protest against any maneuver that tends to expel from the family of the League of Nations any member of that family."

In March of 1938 the vigorous voice of the Mexico of Lázaro Cárdenas was again heard in the League of Nations. It was over the invasion of Austria. Hitler had been testing the terrain. At that time he was more prudent than one would believe from some accounts. It was only when he noticed a lack of resistance in the opposition that he moved into action.

Later Isidro Fabela told me: "I was at the head of the Mexican delegation in Geneva and I realized with sorrow and surprise that no member of the League was intervening in any way in favor of Austria. In view of the fact that President Cárdenas had instructed me to be faithful to the principles of the Pact; in view of the fact that in the cases of Ethiopia and Spain Mexico had been the only State to fulfill her duties by protesting against the conquest of Ethiopia and against foreign intervention in the Motherland, and judging that my obligation was to place on record once more my Government's support, in fulfillment of its duties, I sent to the Secretary General of the League of Nations, Mr. Avenol, a note urging him to inform all member states, having also informed the world press, so that everyone would know that Mexico condemned the suppression of Austria as an independent state."

Seeing what now happens in the United Nations and the warnings heard about the importance of preventing the United Nations from following the same unfortunate path of its predecessor, the League of Nations, the vision of Lázaro Cárdenas with respect to neutrality is clearer than ever. The Mexican president made use of the Spanish War to denounce the hypocrisy behind which the opportunists of neutrality took refuge, trying to escape the duties imposed on them by the Pact, the Charter of that time. Cárdenas argued with great logic that if the Pact established a clear separation between the attacked states, to which all moral and material support should be given, and the aggressive states, against whom the League should apply economic and financial sanctions, what right then did the Council and the League Assembly have to declare that the member states were neutral in the face of the international struggle that was developing on Spanish soil?

I based myself on the reasoning of President Cárdenas when Edouard Herriot, the great French parlimentarian who represented France in the League, advised me privately in Geneva to demand "international justice." I said somewhat ironically that I was more modest and that I was content to ask for the fulfillment of the Pact, which is what the Mexican delegation was doing, on instructions from Cárdenas.

One cannot evoke the exemplary international policy of Lázaro Cárdenas without mentioning his battle against the abuses of the oil companies. In this battle Silva Herzog played a major role. In the report drawn up under his direction it was clearly established that the companies, in spite of the substantial benefits that they had obtained, had never carried out in Mexico a single undertaking of any social character. It was pure exploitation without a sign of compensation.

The oil companies had been accustomed to dictating the law and they did not believe that Cárdenas would dare to go as far as expropriation. The president had tried, in fact, to reach a compromise with them. It was useless. The spokesman for Standard Oil of New Jersey rejected in New York the conciliatory gesture of Cárdenas, declaring: "As far as we are concerned, we now have nothing further to do; the next step is up to the Mexican Government to take." And the Mexican Government took it.

On March 18, 1938, President Cárdenas announced over the radio to the Mexican people the expropriation of the oil companies. He spoke in defense of sovereignty and of the nation's dignity. Against the defeatism of certain Mexican circles accustomed to the idea that a Latin American country could not exist except with the approval of the United States and under the sign of the dollar, Lázaro Cárdenas appealed for the support of the masses. It was his way of governing. "I ask of the entire nation a moral and material support sufficient to carry out a decision that is so justified, so momentous, and so indispensable. The Government has already taken the needed steps so that there will be no diminution in the construction activities that are occurring throughout the Republic, and for this, I ask the people for full confidence and complete backing for the measures that the Government will have to dictate. Nevertheless, if it should be necessary, we shall sacrifice all the construction activities which the Nation has undertaken during this period of Government, in order to face the economic compromises that the application of the Law of Expropriation to such vast interests may impose on us, even though the very subsoil of the fatherland will give us all the economic resources needed to pay off the obligation of indemnity that we have undertaken."

The people responded fully and with that valor and sense of grace that characterizes the Mexicans. There was a *corrido* about the expropriation. "The Petroleum Ballad" said in a loud voice that the Mexican people were on Cárdenas' side against the foreign exploitation and against submission to the companies.

Valor paid off. The task was not easy. All the administrators and technicians of the oil companies were foreigners. When they were informed of the exploitation they quit their jobs. They had to be replaced by Mexicans. To make a success of the expropriation became a national obligation. The people pitched in with enthusiasm. The railroad employees vied with one another in working without cease and there was no lack of gasoline anywhere. A hundred thousand Mexicans took to the streets in Mexico City to demonstrate their support of the expropriation. Public collections were organized to bring money to the government. Simple little people brought money, or a little family jewel, or table silver. It was very moving and it brought great joy to Lázaro Cárdenas. Today the nationalized industry is an unquestioned success, with more than ninety percent of the energy coming from petroleum. Cárdenas was one president who fulfilled his electoral campaign promises. In his six years as president he distributed forty-five million acres of irrigated land. Since the Agrarian Law of 1915 there had never been such a distribution of land among the farmers. In 1936 Cárdenas gave an egalitarian thrust to the National Farm Credit Bank, which had paid less heed to poor farmers than had been hoped by its founders, and then founded the National Bank for Credit to Owners of Distributed Lands, set up exclusively to grant loans to those who had benefited from the distribution of land.

When General Cárdenas turned the presidency over to President Manuel Avila Camacho, he gave him a handwritten letter, not at all widely known but which tells a lot about Cárdenas. It said: "Something very important and momentous in the life of Mexico, for us who assume power, is to be sure that, until there is a categorical declaration by the United States Government that it abandons its theory of recognizing the nationality of origin of Americans who move to other countries, we should not admit here new investors from our northern neighbor. If this important matter is neglected, we shall live to regret more illegal claims and serious conflicts for Mexico. Although foreigners, in accordance with our laws, are obliged to renounce all diplomatic claims, what is certain is that the North American governments have not respected this principle, which is the supreme law in our country, and because of this it is becoming indispensable to have in advance an official declaration from the American Government. Our Chancellery should go on working until it achieves absolute respect for the sovereignty of the Nation. If the citizen who succeeds me in the presidency agrees with me on this matter, I ask him to transmit this message to his immediate successor." The advice of Lázaro Cárdenas was gradually forgotten over the years with the result that today foreign investments in Mexico are multiplying and eighty percent of them are United States investments.

Cárdenas established many records. One was that in the six years of his presidency there was not a single political prisoner. He opened his country's doors to the greatest influx of political exiles of all times and thousands of Spanish Republicans found a second home in Mexico. Cárdenas told me once that the only limitation was transportation. "If I had had the ships I would have brought to Mexico all the Spaniards lost in the French concentration camps." Among the exiles was the director of the Museum of Natural History in Madrid, who on embarking for Mexico at the age of eighty-nine answered a question as to why he was leaving Spain: "Why am I going to Mexico? To die with dignity."

We happily accept the judgment of Silva Herzog: "For us Cárdenas was the Mexican politician with the greatest international influence. He was a very great President, the only one to equal in stature the distinction of Benito Juárez." In the history of Latin America he stands beside José Martí of Cuba and he precedes Salvador Allende of Chile who, as these words are being written, is his country's great hope. Following Cárdenas' example, Allende called the day of the nationalization of copper the "Day of National Dignity."

I love Mexico today with the same loyalty as in the days when I had the honor of representing Spain there. But I miss the revolutionary passion that I witnessed. Nowadays there is an attempt to revive it, by Silva Herzog, by the poet Octavio Paz, by the novelist and dramatist Carlos Fuentes, and by many young people who let me know the strength of their support for our struggle for freedom in Spain.

SIXTEEN

The New China

President Nixon's visit to Peking in February 1972 had consequences that will be appreciated fully only at some time in the future. But one immediate consequence at least was to reveal to Americans the China of Mao Tse-tung. If a book were printed in two columns, with one column showing all that had been written and said in the United States about China since 1949, the year of the liberation, and the other column showed all that has been written and said since Nixon's visit, the difference would be startling. Americans are finally learning something about Mao's China, although it is a very limited amount. There are still many things in China that are not understood by Americans, beginning with their experts, the Sinologists.

The Americans are not the only ignorant ones. A few days after the publication of the photograph of Chairman Mao shaking the hand of President Nixon, I met in the Palais des Nations in Geneva a member of the Secretariat who up to then would have been classified as pro-Chinese. He said: "I no longer believe in God or in Mao. I no longer believe in anything."

In words less shocking, in French, British, Italian, German newspapers, or on the radio, from the pens or the lips of well-known leftist writers, many of whom I know well, came comments that reflected the same disappointment. An ill-contained irritation on seeing the major representative of American imperialism welcomed in revolutionary China with somewhat open arms. They thought that China was sacrificing her principles for the benefit of her national interests.

It was not the first time that enthusiasm for China was followed by disappointment, or that pessimism was followed by the success of the Chinese Revolution. Something similar happened with regard to the Cultural Revolution. An American intellectual with whom I had often exchanged impressions of China and who shared my admiration and friendship for the late Edgar Snow (and *there* was a man who knew China well) said to me: "Don't talk to me any more about China. A country that keeps its schools closed for two years no longer appeals to me." Other China admirers argued with me when, on my return from there in 1967, at the height of the Cultural Revolution, I disagreed with their predictions that China was being ruined. In both cases, and in others that I could cite, the error lay in failing to understand the China of today, failing to distinguish the primary from the secondary.

Dr. and Mrs. del Vayo with Premier Chou En-lai
and other Chinese notables

As the influence of China in world affairs is only beginning and as China in the coming years will be called upon to play a more and more important role in international politics and in the ideological sphere, it seems to me useful to present here my experiences during three visits to China in 1957, 1961, and 1967.

I had read everything I could about China in all the languages that I know. But in my three visits I tried to see things with my own eyes. I saw not only the landscape of a country that had a charm immortalized by the paintings of many dynasties, not only Peking, which is for me the most beautiful city in the world, constantly enriched by the planting of thousands of trees and the construction of many buildings, yet without losing any of its unique character. What I tried to see and sense was the nature of the Chinese people, in order to have a basis on which to build a vision of China that would be valid today and for many years to come.

I therefore visited, on my three trips, large parts of China, in the company of my wife, who is an excellent observer. But many other people have made extensive visits to China. The point is not who has traveled the most miles or the most thousands of miles. The point is not who has interviewed the greatest number of dignitaries. The point is to get to the heart of the Chinese Revolution and to find in it what is new and important in the world Communist or Socialist movement.

To reach that knowledge of China, I had the advantage of enjoying the trust of the Chinese, a trust that increased from one visit to the next. Everyone knows that courtesy and tact are characteristic of the Chinese people. A foreign visitor can be assured of being received politely. But trust is something else. China's experience with foreigners, a centuries-old experience, has made the Chinese generally suspicious, with very good reason. But when they trust someone, all reservations disappear. This is why, on my visits, I was able to talk with all kinds of people, from Chairman Mao down to a Chinese whom I met in the street, who happened to speak a language that I knew and with whom I walked along as though we were old friends, he asking me how old I was and what I was doing in China.

A difference between Peking and other cities in the Socialist world is the ease with which one gets to know people in the Chinese capital. I have been in the National Hotel and other hotels in Moscow, and it would never have occurred to me to go from one table to another to chat with people eating there. But in the dining room of the Hotel Peking I went to the table where the wife of Ernesto Guevara was sitting (Ché was still alive then) or to a table where there was a group of Australian doctors who had come to study health conditions in China and who exchanged impressions with me.

My wife and I spent many days in the Peoples Communes, not just one day or overnight like other foreign visitors. We lived the life of the Chinese farmers. We slept in a "tank," which is an enormous clay bed, easily built up again when it wears down. Underneath it there is a huge tube bringing warm water from the kitchen, an arrangement that supplies a very effective heating. We took our meals with the family, nourishing, varied, and delicious food. To his rice and to the vegetables that have flooded China thanks to the communes, the Chinese farmer has learned to add fish, which he raises in pools built to provide against a year of drought. Drought and floods were once the plagues of China.

The millions of lives lost as the result of the catastrophes of nature are today a thing of the past.

We had two very good interpreters. On the first visit we had Chin, who spoke excellent English; on the other two visits we had Tang, whose Spanish was very fluent. My wife discovered that he had learned it with a schoolmate of our eldest son. The schoolmate was teaching in China. When we arrived there in 1957 more than sixty Spaniards were in Peking, working in radio, in publishing houses, teaching Spanish. They held a dinner for my wife and me that was attended by the poet Rafael Alberti, his wife María Teresa León, also a writer, and their daughter, also a poet. They were on a visit to China. The Spanish workers had come from the Soviet Union when there were good relations between the two giants in the Socialist world. Then, when the break came, the Spaniards, who were happy to work in Peking and who were very well treated by the Chinese, were ordered back to the Soviet Union. But they left behind students like Tang, very well trained, and today the number of Chinese who have mastered Spanish has increased considerably.

In the commune, the wife of the head of the family, who was also the head of one of the production gangs, was entirely at our disposal. We visited everything throughout the commune and since we were on the go all day, a "doctor," one of those young girls studying medicine who were beginning to practice out in the country before finishing their training, used to come to take our blood pressure each morning and to assure us that our health was not suffering from the beating that we were giving ourselves. At night after supper other commune families would come to see us, and the young people were especially interested in being able to talk freely with a foreign friend. I gathered a huge quantity of notes, enough notes to produce a whole book just on this one commune.

No one can put up a false front for the length of time that we were in China. And those who, on reading this, think that it was all well-contrived propaganda and that we were just two gullible tourists who swallowed everything are completely wrong. It is on the actuality of hundreds of millions of Chinese farmers, won over to the "thinking of Mao," that the solidity of the Chinese Revolution is based, a solidity that was demonstrated during the Cultural Revolution. Those who predicted that China would collapse because of the gigantic shock of that revolution underestimated the strength that came from the unconditional support that the great majority of the Chinese people, who are farmers, gave and give to the leadership of Mao Tse-tung. The Soviet Embassy in Peking had a staff of more than a thousand. There were two thousand eyes looking in all directions. Looking but not seeing at all clearly.

When I was in Peking in 1967, in the midst of the Cultural Revolution, I learned that the Soviet embassy was counting on the victory of Liu Shao-chi over Mao Tse-tung. I, who noticed everywhere I went in China the immense popularity of Chairman Mao, could not understand the lack of sense of reality of the Russians. Five years later came details on the fall and death of Lin Piao, the former defense minister and one-time heir apparent to Mao Tse-tung, who died in a plane crash in September 1971 while trying to escape to the Soviet Union. Lin had enjoyed the friendship of Moscow since the moment when he turned against Mao. Lin paid for his rebellion with his life. But Liu Shao-chi had sent trucks filled with his armed supporters to Shanghai to crush the supporters of Mao Tse-tung. I had the story from workers in the port of Shanghai. Yet Liu was still alive, "being re-educated," according to a Chinese friend. That he should still be alive is one of those aspects of the Chinese Revolution that is incomprehensible to many people. But that's the way it is.

One night a farmer came from a neighboring commune to visit the family who were our hosts. He had gone with a delegation from his commune to visit Chairman Mao. The farmer was unusually tall, very handsome, with the brilliantly white teeth that are the envy of foreigners. He was accompanied by his daughter, about fifteen and very pretty. For this occasion she had changed her blue cotton jacket for a multicolored one. She told us that she was studying to prepare for the Special School of Geology in Peking, which we had visited. The petroleum boom was beginning in China, and getting to be self-sufficient in that most important branch of the economy was a goal that seemed to have a special appeal to young people.

When the girl had told us about her plans, I asked her father about his impressions of his visit to Chairman Mao. "He is the simplest man that I have ever met in my life. He is just like one of us and he is very well-informed about our problems. In our commune, and it is a small commune, we have eight handwritten notes from Chairman Mao telling us how to solve our difficulties, not just about the crops and about how to feed the commune. He has spoken to us about the revolution and about the necessity, for the future of socialism, that China be faithful to its principles. She must be so not only for her own sake but for the sake of the whole world. She must not sacrifice her revolution for the material well-being of the individual. Material well-being is important, but principles are more important. And Chairman Mao spoke for a long time against egotism. Egotism and a truly socialistic society are incompatible, he told us. Chairman Mao was very happy when we told him that, by increasing our production each year, we hoped to be able to help other peoples who still were in our situation before the Liberation, oppressed and starving." For me it was fascinating to hear a farmer, who generally thinks only of his work and his earnings, talking about his duty to help other peoples. This attitude is essential to an appreciation of the role that China is going to play in the coming years with relation to the "third world."

In the 1970s China has become the Communist world's principal supplier of economic aid to developing countries, greatly outstripping the Soviet Union. According to a source not suspected of sympathy for the Chinese Revolution, the U.S. State Department's Bureau of Intelligence and Research, Chinese commitments to developing nations reached 709 million dollars in 1970, compared with 204 million dollars by the Soviet Union. But in 1972 the increase in Chinese aid to the "third world" was even greater.

This confirms what Chinese economists told me the last time that I was in Peking. They insisted that, to the extent that the growth of the Chinese economy permitted it, the aid to the developing countries would increase more and more. And China would not stipulate that a country that received aid be in favor of the politics of the Peking Government. In fact, Malaysia and Turkey received emergency relief even before they established diplomatic relations with the People's Republic of China. As this is being written, Peking is considering a vast plan of aid to the Latin American nations, and the Venezuelan Manuel Pérez Guerrero, Secretary General of the United Nations Conference on Commerce and Development, has been invited to visit China.

The stories, the human and picturesque side, living with the farmers as we did, were of more help to us in understanding the Chinese countryside than a conversation with the Minister of Agriculture and all the statistics put together. I reached conclusions important for judging the future of China: the farmer did not view his commune from a purely local or personal angle, as a mere improvement in his living conditions, as a great improvement, in fact, compared with the life that our host led before the revolution. He told us about this in great detail in the days that we spent in his house, a house that really belonged to him, together with hens and a couple of pigs. He saw the commune as a very small cog in the wheels of the revolution, but essential to it.

When these farmers talked to us about how, on rocks that had never seen grass, they had planted trees that now produced delicious fruit, or how men, women, and children had lugged wood to build a new workshop from a forest some miles away, they felt sure that they were serving the cause of the revolution and that they were acting in accordance with the thought of Chairman Mao. They told themselves that their successful efforts, multiplied by the efforts of hundreds of millions of other Chinese, in agriculture as well as in industry and mining, assured revolutionary China of being one day the leading Socialist nation of the earth.

Certain mocking comments were made abroad about the thoughts of Chairman Mao and about the little red book of quotations, the constant reading of which seemed to certain foreign intellectuals too boring for words. But these had penetrated so deeply into the Chinese mind that there was no turning back. In short, I can conceive of no greater possible error of judgment than the one committed by those who speak of a different China after the death of Mao. I feel quite safe in predicting that after the death of Mao, China, instead of following Russia and moving toward compromise, will be just as revolutionary as the China of today. It will be revolutionary enough to allow for readjustments in conduct that will not change in any way the essence of revolutionary China. This was true during the sensational visit of President Nixon to Peking, so wrongly judged by so many.

Does all this mean that everything in China is perfect? The first people to be deeply dissatisfied by what they have accomplished are the Chinese leaders, beginning with Mao and followed by Chou En-lai. And here I should like to add my personal observation. I had met the Chinese prime minister on several occasions during my different visits to China. But it was a whole evening spent at his home in 1957 that enabled me to form for myself a personal idea of the man who assures the forward march of China across all the crises and all the storms. His portrait is familiar now to millions of Americans who saw him on television during a week in Peking, in Hangchow, in Shanghai, accompanying President Nixon. Everyone knows that he comes from a family of Mandarins. There is unanimous praise of his distinction and his manners. To me, the most expressive thing about him are his hands. I watched them during our long interview. I noticed them again in 1961, when from the capitalist press box I saw them resting on his desk during the 22nd Congress of the Communist Party meeting in Moscow. I mention the capitalist press box because when I showed the Soviet controller my credentials as a correspondent of the *Nacional* of Caracas, he said: "This one to the capitalist box." There was a different press box for Communist or Communist-sympathizer journalists.

From my seat I observed Chou En-lai, whose entrance into the hall had been greeted by a rousing ovation. The Chinese prime minister applauded in turn the report read by Khrushchev, until he began to attack Stalin and Albania again, and entered on an area where Chou En-lai could not accompany him. Stalin could not be especially attractive to Chou En-lai, for he had been fundamentally opposed to Mao and to Chou. As is well-known, during the Second World War Stalin had supported Chiang Kai-shek. But the same thing happened with Chou En-lai and with other Chinese leaders that happened, as I have said, with Beatrice Webb, with Isaac Deutscher, and with Georg Lukács. Although they were not pro-Stalin, they were aware of the services rendered by Stalin to his country and to the revolution. That day, for the first time, I had the feeling that an ideological antagonism had been opened between China and the Soviet Union that would be very hard to heal. This surprised me at first because I was returning from my second visit to China and there I had not heard, in 1961, a single word against the Russians.

The evening spent in 1957 with Chou En-lai at his home, a home with a garden in which we could admire some Chinese trees that we had not seen before, produced a shift in my thinking that was of great value to me, because of the frankness with which the prime minister expressed himself on a great variety of topics. As our conversation began he took out a small notebook in which he had noted down some of the things that I had said in my series of lectures at the Chinese People's Institute of Foreign Affairs. That a man with the duties and responsibilities of the prime minister should find the time and the inclination to note down in that way my modest opinions on world affairs was for me a revelation of the personality of Chou and of the attitude of China toward those foreign visitors in whom it had faith.

One part of that interview, the part intended for the public, appeared in my book *Reportaje en China*, published in Mexico. I reread it as the result of the publication of the Shanghai communiqué, following the visit of President Nixon to China. The sense of continuity is striking and it justifies the opinion, formulated by some shrewd observers of that extraordinary event, that "China has not changed." Among the commentators to whom I refer there were three ex-premiers of France, Edgar Faure, Maurice Couve de Murville, and Pierre Mendès-France, the latter just back from China.

In 1957 Chou En-lai was already talking to me about the American people in the same terms as those of the Shanghai communiquè. Some days before we were received by the prime minister, we had returned from a trip in which we had seen most of China. I had visited the great steel factories in the interior, which for that epoch were very impressive and which have since been extended to various parts of the country. I had toured the coal mines, where I had talked directly with engineers who spoke English and who were beginning to experience a mounting production that was consolidated in later years. I had visited jails, factories, schools, I had talked with hundreds of people, with the chief of police in Shanghai who, using photographs, had shown me the difference between his Shanghai and the Shanghai of the 1930s, which attracted all the sensation-seekers and which was the scene of fabulous kidnappings of Chinese millionaires. Among these was the father of the vice-mayor of the city, an old industrialist who was very enthusiastic about the new regime. We dined with him in his house filled with treasures. There were jewels of jade and ivory, pictures of great value, rare books found in private houses by the Red Guards during the Cultural Revolution and turned over scrupulously to the local authorities. I had lengthy talks with the dockworkers in Shanghai and I talked again with their leaders in 1967, during the Cultural Revolution. They described for me with no inhibitions at all the violent struggles that had occurred in China's first port between the supporters of Mao and of Liu Shao-chi.

Del Vayo and Chou En-lai, Peking, 1961

I returned enthusiastic from the great trip through the interior. Chou En-lai listened to my enthusiasm with indulgence, but he felt it his duty to restrain me. He made a sober analysis of efforts and results. This statesman, whom Edgar Faure did not hesitate to present as a real expert in negotiation and as a realist of the first rank, revealed himself to me that afternoon with all his imposing personality. During my long newspaper career I have interviewed the most important figures in world politics, but I have never had a franker or more enlightening conversation. China, insisted Chou, was a very backward country. The task that it faced was enormous. It would be carried out without self-deception and with determination. He found much justice in a conclusion of mine, which I reached as the result of my travels: "I am convinced," I told him, "that in a nation so vast and with such varied regions no method of coercion would be effective. Even if the Chinese government had an army and a police force that could watch over the movements of all the people and try to make them work by force, it would not achieve as much as it is now achieving by having attracted the support of the Chinese people for the construction of a Socialist society." Chou En-lai told me that mine was an exact and adequate definition of the situation.

Perhaps with other words, but with the same idea inspiring these words, the Chinese prime minister already had said in 1957 the same thing that he says and repeats today: "that China was no great superpower, that it could not become one, that it did not wish to be one. It would always insist on equality of rights among the great nations and the little nations and on the defense of the principle of national independence, for the weaker as well as for the stronger." "What we have done," said Chou En-lai, "is to give to each Chinese, even to the poorest one, the one that foreign exploiters scornfully call a 'coolie,' a sense of human dignity, personal dignity and national dignity."

In my first visit to China I sensed to what degree that observation of the prime minister was correct. I had at my disposal, thanks to the kindness of the institute where I was lecturing, a car and an inexhaustible driver. As we wanted to see everything and to talk with the greatest number of people, we were always on the road. One of the meetings that we attended was with some Chinese-Americans who had come from the United States, where they had been highly successful, to help the Chinese government in its national effort. This was for me a great demonstration of the patriotic feeling in today's China.

Since we had kept our driver up until all hours of the night, we decided when we left China, that we wanted to give him some token of our gratitude. I knew that tipping was not allowed in China. But I thought that I might buy a gift for him or for his children. I talked about this with a professor of English at the University of Peking, one of my Chinese friends. He said no gift; "but when you say good-bye to the driver at the airport shake his hand." "But I've done that every night when we get back to the hotel." "Well, then," my friend suggested, "hold his hand in your hand just a little longer than usual and he will understand."

We had abundant evidence of that fineness in the simplest people in China. In a hotel in the interior three girls had waited on us, trying to make our stay as comfortable as possible, and succeeding admirably. Most of the provincial hotels, by the way, have been built under the new regime. They are all models of cleanliness and their service is outstanding in speed and courtesy. The hotels are numerous but still insufficient to serve the tens of thousands of foreigners who would like to go to China. In that hotel where we stayed we could not tip the three girls who were as kind as they were efficient. But my wife treated them with an affection to which they were very sensitive. On the day we left, we were surprised and touched to see the three girls at the railroad station, come to say good-bye to us.

My sympathy with the Chinese people did not prevent discussions in which I supported my points of view freely, as freely as the Chinese supported theirs. This occurred in Peking after my lectures at the Institute of Foreign Relations, in the question and answer period, and it occurred in my trips throughout the interior. The audience at my lectures was composed mostly of Chinese specialists in the subjects that I was discussing. I felt just as free to speak my mind as if I were lecturing at a university in the United States or at Chatham House in London. If my Chinese listeners disagreed with my point of view, they felt equally free to contradict me, but always with that politeness that is their characteristic. I remember especially my conversations with political-military experts to whom a foreign visitor rarely had free access. During the Cultural Revolution I had a conversation with two such experts that lasted five days, morning, afternoon, and evening.

A theme that frequently came into our conversations in Peking as well as in the interior was that of the relations between China and the Soviet Union. I had been able to follow the period of friendship as well as the various phases of its deterioration. In 1957, wherever we traveled in China, one of the most important buildings in each city was dedicated to Chinese-Soviet Friendship. The Soviet experts and their families were treated with special consideration. The best hotel rooms and the best lodgings were for them. Although the Russians who were working in China treated foreigners with great reserve, it was not hard to see that they were happy to be in China and to make their contribution to the creation of a new Socialist state.

I talked with the Chinese engineers who were working with Soviet engineers to finish the first great bridge across the Yangtse River in 1957, the bridge that was going to unite Northern and Southern China, and which was so important for the development of Chinese economy. Years later, the Chinese were building another great bridge all by themselves. They had learned how to build bridges with an ease and a swiftness that is characteristic of them. But in 1957 Chinese and Russians were happy to be working side by side in an enterprise as formidable as erecting a bridge over a river immensely wide and immensely deep.

Later, overnight, Khrushchev, with his well-known impulsiveness, withdrew all the Soviet experts and decided that Russia should not aid China in mastering atomic technology, which China proceeded to master by herself. This was the beginning of a deterioration in Sino-Soviet relations that at times has taken an extraordinarily alarming turn.

I tried to argue that, no matter how concerned the Kremlin was at suddenly finding in China a nation that challenged the exclusive Soviet leadership in the Communist world and that was attracting many of the countries of the "third world," it was unthinkable that Russia should attack China. But what happened in Czechoslovakia and the Brezhnev doctrine of limited sovereignty only increased the suspicions of the Chinese and strengthened their defenses against any eventuality.

This is what has led to the building of an underground China in anticipation of an eventual Russian attack. Today that defense against an atomic attack is developing systematically. I heard the former French prime minister, Pierre Mendès-France, who was in China at Chou's invitation, say how impressed he had been in 1972 by the Chinese leaders' conviction that Russia would attack China at the first opportunity.

China does not want war but she does not fear it. Viewed objectively, China becomes more and more difficult to conquer as she becomes an important atomic power and as her political power increases in the United Nations and throughout the world.

In the interior I had become convinced that there was a farmers movement definitely committed to Mao and firmly opposed to any attempt, during Mao's lifetime or even after his death, to shift the Chinese Revolution toward the right or toward "revisionism," to use the current term in Peking. And the Chinese factory workers, if possible even more than the farmers, were completely devoted to Mao and his ideals, as far as I could judge. As they frequently told me, the red flag could never be red enough. This might be just a phrase, but there were events behind the phrase that made it a truth.

When I visited the factories in 1957, what most impressed me was the transformation of old workshops into modern factories. There was an emotional dedication in it. I could not imagine workers from other countries patiently rebuilding machinery that seemed unusable and delighting to see it again able to contribute to the immense task of putting the Chinese economy, still so weak, "on its two feet," which was at the time a popular slogan. I talked with the ministers and the top officials of the government most directly involved in carrying out the Five-Year Plan and with the principal economists, many of whom knew English. The idea that they all had in common was that it was of first importance to build some economic base for China, even though a very modest one, that would make her self-supporting. This insistence upon economic independence at times seemed obsessive. But in view of the American embargo and the Soviet sabotage after the break, the goal now seems sensible and intelligent. Whatever happened, the survival of Communist China was assured. To destroy her it would be necessary to bomb her, and even that would not succeed.

In 1967, at the height of the Cultural Revolution, what most impressed me on my visits to factories was the complete confidence of the workers that they could fully carry out the directive of Mao to use their individual capacity and imagination to increase production and make goods cheaper and better. The workers explained this to me, showing me the machinery, the nature of the technical innovations that they had introduced and the resultant advantages. The workers and the engineers managed the factory through a Revolutionary Committee. The committee studied the workers' proposals and put into practice the ones that looked promising. There was keen competition for new ideas. With joy they showed me a locomotive that they had built according to the workers' specifications, a locomotive that replaced an inferior one built in the Soviet Union and that had cost them three times as much.

The Chinese worker puts more emphasis on benefits to his country and to the revolution than on his own personal advantage. The union leaders told me that their big problem was not a shorter work day or higher wages or strikes. Their problem was to get the workers to stop working occasionally and take a rest. The periodic pause for breath had to be strictly enforced.

1961

From our second visit to China, in 1961, I am going to set down the basic aspects that indicate the true situation of the country at that moment. We shall have to omit from this commentary the new productions of the Peking Opera, the modern ballet seen in the new Palace of Nations, the hours spent in film studios, the cordial atmosphere toward Spain, toward the cause of freedom for the Spanish people, the Foreign Affairs Institute, where I gave my lectures, the visits to teaching centers, from which come the technical and professional cadres that assure the national development, together with the decisive contributions of the laboring, industrial, and farm classes, the descriptions of the interior landscape, the lakes and the parks, still so enchanting, and above all, the street life, so full of vitality. All that and much more has to be put aside in order to face the central problem of the practical development of the three fundamental directives of Chinese politics in these recent years, which have provoked such a lively debate outside of China: the general line for Socialist construction, the great leap forward, and the Popular Communes.

Especially with regard to the latter there had been much discussion abroad, with most opinions, including those of the left, strongly critical. In general it must be said that the Chinese Revolution has received from the foreign press and commentators on international affairs, in newspapers, on the radio, and in books, a treatment even more hostile than that accorded to the Russian Revolution up to the Second World War.

The main itinerary for our trip to the interior, indispensable to complete whatever we might gather as information in Peking itself, would be visits, for purposes of comparison, to places that we had seen in 1957, added to places where we had not had time to go, like the province of Ah-hui, one of the most poverty-stricken before the proclamation of the People's Republic.

In Nanking I met my old friend Wuang Chao Treuen, who in 1957 was the representative there of the Institute of Foreign Affairs. Since then Mr. Wuang had been elected vice-mayor of the city. So I had an opportunity to visit it again in his company and to obtain from him at first hand much valuable information.

As on many other occasions when I met Chinese officials, and as I have already said, in my conversation with the vice-mayor of Nanking I was able to note how the authorities, and the higher their rank the more it was true, combine a legitimate satisfaction for what has been accomplished in little more than a decade with a readiness to admit the errors that have occurred in the application of this or that project. The procedure that usually ends each visit to an important enterprise, industrial, agricultural, or cultural, and according to which the foreign visitor is urged to give his frank opinion and to criticize, if necessary, what he has seen or to give observations that he deems pertinent, is not merely an example of traditional Chinese courtesy. It is part of the very manifest eagerness to excel, to correct defects that can be noticed not only by themselves but by foreigners who, through having visited other countries, are in a position to make interesting comparisons or to offer suggestions that might help them to perfect their work. The criticisms are fewer than in 1957 because with each passing year the technical cadres are more numerous and better prepared, but even today one frequently hears an engineer who runs a factory, the director of an institute of specialized education, or someone who is in charge of an agricultural fair say that China is still a technically backward country and that they have much to learn.

In 1957, during my first visit to Nanking, the total value of industrial property there had increased fourteen times over that of 1949. Three years after that visit, in 1960, this advance had doubled. This fact is interesting because it proves that, even during a period of calamities of nature, with their adverse consequences for the economy of the country, there have been several branches of production in which it has been possible to continue advancing.

Nanking, like Peking, has benefited from the planting of trees. Within two years the system built around the most powerful rivers with the most destructive outpouring, the Yellow River, the most terrible of all, the Yangtze, and others will be able to reduce by a fantastic degree the damages of floods and droughts. One must give time to time. But one thing is sure. Even under the most fortunate circumstances the national hydraulic system takes a great deal of time to make its benefits felt in a country as vast as China. That is where the People's Communes, taking the problem at the local level, cooperating with the state in this struggle of transcendent importance for the future of China and the welfare of her people, render an inestimable service.

A visit to the hydraulic system built in the province of Ah-hui allowed us to see the change that has taken place in this province, which we previously described as one of the poorest in China before the proclamation of the People's Republic. Its capital, Ho-fei, had 50,000 inhabitants in 1949. In 1961 its population exceeded half a million. It was not only its demographic growth but its industrial and cultural development that gave an impression of how China advances. We passed along what had been, twelve years before, the great Ho-fei Avenue. It has been left there as it was, not as a contrast but simply because the hour has not come for it to be incorporated into the current project to build a few more blocks of workers' houses. The "grand avenue" of yesterday seems today just a mudhole. Nine new paved avenues answer the needs of a population multiplied by ten.

From the balcony of the Peace Hotel of Shanghai I saw the port with double the traffic that it had on my previous visit. What we were seeing allowed us to appreciate the rhythm of the New China and better to capture the real significance of what we had heard in conversations with the principal planning experts, among whom I mention very especially Mr. Yung Lung-kuei, Vice-Director of the Institute of Economics of the Chinese Academy of Sciences, for the interview that he so kindly gave me on one trip. For a comprehensive view, the best thing is to sum up generally, as they were expressed to me, these appraisals of the Chinese economists and planners who were so eager to answer my questions with impressive frankness and to clarify the points most frequently discussed concerning the situation today.

To evaluate exactly what was accomplished in the course of only two Five-Year Plans, with the Third Plan appearing in the perspective of an extraordinary apprenticeship in the field of national construction, it is essential to recall what the situation was in China in 1949, when the People's Republic was proclaimed. During its many years in power, the government of Chiang Kai-shek had not carried out a single fundamental reform. Of the eighteen hundred foreign enterprises, including factories, mines, businesses, and ships, that gave Old China its well-known colonial character, only a few are still functioning today, and even these have had to adjust themselves to the laws and politics of the government. Everything has passed into the hands of the people.

The first thing that the People's China faced was the problem of the land. The feudal land system was entirely destroyed. But the Agrarian Reform kept the agricultural realities in mind and avoided hasty measures. For example, the former landowners were allowed to become associated with the new common collective farming, provided that they had not been found guilty of cruelty to the peasants, of crimes against the nation, or of collaboration with the Japanese aggressors. The same criterion of differentiation between elements of the old society, in order to involve it in the major task of national construction in a country so backward economically, led to the division of the bourgeoisie into two categories: bureaucratic capitalism and national capitalism. The first once served the interests of imperialism and under the Kuomintang regime of Chiang Kai-shek it devoted itself without restraint to enriching itself, paying miserable wages, exploiting female and child labor as in the most abject colonial slavery.

The property of the capitalists of this first type, the bureaucratic bourgeoisie, was confiscated on the spot and without compensation. With all that property in its hands, the Chinese people were able to face the American policy of embargo. With the national bourgeoisie, which had shared the national concerns of the Chinese people and had not sold out to foreigners, a different policy was pursued, and they were given all kinds of facilities to become a part of the new regime. It was the first phase of the democratic revolution. If this had not gone forward progressively, trying to regroup the greatest possible number of the Chinese people around the transformation in progress, it would have prevented, or made extraordinarily difficult and bloody, the transition to the socialist revolution.

To understand the China of today it is necessary to keep in mind this advance by stages. Thus what frequently seems to foreign observers a serious reverse, a disastrous step backwards, is in reality only a new proof of the capacity of the Chinese government to combine the revolutionary and the practical.

One example of this capacity is the socialist transformation of the national bourgeoisie. It is pertinent to emphasize here the patriotic element that usually accompanies great historic revolutions. The leaders of the Chinese revolution, headed by Mao Tse-tung, kept in mind that the

234

national bourgeoisie, as distinguished from the bureaucratic bourgeoisie, had been on their side in the war with Japan, had been eager to see the country prosper, and had frequently condemned the Kuomintang for the weakness of its opposition to imperialism. In a certain sense they too had been the victims of the Kuomintang, which preferred to divide commissions and benefits with the great foreign companies, neglecting the more modest Chinese industries and the interests of the average business. When the present regime came into power, the national bourgeoisie supported it and joined the Democratic Popular Front. Its factories, its machinery, its knowledge of business were useful to the Chinese people, and the government adopted toward them a parallel policy, on the one hand watching them carefully, since after all it considered them capitalists, in order to eliminate any attempt at exploitation, and on the other hand associating and re-educating them by making them understand that only a socialist economy could move China ahead and make of her a truly great nation. "That does not mean," observed Mr. Yung, "that we did not have to struggle with the national bourgeoisie, but the struggle was carried on in a civilized way."

Some of the members of that national bourgeoisie are today ministers or vice-ministers of the republic. The minister of light industry is a former capitalist from Tienching. The vice-minister of the textile industry, at whose house I dined in 1957, as I mentioned, is the former vice-mayor of Shanghai.

With the experts and with various members of the government I spoke of the great leap forward, asking them all kinds of questions about this other development so much discussed abroad. During the five years of the First Plan ten thousand enterprises, large and small, were undertaken, among them nine hundred major projects. At that time many were begun with the aid of the Soviet Union and other socialist countries.

"But, in order to take care of all that we are building and projecting we would have needed an enormous and continuous contingent of foreign experts. We had to develop our techniques and extend the base of our production. After the end of the first Five-Year Plan, we were faced with the need to accelerate the pace. We had succeeded in raising the standard of living, but it was still primitive, in spite of all our efforts. The great mass of the people wanted to see, in a relatively short time, China transformed into a prosperous country. To accomplish that we needed peace and hard work. And so was born the great leap forward."

What were the results? On this point the authorities that I consulted were unanimous in giving a special importance to advances in the steel industry. In 1958 steel production increased by eight million tons; in 1959 it reached the figure of 13.5 million (I remembered that in 1957 they had told me that by 1962 they hoped to reach 12 million). But in 1960 they were already producing 18 million tons, with a consequent influence on machine production of enormous importance for the rest of industry and for agriculture. In 1962 the production of steel would increase even more. "We can now make the equipment, the machines, and the instruments that we used to have to import."

It is appropriate here to tell something which, although it is irritating, shows the consequence of the embargo imposed by the United States, which was intended to isolate China but produced the opposite effect. In 1957 we had met, aboard a ship crossing the Yangtze, the famous doctor Wu Hoan Hsing. We knew that he was now director of the new cancer hospital in Peking. This hospital, like the new maternity hospital excellent in every way, attracts the interest of the various medical missions in the country. The opinions of the foreign doctors are of exceptional interest since they are expressed by people who do not belong to any political party. When they praise what has been accomplished under the new regime in the fields of public health, hygiene, and the struggle against epidemic diseases, they do so with a strictly professional and scientific point of view. From one of these doctors who had been traveling extensively throughout the interior, I heard authoritative evidence that the news published in the foreign press about starvation in China was a pure invention. It had been necessary to reduce the food ration because of deficient harvests, but all the people were being fed.

Well, Doctor Wu, after showing us the huge installations intended for the treatment of cancer with cobalt, showed us a tiny machine that was of great importance for the hospital. At first, they had ordered it from the United States. But the embargo regulations had prevailed over humanitarian considerations. When they failed to get the machine there, they decided to try to manufacture it in Shanghai. And here it was, produced in China. And now they were exporting the machine to other Asian countries. The embargo, instead of stifling China, as had been hoped, has spurred her into developing her own production, in this and in other cases, with a substantial saving in foreign exchange. As for the political embargo, one of the results was that Mrs. Eleanor Roosevelt and other eminent Americans invited to visit China were denied permission to make the trip by the State Department. By contrast I had the honor of greeting in Peking Queen Elizabeth of Belgium and of thanking her for her support of the campaign for an amnesty for Spanish political prisoners. In Peking I also saw British Field Marshal Viscount Montgomery, whose impressions of China on this, his second visit, published in the British press and broadcast by the B.B.C., created a sensation everywhere because the impressions were so highly favorable.

Much has been written abroad about the difficulties that China has had in recent years with floods and droughts of an unusually devastating violence, but with a remarkable lack of understanding. One can have the most complete information about this or that aspect of the China of today and nevertheless err in focusing on the total situation. It is not a question of being right in saying that the Chinese Government was forced to readjust the rhythm of the great leap forward as a result of the difficulties created by calamities of nature. Or whether it was forced to introduce new norms in the functioning of the People's Communes. The government, its experts, and the Chinese press have been the first to admit that, after twelve years of tremendous effort, a readjustment in the rhythm of national construction, keeping in mind the new circumstances, was obligatory within the framework of a realistic policy.

It is not a question of wanting to demonstrate, on the basis of these or other figures, as some of the foreign writers who have recently visited China or who have gathered their material in Hong Kong have been doing, that the balance between agriculture and industry, especially heavy industry, has not yet been found. Or to try to prove that in this specific branch of industrial production or in that specific aspect of agriculture what has been achieved does not correspond entirely to the expectations of the planners, although in other expectations they have gone beyond their goals. All those very serious studies of the experts and the Chinese authorities, and the declarations of the principal leaders, as well as the conversations that one may have had with them, offer the most authoritative testimony.

Working as no people would be thought capable of working, in a way that would be impossible without a very extensive and solid support from the masses, not letting herself be disheartened by difficulties and momentary obstacles — it was not in vain that Mao Tse-tung and his comrades made the Long March — China entered its third Five-Year Plan, which is going to have great importance for the development of its economy, having already created the basis, the solid foundations, with which to multiply her achievements since 1949.

It is these essential elements of the present situation in China, and not the secondary elements of a partial retreat in the rate of production, or the disappointing harvest, that must be kept in mind in writing about China if we are to place in true perspective the future that is destined for a nation called upon to have an increasingly decisive influence on the balance of power, and the correlation of world forces.

On this trip I had a most unusual and interesting encounter, which led to a two-hour conversation, with the last Chinese emperor, Pu Yi, who ascended the throne at the age of two. He told me his whole life history and that of the dowager empress, Tzu-Hsi, who died in 1908. I had been looking everywhere for portraits of this remarkable woman, whom Chinese patriots called "the spirit of evil," for she was as scheming and dominating in love as in politics.

The former emperor began by saying: "I let myself be used by the Japanese as a puppet in setting up the hoax of an independent Manchukuo. In any other country I would have been shot. Here I have been allowed to live and work." He worked first as a gardener. When I met him he was working in the library and writing his memoirs. He was proud of what China had accomplished since the Liberation.

He naturally knew the history of all the dynasties. He said there were emperors worthy of comparison with any of the great figures of antiquity or of modern times. One of them was Che Huang-ti, of the year 191, who had the reputation of being a tyrant, a reputation fabricated by the scholars who were offended by his scorn of them. In reality he was a renovator. He wanted to organize the country so that the farmers would own their land and at the same time be reserve soldiers. It is true that he burned the books, but they were books in which the scholars found arguments with which to defend feudalism.

The Han dynasty, he said, had an emperor, Kuang Wu-ti, who created the system of examinations that lasted until 1904. The Han emperors fostered the study of classic texts and the concept of Confucius above the State, a centralized power and an orderly administration.

The Tang dynasty had an empress, Wu Hou, known for her passion for Buddhism and for her energy, which kept her in power until she was eighty. The Tangs gave a great impetus to commerce. From Central Asia the caravans swarmed, with merchants anxious to buy Chinese silks and precious metals. During the long reign of Hsuan Tsung, who was a poet of lofty inspiration, the arts and letters, as well as scientific discoveries, acquired a great splendor. He also was a long-lived monarch; he died at the age of seventy-eight.

The Sung dynasty made the academies the favorite advisors of the sovereigns. One of its statesmen, Wang An-shih, was a kind of precursor of socialization. He freed the peasants from exploitation by the usurers. He was one of the first to give to the State the role of regulator of production.

No dynasty was more national than that of the Ming. Culture triumphed. Under Yung Lo there was published a great encyclopedia, the teachings of Confucius, philosophy, literature, astronomy, prophecy, Buddhism, and Taoism. It was the work of more than two thousand scholars and numbered more than twelve thousand volumes. The fame of Ming ceramics has come down to our times. Its most perfect achievement came from the imperial factory of King-to-chen, in Kiangsi. Their material was very fine, with a bell-like resonance and a blue design that was divine and unmistakable.

The Ming dynasty suffered from the influence of the eunuchs. As the emperor's harem increased in size, so did the eunuchs increase in number and in rivalries. One of the last Ming emperors, who ascended the throne at the age of sixteen, fell under the domination of the famous eunuch Wei Chong-hien, who persecuted the members of the academy, forcing them to seek refuge in the secret societies that were so numerous and so powerful in Chinese history.

Some of these societies were used by the ambitious Empress Tzu-Hsi, especially the Boxers, who at bottom hated her and wanted to dethrone her. She arranged matters so shrewdly that they directed their hatred to foreigners. And when in 1900 Tzu-Hsi appeared before the Great Council to recommend the extermination of the "foreign devils," she had the Boxers on her side. This was the period of the greatest foreign intervention. A German general marched on Peking and Tzu-Hsi had to flee the capital disguised as a peasant woman. Once the revolt was defeated, Tzu-Hsi returned to Peking and, with her best smile, she thanked the foreigners for having permitted her, under most pleasant conditions, to return from her travels to visit her subjects.

Pu Yi told us how the eternal idea of a unified China has been realized since the Liberation. He said that his treatment by the government was not unique, that former Kuomintang generals who had stayed in China had been respected in their private lives and permitted to work for their country in various capacities.

A couple of weeks after our long conversation, at the annual banquet offered by the head of state on the eve of the first of October, the national holiday, the last emperor of China came to our table to drink to our health and to the Spanish people.

In 1967 my wife and I were among the few foreigners living in the Hotel Peking, which on other occasions was the residence for distinguished guests from many countries. The Cultural Revolution had reduced this clientele considerably. Our fellow-partakers of the delicious food and excellent service in the vast dining room of the Hotel Peking were guerrilla fighters. I did not meet a single foreign correspondent at that crucial moment in the Chinese Revolution. This is what gives my personal account of the Cultural Revolution a somewhat exclusive character.

I had been surprised one day by the news that, among the thousands of posters and cartoons that were practically papering the beautiful city, there was one attacking Chou En-lai, not of course in the direct way used by the "Chinese Khrushchev," Liu Shao-chi, but in an irritatingly insidious way. For years, through having met him and followed his amazing achievements, I had had the highest regard for the Chinese prime minister, one of the greatest living statesmen. I asked for a translation of the text of the cartoon. And shocked to the extreme I asked how it was possible that a cartoon of this type could stay up on a wall more than half an hour after it was posted. The answer was that Chairman Mao had called on the Chinese people to express themselves on everything and everyone and that consequently there was no reason for tearing down that idiotic paper. However, the Chinese people esteemed Chou En-lai enough to take the text seriously. It was finally covered by another poster and forgotten.

But a month later, returning to Peking from a trip through the interior, I had for the first time the impression that into the mainstream of the Cultural Revolution there had been introduced elements of a dangerous extremism that claimed to be more Maoist than Mao.

This was a difficult theme to explore. But in my endeavors I had the assistance of a close friend, one of the most ardent followers of Mao Tse-tung, who had taken part in the discussions of certain groups and

The author and his wife in a Chinese garden

who informed me, confident of my discretion, that a few extremists were falsely interpreting the thoughts of Mao.

One of their influential centers of operation was the Ministry of Foreign Affairs. From there, at the head of a group of fanatics, functioned a Chinese diplomat, Yao Teng-shan, who had been chargé-d'affaires in Indonesia at the time of the anti-Communist coup against Sukarno, and who had returned to Peking at the height of the Cultural Revolution, haloed with a hero's fame, and consequently for the moment in a position to play an influential role. He practically took control of the ministry and of all propaganda services. That group was responsible for the attack on the British embassy in Peking and for a series of equally irresponsible actions that were largely responsible for the fact that outside of China the Cultural Revolution was misinterpreted and abused in all the most hostile terms imaginable. Chairman Mao himself told Edgar Snow that this group was the one that intervened in 1967 to prevent Snow's admission to China, a decision that many of the friends of China and of Snow could not explain to themselves.

All these facts are interesting to record because they show what kinds of problems and situations Mao had to confront during the Cultural Revolution, and they make him figure in history as the most inspired politician of all times, controlling the technique of launching a revolution and controlling it in time.

When I returned from my trip through the days of the Cultural Revolution during which I had had the great good fortune to be able to get on-the-spot information on everything I wanted to know, I met, in Paris, Geneva, and New York, friends, politicians, journalists, professionals, and UN delegates in Manhattan who must have thought me starry-eyed when I assured them that China would come out of the Cultural Revolution stronger than ever. Most of them were convinced that China was on the verge of collapse. It was not so strange to hear them express themselves this way at such a great distance from the scene when the Soviet embassy in Peking had informed Moscow that the one who was going to win was not Mao but Liu Shao-chi, the president of the republic.

In the Medical School of the University of Peking, my wife asked a young student if the closing of the school during so long a period of time was not a great handicap to her. "On the contrary," answered the young lady, "during that time we traveled all over China. [This was the students' Long March during the Cultural Revolution.] We have walked hundreds of miles. We have learned to know our country, to work with the farmers, we giving them our experience in matters of hygiene and the avoidance of disease, they teaching us to work tirelessly for the prosperity of the country. All the rest, the scientific medicine, we can learn later. We have time for all that."

An old admirer of China, but one opposed to the dominance of the military over the civilian element, bewailed the fact that "the Chinese army today is running everything." I answered with the experience of my visit to one of the headquarters of the Army of Liberation during which for many hours I discussed everything with generals, with other officials, and soldiers seated around an enormous table. That army bore no resemblance to any other army in the world. It was the people in uniform. It was the army of the least militaristic country in the world.

The Cultural Revolution was clear proof of China's ability to survive the greatest shocks. The revolution was not a single earthquake; it was a series of earthquakes. Any other nation would have foundered amid such a storm, deliberately unleashed. But not a nation with a helmsman like Mao. The song that we heard so constantly in 1967, "And Chairman Mao is a great helmsman," sums up one of the most perilous human experiences and one that ended with complete success.

China emerged surer of herself than ever. But without arrogance. Because arrogance does not go with China's character. And today, as I write this chapter, the official voice of Peking keeps repeating that China does not want to be a superpower. Mao Tse-tung says this. Chou En-lai says this. They have no desire to see the double hegemony of the United States and Russia, which they have so often denounced, replaced by a triangular hegemony, adding China to the other two. On the contrary, she sees herself struggling together with all nations, the smallest on a level with the greatest, for a better world.

It is my ambition and my plan to write a book about China that will be extremely simple and that will give an exact idea of the situation today and of the perspectives that are opening up for that great country. I have already published two such books in Spanish and I intend to spend several months in China in the spring of 1973 to bring everything up to date. It's not that there aren't books and essays of high quality on the different aspects of the Chinese Revolution. There are the works of Edgar Snow, those of Han Suyin,* and very recently the book by the Italian Maria Antonietta Macciocchi, *De la Chine*, which was widely praised by French critics, in addition to interesting reports like that of Robert Guillain in *Le Monde*: "China after the Cultural Revolution." But the book that I want to write must be so easy to understand that it can be read to an illiterate Andalusian farmer or a Bolivian miner and they will understand it.

The picture of an indestructible China made inevitable her admission to the United Nations during the twenty-sixth session of the General Assembly. The whole session revolved around China. I heard every speech made on that occasion. The Assembly was in favor of China from the beginning. Each speech in favor of the admission of China was received with the applause of an enthusiastic majority. Each speech supporting the desperate attempt of the United States to save at all costs the phantasmagoric membership of Chiang Kai-shek was received with a coldness that anticipated the defeat reserved for Ambassador Bush's delegation.

The Chinese victory in the United Nations was so resounding precisely because up to the last moment Ambassador Bush was convinced that he had a margin of five votes with which to impose once more the artificial

---

* In March, 1972, I heard Han Suyin, at the close of the speech she made in Geneva, answer all the criticisms aimed at China from the left as a result of Nixon's visit to Peking. She was as effective as ever.

demand of the two-thirds rule, which in the past had prevented the entry of China into the United Nations.

It was a victory not only for China but for the United Nations. In an organization that had been in poor health for years and that not even the celebration of its twenty-fifth anniversary had managed to revive, there suddenly entered a current of life and hope. That's why there was dancing in the aisles of the United Nations on the night of that historic vote, October 25, 1971.

The same atmosphere of satisfaction and hope in the future of the United Nations prevailed on November 15, the day on which the Chinese delegation made its entrance into the United Nations, greeted by fifty-five speeches of welcome. An interesting detail: the Chinese press published long extracts from all the speeches and their authors therefore suddenly had an audience of eight hundred million readers. The Chinese delegation was very well chosen. It was headed by the vice-minister of foreign affairs, Chiao Kuan-hua, who worked closely with Chou En-lai, and it had Ambassador Huang Hua as the permanent representative on the Security Council.

I had stopped to have lunch with Ambassador Huang Hua in Ottawa, at the Chinese embassy, on the very day of the United Nations vote to seat China. I was returning from a Canadian conference in support of Spanish Republican resistance. And that same afternoon I flew back to New York to be a witness to the admission of China to the United Nations. Huang Hua is one of the best Chinese diplomats. On the Security Council, he will have in the years to come abundant opportunity to make China's influence felt in the organization. On the Security Council, Chiang Kai-shek's representative, conscious that he was representing very little, was, as a permanent member, negative, nonexistent, politically dead.

But the revolutionary China that Huang Hua represents in the United Nations could not be more alive. The speech of Vice-Minister Chiao Kuan-hua, in answer to the welcome from the delegations, already gave some idea of what China is going to accomplish in the United Nations. "He said it all," commented a Western delegate when the session ended. What Chiao said was that China would never act like a great super-power. That in her eyes the smallest nation should be treated, in matters concerning her national independence and economic interests, just like the largest nation. This moment marked the end of what had been for many years the "bi-polar world." Chiao said that China would never be the first country to drop the bomb, nor would she ever use any ideological excuse to invade any country. But that she would aid, to the limit of her economic capabilities, all countries that needed assistance to become truly independent and free. The "third world" had found its leader.

This was a speech completely in the spirit of the United Nations, in defense of the Charter, and in the service of peace. It was the herald of an activity in the United Nations exactly the opposite of what China's opponents had predicted. Aid to developing nations and disarmament are the two themes that in the next few years are going to make of the United Nations something more significant than the scene of the power struggle or a mere social club.

SEVENTEEN

Women and Revolution

In March of 1971 my most interesting imaginary interlocutor was the Paris Commune. No place was more appropriate than the French capital to analyze correctly the historical impact of that great revolutionary event of a century ago. There were dozens of unpublished documents, such as the "souvenirs" of the "Vierge rouge," the Red Virgin, Louise Michel. In the court of justice she was fantastic. She declared: "Since it seems that any heart that beats for liberty has the right only to a little lead, I demand my share."

A member of the Communist International, Louise Michel fought to die, not to live. After shifting from one barricade to another, from her 152nd Battalion to the Battalion of Théophile Ferré, her lover who was executed at the age of twenty-five, she defied the judges so resolutely that they finally lacked the courage to condemn her to death. And what did she shout in their faces? "As for the burning of Paris, yes, I took part in it. I tried to set up a barrier of flames against the invaders from Versailles. I had no accomplices. I did what I did all by myself, to carry out my own wishes." Victor Hugo was much moved, but he feared for his life, and he wrote her: "You told lies not to save yourself but to harm yourself. You are terrible and inhuman."

Louise Michel was an anarchist under the spell of Prince Kropotkin, with whom she was associated in London. But she was above all the complete revolutionary. Before she died in Marseilles at the age of seventy-five, she heard the news of the outbreak of the first Russian Revolution in 1905. She wrote: "I feel it rise, widen, expand, the Revolution that will sweep away the Czar and all his Grand Dukes, and then will shake to its foundations this enormous death house." Verlaine dedicated a ballade to her.

How to write the history of the Commune in 1971 was one of the themes to which I directed my attention in the spring of that year. It had been one of the most vigorous expressions of the revolutionary and patriotic feelings of the French people. It is essential to stress the patriotic element, because the uprising of the masses of the people a century ago meant the condemnation of the government of Thiers and of his policy of capitulation to Bismarck. The centennial celebration in Paris had not been worthy of the occasion. One of the reasons for the tepidity was the weakness of the French left as a whole following the disillusion produced by the loss of the opportunity offered in May of 1968. At a

Dolores Ibarruri — "La Pasionaria" —
heroine of the Spanish left

meeting of French intellectuals, I heard: "The place where the commune is alive is China. It was in China that the Paris Commune was celebrated with the greatest warmth."

The Commune personality to whom most attention was paid a hundred years later was Louise Michel. She was the worthy heiress of the women of the Great Revolution of 1789 to 1794, women who were in its vanguard, as the historian Michelet made clear. For Michelet, the revolution was Woman. As long as the women did not enter the fighting, there

248

was no true revolution, according to Mirabeau. And in her turn Simone de Beauvoir would say: "One is not born a woman, one becomes a woman."

The theme was timely because, coinciding with the centenary of the Commune and the Frenchwoman's participation in it, certain sociologists and anthropologists, among them the Canadian Lionel Tiger, author of *Among Men*, had responded to the American Women's Lib movement, placing the emphasis on the biologically transmitted origin of masculine behavior.

To pile up the arguments against the claims of Women's Lib, some go back to the very beginnings of human history. In the earliest civilizations, hunting and fishing, the main sources of subsistence, were almost exclusively assigned to men, assert the enemies of Women's Lib. The woman who hunted was exposed to many dangers, to miscarriages, to being wounded. Therefore, according to this theory, the humanitarian feeling of men limited woman's activities to taking care of the children and the home. Aggression and war were for men. For them, too (and this is a humorous aspect of these antifeminist theorizers), was reserved the drinking of alcohol, the masculine attribute par excellence.

The predominant role that some women play in certain countries, Madame Bandaranaike in Ceylon, Madame Sun Yat-sen in China, and, in the recent past, Eleanor Roosevelt, is explained by their being widows of great personalities. In contemporary European governments, women function only as a decorative element. Ignored in this analysis are the women who fight in the Vietcong ranks or who are the Vietcong spokesmen to the world, for example, the brilliant minister of foreign affairs, Madame Binh, who plays a role of first rank in today's diplomacy. And no account of the war in Spain would be complete without describing the exploits of the famous Dolores Ibarruri — "La Pasionaria."

But when we look back to the eighteenth and nineteenth centuries, the kind of thinking that we have just described reveals its errors and its weaknesses. The eighteenth century fully recognized the existence of women as a social group. In 1777 the Prize of the Academy of Besançon was conferred upon the future Madame Roland, who became one of the greatest intriguers of the Revolutionary period and the implacable foe of Robespierre. A *Memoir by the Feminine Sex against the Masculine Sex*, protesting the laws that prevented women from becoming magistrates and financiers, appeared in the last years of the *Ancien Régime*. It was the start of the struggle against discrimination. Even if in the Assembly of the Third Estate there were only two women working-class deputies, the representatives of the women who worked in the fish markets and the fruit markets, a pamphlet of the time recalled that the "prince of Human Genius," Aristotle, recognized that women had the right to use the laws of reason to make the truth prevail.

Women passed from theory to action in the first days of the Great Revolution. They took up arms to attack the Bastille. A week later the *National Gazette* listed the names of the heroic women. It was women who tied the ropes to the cannons that were moving toward Versailles. They were proud of having forced the king to move to Paris, whereas the men later let him escape. Next to the political struggle was the struggle against the denigration of women. Anonymous or even signed pamphlets spoke of thirty thousand young women engaged in prostitution. There was an exposé of the cruel lot of the ill-married woman. There was a demand for concrete legislative measures to protect women.

The efforts to assure political equality for women and men were renewed in the course of the revolutionary process, with alternative failure and success. In the *Société fraternelle des Jacobins* the women took part, under the same regulations as the men, in the administration of the society. The Secretariat was assigned to four men and two women. The traditional titles of Monsieur, Madame, and Mademoiselle had yielded to those of Brother and Sister. The mixed clubs, those that admitted both women and men, were defended in Marat's *L'Ami du peuple*.

In the French Revolution woman was the symbol of impassioned patriotism. When war was declared in 1792 she worked with complete devotion for the army. Women were called the knitters because they never stopped knitting, either in the courts of the Convention or in street meetings or beside the guillotine. Even before the appearance of the decrees summoning all the people to arms, women considered themselves mobilized.

EIGHTEEN

Portrait Gallery

Franco's dictatorship has had a disastrous effect on the intellectual life of Spain. It has destroyed the university as a center of liberated thinking. For a couple of years it has not functioned normally. Whether in Madrid or Barcelona or Seville or Bilbao, it is a university occupied by the police. Students and professors are the object of frequent outrages. An entire class of medical students lost a year in 1972, and this loss is especially grave for the health of the country. But all that police politics has not succeeded in diminishing the fighting spirit of the students.

The dictatorship has not been able to prevent the emergence of writers, especially young poets and talented artists. Many of them, opposed to the dictatorship and with the courage to gather clandestinely in the Montserrat Monastery near Barcelona to protest against persecution and torture, are in their turn persecuted, in danger of imprisonment or heavy fines. One constantly misses the strong and original literary personalities that we had before the dictatorship: an Unamuno, a Valle-Inclán.

I knew Miguel de Unamuno in Salamanca, which is where he had to be seen not so much because it was his intellectual fief, his university, his life, but because he had identified himself completely with a city that is among the most impressive in Spain. I met him when I went to Salamanca to do graduate studies in law, a lawyer with no future and with no illusions, for I never expected to practice law. When as a political exile in New York in need of money I tried to act as a legal counsel for an important office for Latin American affairs, the American legal authorities decided against me, since I had not had my legal training in the United States.

I saw Unamuno again during the First World War. With José Ortega y Gasset, he had been trained as a scholar in Germany, although his favorite philosopher was not Hegel or Kant but Kierkegaard. He had sided with the Allies, and this was another reason for my attraction to him. But the time when I was closest to Don Miguel was in Hendaye during his political exile. The stupid sentence imposed on him — a two-year exile — by Primo de Rivera, a dictator, but so humane in contrast with General Franco, got me put in jail. I protested in a speech at the end of a huge banquet in Madrid and I spent that night in the Model Prison, which was a model only for the considerable number of rats in it.

My jail sentence because of Unamuno resulted in the great writer's showing me a special affection and letting me stay with him in Hendaye, his place of exile, each time that I crossed the frontier on my way to Paris on missions that were ostensibly journalistic but actually political. In order to talk at length with him and to bring him the latest news from Spain, I had to delay my trip for several hours. When I would get to Hendaye after dinner Unamuno would be playing cards, usually *mus*, a Spanish game that demands great concentration. And he not only wanted to show his skill but win a little money. In addition, he wanted to be alone with me, and his favorite walk was along the beach, one of the longest in France, and one that had a view of Spain. He had to look at Spain every day. His nostalgia was boundless and I have often wondered if, instead of being a refugee two years, he had suffered through an exile of over thirty-four years, his heart would not have burst with grief.

From our conversations in Hendaye I am in an unusual position to testify in the argument, opened again and again, as to whether or not Unamuno was a man interested in politics. He was so, to an extreme degree. In one of his essays he had written: "I shall never tire of repeating it — because it is well known that if I have a weakness it is repetitiveness — politics is one of the best points of view for facing up to any problem. I, for example, believe that I am one of the Spaniards who has played most politics in my country and yet I do not appear as an affiliate of any political party. Where there is not an intense political life, culture is floating, rootless." And it was politics, more than his novels, his poetry, and his plays, that made Unamuno a world figure in those days. His sentence of exile brought forth a series of protests from intellectuals everywhere, beginning with Romain Rolland.

Unamuno exerts an impressive influence on young people who were not even born at the end of the war in Spain. A new review in Spanish, *Atalaya*, founded in Paris by those young people in 1971, has as its motto these words of Unamuno: "Culture is one thing, Light is another. That's what we must have: Light."

Unamuno's work with every passing day is more appreciated inside and outside of Spain. Jean Cassou, a novelist and one of the best French critics, with whom I now talk about "our Spain," because for him Spain is his second country, writes about Unamuno: "To Shakespeare, to Pascal,

Don Miguel de Unamuno at the University
of Salamanca, 1933

to Nietzsche, to all those who have tried to retain in their tragic personal adventure a little of this humanity that slips away so swiftly, Miguel de Unamuno comes to add his experience and his effort. His work does not pale beside those noble names: it means the same desperate eagerness."

Unamuno's work began, in 1895, with the publication of five essays that he called *About Traditionalism* and which are an interpretation of the Spanish soul. His first novel, *Peace in War*, appeared two years later. It is a historical novel of the Second Carlist War, which he lived through as a child. He believed in telling about life. "To tell about life," he wrote, "is this not perhaps a way, and perhaps the most profound way of living it?"

Unamuno said of Clemenceau: "This lad of eighty-five," who, on being asked if he was going to write his memoirs, answered: 'Never, life is made to be lived and not to be talked about.' " Unamuno comments: "And nevertheless Clemenceau, in his long Quixotic life as a guerrilla fighter with his pen, has done nothing but talk about his life."

Unamuno was a playwright, especially great in his *Nada menos que todo un hombre* [Nothing Less Than a Whole Man], and a poet. He read me his last poems, walking along the beach at Hendaye. His second book of poems, *Rosary of Lyric Sonnets*, could have been called tragic sonnets. And then, "El Cristo de Velázquez," one of his best. He wrote marvelous interpretations of the Spanish countryside. He called them "a kind of poetic soul landscapes." *Mi España*: Salamanca, Bilbao, Cáceres, Zamora, Oviedo, Córdoba — the light of Córdoba, unique in the world, and of course, Toledo and Avila. He felt the need of crying out, in a lyric form, against the pain of his exile and his faith that Spain would finally rise against the dictatorship. This is what makes Miguel de Unamuno one of the poets closest to the present anti-Franquist Spanish youth.

Another of the pre-war Spanish authors who continues to enjoy great popularity under Franco's dictatorship was Ramón del Valle-Inclán. If he had been alive today the Franquistas would not have dared, as they have dared, to name a Madrid theater after him. He would have presented the regime as the most amusing *esperpento* (grotesque tale) of his collection. In the *esperpento*, a genre exclusively his, the romantic author of the *Sonatas*, which were dedicated to the four seasons of the year, put all his sense of the comic and the grotesque, making fun of the sacred Spanish institutions, the army, the monarchy. He would have written a fabulous *esperpento* about the Caudillo, about his wife Carmen de Polo, about his daughter Carmencita and about the Matesa, called even by Franco's associates the scandal of the century, and about Juan Carlos "the Brief."

My youth was associated with walks with Don Ramón through the streets of Madrid, at all hours of the night, listening to his inexhaustible and inimitable mixture of truth and fantasy as he invented a world to his own taste. He was a figure known to all. A long beard, abundantly flowing hair, a body as thin and bony as Don Quixote's, and one-armed like Cervantes. There were countless stories about how he had lost his arm in imaginary heroic deeds. The true cause of the loss was a literary dispute in a café, where he was defining the value of a book or a painting and was accepting no other interpretation. A blow with a walking stick, delivered by Manuel Bueno, an insulted critic, led to unexpected complications and the subsequent amputation.

But Valle-Inclán preferred to locate the accident in one of the battles laid in Spanish-speaking America, part of his literary work so marked with his genius that one had only to read or hear a sentence to know who the author was. He was a potential warrior, telling the story of the Carlist Wars as if he had taken part in them, and he was passionately devoted to the Allied cause in the First World War.

One night at the café gathering that I used to attend there was a discussion of how much distance a French infantry soldier could cover as opposed to a German soldier. None of us who were there knew the answer, except Don Ramón. But the distance that he gave seemed so exaggerated that it roused some objections. Valle-Inclán did not yield and, as a clinching argument, he challenged the others to test the truth of his assertion. He proposed at midnight that we walk from Madrid to Toledo. I, trying to think how to dissuade him, offered to accompany him. We walked about a half an hour and suddenly I pretended that I had lost him. From around a corner I saw him step into a hired carriage to return home. But I was sure that I would hear him tell, the next night at the café, how he had reached Toledo on foot before noon and then returned by train.

During the dictatorship of Primo de Rivera I was a witness to Valle-Inclán's unquestionable personal courage. He defied the censorship, publicly insulted the dictator, but did not succeed in being jailed. During this dictatorship there was abundant use of the psychological warfare about which there is so much talk today. The most effective weapon was the witticism, the biting joke, the popular verse. To ridicule the generals in power and the civilian ministers who were a blind for them was in the long run to ensure the fall of the regime.

Valle-Inclán was one of the stimulators of this intellectual guerrilla warfare. Every event might offer an opportunity to attack. He undertook to organize a banquet for me to celebrate the publication of a book of mine on Russia. The merit of my *La Nueva Rusia* [The New Russia] is that it was the first study on the subject published in Spanish.

Valle-Inclán had read my book, which was an honor for me. If he didn't like a book he could easily find, just by flipping pages, enough arguments to destroy it. But he was in favor of Russia and he was in

257

favor of the book's young author. And so his speech in my honor was brilliant and filled with barbed allusions to "the New Spain," the Spain of Primo de Rivera.

With each passing year the intellectual opposition got wider and stronger. Just as in 1972, in the last years of the Franco regime, Spanish jails were filled with students, so in the 1920s the university had been in the vanguard of the struggle against a more flexible type of dictatorship. But despite its flexibility, the students were no less clobbered by the police then, although they were not tortured as they have been under Franco. The Spanish dictatorship of the twenties had not had the benefit of instruction by the efficient officers of Himmler.

The opposition, under both dictatorships, included a certain number of members of the legal profession. In 1971 forty prominent Spanish lawyers protested against a new law of public order, which strengthened considerably the character of the law of 1959. The approval of the project submitted to a Parliament created by Franco for this purpose meant that the state of emergency decreed in relation to the Burgos trial became the norm. The police became a political pressure group. On the eve of the fall of Primo de Rivera, the law schools in the principal Spanish cities felt obliged to take a position similar to that of the lawyers of forty years later. This shows how brief the periods of liberty have been in Spain.

Valle-Inclán took advantage of a meeting of professors and lawyers to launch a very amusing and sarcastic attack against the government. Some minister said that it was time to silence him and that he ought to be arrested. But Primo de Rivera understood that persecuting him would only aggravate things, and so the error committed in the case of Unamuno was not repeated.

My friendship with Unamuno had as a complement the friendship that tied him to his translator into German, Doctor Otto Buek. He was a fabulous person. If instead of giving life in several languages to the works of others he had just applied his talents to his own creative powers, Doctor Buek would have produced great works. But he enjoyed being the interpreter of contemporary Russian thought and he translated into German (for the well-known Pipper Publishing House of Munich) Gogol, Dostoevski, and other nineteenth-century novelists. He also translated from the Spanish, especially Unamuno, whom he admired as a thinker and a novelist. Years later, well over ninety, he used to consult me about an occasional word that eluded him in Rubén Darío, whose poems he was translating for his own private pleasure.

My acquaintance with Doctor Buek dated from my student years at the University of Leipzig. After World War II I met him again in a café frequented by writers. He loved the café life and although he was lodged in a chateau for elderly people near Paris he would escape as often as he could, take a taxi, and meet me in the Café des Deux Magots. In Leipzig he had introduced me to Franz Werfel, then a more fighting type than when he wrote his novel about Lourdes, and to a great number of young writers, and he talked to me about Thomas and Heinrich Mann, whom I was to meet later.

Doctor Buek was Russian, born in St. Petersburg and trained in Germany, at the University of Marbourg, where he had known José Ortega y Gasset. He had studied there with Professor Hermann Cohen, a Kant scholar. But for me he was completely Russian, originally imaginative, a great conversationalist, knowing everything, philosophy, science (Einstein used to say that Buek was one of the few people at the beginning who had understood the theory of relativity, and he made a film on it), theater, music — he played the cello and I took him to a dinner arranged in Paris after the Second World War for one of his great favorites, Pablo Casals.

In 1916, when I went back to Germany, Doctor Buek was one of the regular attendants at one of the cafés of the Kurfürstendamm, the gathering place for the opponents of the war. Among them was the poet Johann R. Becher, who was later the minister of culture in the government of East Germany. At the end of the war, in 1920, when I was organizing the services in Berlin for the *Nación* of Buenos Aires, taking on the correspondence for Central Europe and Russia, I invited Doctor Buek to be my collaborator. I was later associated with him in several literary projects. He was my traveling library. There was scarcely a topic about which I consulted him on which he could not be informative. In return he listened avidly to my impressions of my trips to Russia, my meeting in Moscow, for example, at Maxim Gorki's home, with Romain Rolland and a discussion that followed about Russian literature since the Revolution. Doctor Buek was much interested in Mayakovski and in Bebel.

We generally talked in German, but we shifted to Spanish whenever we felt it safer. Just after the German occupation of Paris, it was not advisable in a Paris café or restaurant to be overheard talking in German. Through Doctor Buek I made contact with the Russian intellectual emigrés who, late in 1922, reached Berlin, where there was a great increase in houses publishing books in Russian. With most of the emigrés it was impossible to talk politics but through conversations with them I could keep up to date on Russian literature, which had always had great interest for me. In Berlin they were reprinting Turgenev, Tolstoi, Dostoevski. They were publishing art magazines like the very luxurious *Jar Ptitsa, Firebird*, and literary reviews like *The Epic*, in which Biely put down his memories of Blok. Our meetings were stimulating but they had a quality of unreality, since some of those emigrés were gambling on the collapse of the Bolshevik regime and thought that they would be home again in a couple of years.

Doctor Buek was not very patient with them. Even the philosopher Berdyayev, who did not believe in a counterrevolution and who rejected the idea that Russia could be saved from outside, irritated him with his theories that Russia suffered, in the years immediately after the October Revolution, because she had never in the past experienced either the Renaissance or humanism. Doctor Buek felt closer to the 'Eurasians,' a group that conceded that the revolution had brought to Russia the benefits of a rational economy and some writers like Remizov, whose inspiration was popular folklore. But Buek was to the left of all of them.

The political evolution of Doctor Buek is somewhat like that of Bertrand Russell and Beatrice Webb. His philosophical training, his whole nature, predisposed him not to go politically beyond the limits of a humanitarian liberalism. And yet his intellectual honesty, his intelligence, and his immense historical culture gradually pushed him toward socialism. He studied the original texts on the course of the Russian Revolution and he became, in the discussions that I attended, a debater hard to defeat because of his superior knowledge of the facts.

I have never seen a man of his age with more youthful eyes, blue and kindly. But he was capable of great explosions of rage when he encountered a pretentious intellectual. He had amusing quarrels with Professor Nicolai, who had signed, with him and Einstein, in 1914, the first public document against the war, but who had changed into a rabid anti-Communist and anti-Soviet. He was teaching in Chile, he came to Paris on vacation, he sought out Doctor Buek, took him to dinner, and they spent the night quarreling. Discussing with me his arguments with Nicolai, Doctor Buek said that he was completely gaga. Nicolai must have been eighty-eight years old at the time and Buek was eighty-nine.

The pleasure in translating poetry that came to him in his last years transformed him into a poet. He wrote political poetry, satires about imperialists, the illusion of democratic liberty, ballads that he recited from memory with extraordinary style and enthusiasm. He was one of the companions of my life whom I have missed the most.

Among the important and active people that I know today there are three quite distinct personalities that have one thing in common: they are superior to the people who are occupying places that they ought to be occupying: Galbraith, Myrdal, Mendès-France.

When I first met John Kenneth Galbraith he was living in a chalet in Gstaad with a spectacular view of the mountains: the Hornberg, the Windspielen, and the Egli. For many years Gstaad has been attracting skiers from all countries. I prefer Saanen, which is a half hour from

Gstaad and has one of the most beautiful valleys in Switzerland. Saanen is more primitive and less pretentious than Gstaad. It has, however, acquired a certain fame in recent years because in the summer, in its church, are held the concerts of Yehudi Menuhin and his sister, Hephzibah, an excellent pianist, and many other notables in the music world. The church in Saanen has very good acoustics. I have heard Menuhin in Paris and in other concert halls, but I prefer to hear him in Saanen.

Hephzi is not overshadowed by the glory of her brother. She plays admirably some of the most delightful compositions of the old Italian music. Married to a British Laborite, Richard Hauser, who was once a prisoner of the Nazis, she is much interested in politics. She is a close friend of ours and a loyal supporter of the cause of the Spanish people. It was through her that I learned that Galbraith was in Gstaad.

I had a long and fascinating conversation with Galbraith about Nixon, Kissinger, the war in Vietnam, about the problems of the developing countries, which he knows not only as a result of his research but from having visited several of them, and especially in India where he was ambassador. Listening to him I thought that a man like him could render a great service to his country in any post connected with the foreign policy of the United States. He is much superior to most of those who are now serving their country.

The point that I make here and that I stress in my conversations with European friends is that the United States has a great number of people who have a very clear view of world problems but whose opinions are ignored by the government. Its foreign policy is influenced by incidents like the insanity of President Nixon in May 1972, when he ordered the mining of Vietnamese ports two weeks before his announced visit to Moscow, leaving diplomats and politicians around the world stunned at such irresponsibility.

United States journalism has had a Walter Lippmann, who, for many of us interested in world affairs, was for many years the best living analyst of international politics. Quite recently Jean Lacouture, a French journalist, a specialist in Asian affairs, found Lippmann the "youngest and keenest" of all the Americans with whom he had talked about Vietnam. Today there are James Reston, Tom Wicker, Anthony Lewis, a whole team on the *New York Times* and another on the *Washington Post* who see world perspectives with an objectivity and a penetration not bettered by any of their European colleagues. And there is Galbraith.

The prestige that J. K. Galbraith enjoys outside the United States was shown when, only forty-eight hours after the *Nouvel Observateur* announced a lecture by him, there was not a single seat to be had. A thousand people stood in line in the street hoping for standing room. It was a panel discussion, and the other speakers were Mendès-France, Michel Albert, Roger Garaudy, and Michel Rochard, Secretary General of the

P.S.U., the Leftist Socialist Party. The *Nouvel Observateur*, which had planned the discussion, apologized for the fact that so many people were unable to get in to hear Galbraith, saying that no one had thought that a lecture delivered in English in Paris, no matter how famous the lecturer was, would attract so large a number of people.

His fellow-panelists had interesting views about Galbraith. For Mendès-France, he was the "militant of democracy"; for Michel Albert, a

John Kenneth Galbraith

"thinker of great stature" (of course everyone knows that Galbraith is more than six and a half feet tall); for Rochard, a "neo-Marxist who doesn't get to the bottom of his ideas"; for Roger Garaudy, "a fertile analyst who turns his back on true Socialism." Nevertheless, all of the other panelists and the audience found him most interesting and they were astounded that some people in the United States should find his philosophy subversive. In Paris, on the contrary, this "grand seigneur" obsessed by "technostructure," according to one of the commentators, sounded not like a rebel but like a scientist coolly announcing the aberrations of capitalism. He argued in these terms with the French participants in the discussion. "You do not seem to be willing to accept change in social phenomena. If Marx and Lenin were alive today, I am sure that they would have accepted it."

Introducing Galbraith to the audience, in which there were a great many young faces, the former French premier, the man who ended the War in Indo-China, Pierre Mendès-France, laid emphasis on Galbraith's influence on American youth. In order to make his ideas known, Galbraith had made himself a writer, a journalist, a pamphleteer. Shunning the academic style, he has sought to explain to his compatriots the problems and the solutions that he proposes. That in itself is a great virtue. But against the influence of what he calls "the giant economic organizations," what Galbraith proposes (in the opinion of his fellow-panelists) is not convincing. As Marx, Lenin, and Rosa Luxemburg have shown, capitalism is characterized by the individual appropriation of wealth and power, the capacity for investment being limited to a few. Turning to Galbraith, he said: "You used the word 'socialism.' But I see no socialism in what you propose. Upon what social force can you rely to fight against a capitalism dominated by technostructure?"

Michel Rochard asked him: "Do you think, Professor Galbraith, that your diagnosis constitutes a challenge to the very nature and forms of power? There is no other solution than the mobilization of the masses against exploitation and social injustice." But Galbraith closed the debate with these words: "I do not accept the capitalist-communist alternatives. I am definitely not a revolutionary. I believe that we can spare ourselves the trauma of a revolution and reach something that will be more satisfactory than either communism or capitalism."

The Myrdals are a couple, tireless in their struggle against racial discrimination, and in their struggle to put an end to the inequality between rich countries and poor countries, and in their struggle for peace. Alva is secretary for disarmament in the Swedish Government and representative of her government at the Disarmament Conference. Each time that I have seen her I have been impressed by the firmness of her refusal to be an accomplice in a hoax that gets worse from year to year, the pretense that we are making progress on the road toward disarmament. This is one of the biggest lies of our time, and one of the most dangerous.

The Disarmament Conference is provided with a round-trip ticket between Geneva and New York, in what I have called "pacifist touring," but in neither place does it accomplish more than an occasional partial agreement on chemical and biological warfare, the fixing of new areas of regional denuclearization. True disarmament is still a chimera. The situation is dangerous and Alva Myrdal sees it very clearly. People let themselves be deceived by those "great strides forward," as was the case also in some ways with the Moscow agreement on the prohibition of nuclear explosions in the atmosphere and with the most recent SALT agreement between the United States and Russia.

Alva Myrdal never forgets that the great opportunity for disarmament was in 1945 to 1946. Nuclear arms were still just beginning. The only three atomic bombs that had been made up to then had been exploded, at Alamogordo, for experimental purposes, and over Hiroshima and Nagasaki, to sow death. A plan to avoid continuing their manufacture had been outlined by Robert Oppenheimer and David Lilienthal and renewed by Bernard Baruch. But all in vain. The two superpowers, the United States and Russia, blamed each other for the failure. The result of that dispute was not disarmament but the Cold War.

Mrs. Myrdal praises Nehru, with whom I also talked in New Delhi on the same subject, because of his efforts to mobilize neutrals and small countries to force the great powers to stop their absurd nuclear race. But if eventual limitations are achieved principally through saving, on one or another side, a few billions of dollars, true disarmament is as far away as when the Conference met for the first time. Only one gain has been made. As long as Alva Myrdal is a member of the Conference, a voice of truth (to which are added those of ambassador Castañeda, the Mexican delegate, and a few other delegates of the neutral powers) will be heard during the deliberations.

My friendship with Gunnar Myrdal goes back to the time when he was the heart of the Economic Commission for Europe. A half hour from Geneva, toward France, was living another of those men who were not occupying the post that they should be occupying, an internationalist and promoter of human rights, as intelligent as he was amusing, Henri Lansier, formerly assistant secretary general of the League of Nations, and in France, his country, professor emeritus at the Sorbonne. Myrdal and I used to lunch with Lansier, a great gourmet, and to talk with him about a world that was getting more unbalanced every day.

Gunnar Myrdal was my favorite candidate to be Secretary General of the United Nations. It is possible that he would not have wished the post. I never talked with him about it. But I did some exploring in the Delegates' Lounge of the United Nations and I realized at once that the United States would never consent to have a man as independent and with such firmly rooted principles as Myrdal in charge of an organization in which the United States held at that time an "automatic majority," an organization that she was accustomed to think of as her own, because, among other reasons, she was paying the highest dues.

Myrdal was a critic of the war in Vietnam and that did not make him welcome in Washington. Again and again I have found Europeans amazed at America's way of thinking about Vietnam. Above all that general cry: "We will not tolerate humiliation." Humiliation by what and for what? The United States intervened in Vietnam against international law, she waged war without declaring war, she mined the ports of a sovereign and independent country, she bombarded the whole country, North and South. President Nixon says: "I shall not allow this or that to be done in Vietnam," and then Americans come out with accusations that the enemy is humiliating them. Humiliating them because the North Vietnamese ask them to fix a date for the withdrawal of American troops and ask them not to insist on setting up as a first condition for continuing the Paris Conference that they should show respect for the phantasmagoric regime of Thieu in Saigon? Humiliate them because neither Hanoi nor Mme. Binh are willing to help the United States to emerge from that blind alley called Vietnamization invented by Nixon, a policy which doesn't and never will work?

A great analyzer of racial questions — his *American Dilemma* is a classic on the Negro problem in the United States — Gunnar Myrdal maintains that today's world is in poor health and is not on the road to recovery. The great conquests in science and technocracy are not being used to promote happiness and harmony among men but to prepare for our destruction.

I always found Myrdal, as well as my other friend Josué de Castro, of Brazil, former ambassador and former director of the OAS, equally interested in the problems of the Third World, the developing conutries, disappointed by the pettiness with which the industrialized countries give aid to the less favored nations. The last Conference on Trade and Development in Santiago de Chile, inaugurated by a frank and brave address by President Salvador Allende, showed that the developing countries were losing patience. Their attitude forced the rich countries to give firmer promises of aid. Myrdal has more than once bemoaned the fact that the expenditure for arms by all nations exceeds the total income of the poorer half of the population of the world.

Another man of exceptional worth, but at present out of work, is the former premier of France, Pierre Mendès-France. Each time that I talk with him I am strengthened in my conviction that, with the death of de Gaulle, he has the best political mind in France. And yet he does not even have a seat in the National Assembly. He was defeated in the last elections.

Pierre Mendès-France was above all else the creator of the peace in Indochina. It was he who freed France from the nightmare that is now weighing upon the United States. He was a man "who knew how to lose," while Nixon is introduced abroad as "the man who does not know how to lose," an attitude that can become extremely dangerous. Mendès-

Pierre Mendès-France

France's determination, when he saw that the Indochina War could not be won, was to end it. To lose in this case is to win. For France it was to win lives, to save money, to put an end to an internal strife that drained energy that could be better used in raising the standard of living, and to end unemployment. Every bit of this thinking applies to the United States in Vietnam. The generals must not be allowed to hamper the freedom of movement of the statesmen. The generals either win the war or if they don't, they must not put any shackles on the peace. If American Presidents had dared to use that kind of language with their generals and with the Pentagon, the Vietnam War would have been over long ago.

Mendès-France has no party behind him, but he does have many supporters, especially among the young. He understands the reasons for their discontent. Instead of offering them commonplaces: "order," "discipline," "sense of responsibility," all mixed with social injustice and with the crudest kind of capitalism, he tries to offer them a Socialist alternative. He has been rather withdrawn from the political scene since the last presidential campaign, but I have the impression that he is preparing for his political comeback, and that he is not just thinking of returning to the National Assembly as a deputy for Grenoble. In fact, he has prepared for his comeback by making a journey to the part of the world where he thinks the most important future events are going to occur, Asia.

Since President Nixon's visit to China there has been a lot of talk in the United States about China and her prime minister, Chou En-lai. The discussion about the Chinese leaders has been usefully rounded out by the impressions of Mendès-France, who knows them well and who has recently visited them. Here is his report: "As in 1954 and in 1958, there exists in Chou En-lai, but probably also in all the other Chinese leaders, a real persecution complex. As a consequence, almost everywhere Chou sees hostile, even threatening undertakings: in Japan, in the United States, and especially in the Soviet Union. The American tide he thinks is now an ebb tide. But not the 'Soviet social-imperialism.' He gives details about 'proofs of Moscow's aggressive intentions.' His tone is harsh and sarcastic." But Mendès-France, as a statesman, admires the Chinese statesman who carries on his shoulders, without a moment of despondency, a colossal task. "Nothing escapes him. He quotes without hesitation figures and technical references about the mounting birth rate in Japan, the particular qualities of the special steels produced in China, in Japan, in Europe, the predicament of Latin America, the Common Market."

Mendès-France did not find Chou En-lai marked by age and work. He was a little thinner, and as distinguished looking as ever. "I hesitate," said Mendès, "to use the word 'aristocratic,' but that's what Chou is, a great revolutionary and a great gentleman at the same time."

It is to be hoped, for the good of France, that the indications of Mendès-France's full return to political life will be confirmed. France will undergo in the next two years a very difficult period. The country, despite the development of certain branches of its economy, is shaken by an undiminished social agitation, by financial scandals, by the vacuum left by the disappearance of General de Gaulle. There is a lot of talk everywhere against the cult of personality. But France without de Gaulle is a proof of the power of personality. At a moment of major crisis Pierre Mendès-France is a great reserve of imagination and political courage.

In my portrait gallery are two Russians: Michael Koltzov and Tron. Koltzov came to Spain during the war as a correspondent from *Pravda*. I had met him in Moscow in 1935, during my fifth visit to Russia. He was in a very strong position as a reporter and editor of several publications. When I asked a friend to tell me whom I could talk to, someone who did not have an official position, which would mean that (except for Litvinov) he would not be able to talk freely, someone who could inform me about several problems that interested me, my friend answered: "Michael Koltzov." And he added: "And he gets along well with Stalin."

But it was in Spain that Koltzov and I really became friends. He saw in me not a member of the government but a fellow journalist, a newspaperman with a temperament like his, and a source of reliable information. I was repaying the debt that I had contracted with him in Moscow. He would come to see me at the War Commissariat or at my home. He was overcome by the emotion of the days he had lived through during Franco's assault on Madrid. He had been captivated by the heroism and the grace of the people. He remembered with joy the organization of a battalion of barbers to cut off the Fascists from their approach to the Manzanares River. "We'll cut the Fascists' 'beards'," they said. He remembered with equal joy Christmas Eve of 1936, in a besieged city, bombarded on all sides, but a city that refused to give up the happiness of hearing guitars, of swapping dances from one country to another with the members of the International Brigade, and the happiness of drinking to a coming victory.

Of the Spanish people Koltzov said: "Suddenly this people who for so long has been vegetating in the lower lefthand corner of the continent, this people that no one had any real knowledge of, a people of dry Castilian plateaus, rain-soaked Asturian mountains, and jagged Aragonese hills, has risen up tall and proud before the whole world. This people is the first, in the third decade of our century, to pick up the gauntlet thrown down by Fascism, this people is the first that has refused to kneel before Hitler and Mussolini, the first to face up to them and to enter into a valiant armed struggle against them."

With that vision of Loyalist Spain filled with intelligence and sensi tivity, Koltzov, in November of 1936, lived through the Fascist attack on Madrid and in his *Memories of the Spanish War* he left a moving and enlightening testimony to his impressions. He gave to the defense of Madrid the importance of a great historical event, which is indeed what it was, the noblest and most heroic among the battles for liberty in the twentieth century. Koltzov made contact with the members of the International Brigade as they reached Madrid to take their very effective part in the defense of the capital. They came from all countries and from all classes: a young British lord who fell mortally wounded at the front, a mechanic who abandoned everything to fight on the side of a people. There were doctors who came to help the wounded, Doctor Barsky from the United States, the Canadian Norman Bethune, who later went to China to help the patriots who were fighting for a free China and who died there. Mao Tse-tung dedicated to him one of his main essays.

From his Moscow newspaper they would telephone to Koltzov, either at the War Commissariat or at the office of the Defense Junta of General Miaja, in order to find out how Madrid was standing up against an attack by forces that were superior in every way. The *Pravda* correspondent described to his readers the jubilation of the people when they saw a powerful Heinkel of Hitler's air force fall in flames, shot down by a *chato* (snub-nose). We were very grateful to the *chatos*, the planes that were all the Republic had, small in size and few in number. What most impressed Koltzov was the spontaneity of the resistance. The Loyalist authorities had no need to appeal to the public to support the war effort. Women and children appeared everywhere to dig trenches. Not even the scarcity of food discouraged people. Koltzov told me later how a house painter, very proud to have been made an artilleryman, told him: "When you're fighting you don't feel either hunger or cold." And the cold began to be felt in Madrid as November advanced. On the twenty-sixth the Fascists, who had sustained many losses, began to lessen their attacks. But not for long. Franco had issued orders that Madrid was to be captured at all costs. The defense was organized on solid bases. With his journalistic vision Koltzov had discovered on General Miaja's staff a modest but extraordinarily competent officer, Vicente Rojo, who was to become one of the most prestigious figures of the Republican Army. At the end of the war Negrín named him chief of the general staff. Koltzov called Rojo to the attention of the journalists of the Madrid press and his name began to be mentioned. Koltzov was alert to everything. He was preparing for the evacuation of the Spanish anti-Fascist intellectuals in case the offensive drive of the Franco forces, led by General Varela, captured Madrid. Koltzov had a friendly quarrel with the poet Rafael Alberti and his wife, María Teresa León, who wanted to stay no matter what happened. Koltzov objected: "That's nonsense. The revolutionary is not an animal led to slaughter, he's not an unresisting fanatic, he's not a suicide. As long as possible he fights, he attacks, he resists. When it is no longer possible, he retreats, saving his strength, he hides, he flees. But, at the first opportunity, he resumes the fight, he continues it, he attacks again."

Koltzov was worried by the possibility that the Fascists would get their hands on the members of the Alliance of Madrid: intellectuals, writers, painters, composers, scientists, and their wives and children. He was worried about Antonio Machado. I used to talk with Koltzov not only about war and politics but about literature, about poetry. I talked to him about Pushkin. He talked to me about Machado. He was a great poet and Koltzov agreed with me when I said: "His greatest poem was his conduct during the war."

There were days when the situation of Madrid was very grave and others when the Loyalist forces not only defended themselves but attacked. And then, in the middle of March, not separate Italian companies but a whole expeditionary army corps led by General Manzini tried to put an end to the resistance of Madrid, attacking from Guadalajara. They were completely repulsed and shattered. Ernest Hemingway said to Koltzov: "This is a genuine rout, the first major rout of international Fascism. This is the beginning of the victory over Fascism." Koltzov answered modestly: "Let's be grateful for the beginning." Koltzov was completely on our side, an inseparable part of our war. I was understandably horrified when I learned, from my exile in France, that he was in danger of being purged and that Maria Osten, the German writer, a friend of his and of all of us, was going to Moscow to see what she could do to save him. He was arrested by the Soviet police and the circumstances of his death in 1942 I could never find out when I went to Russia at the end of the Second World War. Afterwards they rehabilitated him and his complete works were published in Russia. But the elimination of such a magnificent man I could never understand, or forgive.

Tron was to me a Russian in spite of his American nationality. Perhaps the magic of his personality lay in the union of a Russian dreamer with a General Electric technician. Tron was what would be called today a technocrat, but a technocrat with a soul. Not one of those technocrats who are so abundant in today's world, including those of the *Opus Dei* in Spain, pretentious and unbearable, who think they have found the way to stop the revolution by making men into robots and replacing politics and ideology by a computer. Tron was a builder, a creator, with the drive of a Cecil Rhodes, not in the service of imperialism but of socialism.

Tron immediately answered the appeal of Lenin, for whom revolution and electric energy went hand in hand. Tron built the first great dam in Soviet Russia, establishing the base for what would become Russian planning. He was a planner in the grand style. After Tron returned from

India where he had gone at the invitation of Nehru, I talked with him for hours in New York; he said that in spite of everything the idea of planning was progressing in India. Nehru himself had told me in New Delhi that the only thing about which he felt satisfied was that the Indian people were beginning to feel planning-conscious. Tron got along well with Nehru. I don't know exactly when Tron died. He was already ninety when he promised me to come to Madrid to help us with the planning of post-Franco Spain.

Recently I made contact with Tron's widow, many years younger than he. She could not get used to seeing his chair empty. I would like, on the basis of whatever papers Tron may have left, to reconstruct the vision of the world of tomorrow by one of the men who had a clear concept of the future, whether of the Third World or of China.

But Tron foresaw all that is happening in China two years after the proclamation of the People's Republic in 1949. His reasoning, to anticipate its successful development, was sound: "Mao and Chou are men in whose veins runs the oldest civilized blood in the world. They are immensely intelligent and at the same time very human and with a firm faith in the Chinese people. With that intellectual and revolutionary equipment they can go anywhere."

I hope that Mrs. Tron will imitate Helen Kazantzakis, the widow of the author of *Zorba the Greek*. She is one of the people that I most enjoy seeing in Geneva because through her I can experience the endless pilgrimage of her husband through the world at the same time as I follow the effort of the Greek people to free themselves from the rule of the colonels, whose continuance in power contradicts the constant declarations of Nixon that one of his goals and part of his understanding with the Soviets is to guarantee "to the smallest nation the right to establish in its territory whatever regime its people may prefer." Yes, but only after the regime has been approved by the American ambassador.

In the course of writing this book I have insisted, in the light of recent events, that in the decade 1971–1980 there will be profound political and social changes in the world, and that the protagonists of these intense shocks are going to be young people, with the youth of Spain playing a principal role. The case of these young Spanish men and women, who become with each passing day a greater headache for the Franco regime, is particularly interesting. They were not even born when the Spanish War broke out. They have grown up in the midst of a Franco propaganda that has never stopped trying to persuade them that the type of "organic democracy" set up by Franco is of great originality and the one that functions best. But they were never won over by Franco. I repeat that this was one of the arguments of Nehru when I saw him in New Delhi. He said: "Hitler had the German youth with him, and Mussolini the Italian youth. Franco has not succeeded in attracting the Spanish youth. That fact is very promising and very important for you."

But it is not only Franco who failed to win over the young people to his cause. The old parties of the anti-Franco opposition with their in-fighting and their blindness toward the direction in which the world is moving, have also failed to attract the young people. And this is a good thing, for they would have paralyzed them. The young people have become leftists, militants. They have understood that a dictatorship like the Spanish one can't be humanized or liberalized. The only way to respond to the violence of the regime is with the violence of the masses. Although the only weapons they have are the paving stones that they tear from the streets, the young people stand up to the Civil Guards and the police.

This is extraordinary and highly encouraging. Young Spanish students and workers, when I have met them abroad, show a fighting spirit mixed with a keen political sense. They have trained themselves; they are self-made politically. They have a thirst for information. At times they return to Spain, at considerable risk, loaded with books on socialism and current problems in international politics. The prevailing current in Spain today is a Socialist current, in the widest sense. It includes an interest in the Chinese experience, the Cuban Revolution, the Tupamaros, Allende's leadership in Chile, and liberation movements everywhere.

In order to appreciate accurately the foreseeable future of Spain one must reckon with the Spanish youth. Yet in the accounts of Spain in newspapers or in books that have been published in America and Europe in recent years, more attention is paid to this or that personality or this or that party or movement from the past, than to the young people who are the ones who will build the Spain of tomorrow. I work with the youth and they are the basis for my optimism about the future of Spanish democracy. It is to them that I shall devote all my energy when I finally return to my country.

A proof of the keen political sense of Spanish youth is their position with respect to the decision: monarchy or republic. It might be supposed that, never having known the republic and some of them being very leftist, even Maoist, the form of government would be of no importance and that they would be interested only in social revolution. But no. They are perfectly aware that the assumption of power by Prince Juan Carlos, designated by Franco as his heir, would postpone for a long time the political evolution of Spain. And they are fighting just as resolutely against Franco as against Juan Carlos, whom they call "the puppet." The youth denounce the absurdity of certain foreign commentators who, hav-ing a bad conscience about Spain, picture her as on the way to becoming humane and liberal under the reign of Juan Carlos. This is ridiculous because Juan Carlos has no personality or force of his own. He is Franco's creature, publicly committed to follow the ideology of the Movement, of Franco. The day that Juan Carlos becomes king, he will be able to do only what is imposed on him by those reactionary forces in Spain, in the army, in the bourgeoisie, that constitute his only support. It was because he was a slavish follower of Franco that he was chosen instead of his father, Don Juan, who was the legitimate claimant to the throne. Juan Carlos is not only an incompetent but a usurper, a usurper against his own father, which does not help him in a country like Spain, where family ties are very strong.

Juan Carlos is a pitiful creature. I have this from someone who knows him well, the Duchess of Medina-Sidonia. The duchess is the first aristocrat of Spain, several times a Grandee of Spain, with titles more ancient than those of the Duchess of Alba herself. Once imprisoned by Franco, the Duchess of Medina-Sidonia now lives in Paris. With her I have taken part in several political actions and especially in the Toronto Conference in the fall of 1971 organized by the Canadian Committee for Democracy in Spain.

The political evolution of the duchess is remarkable. When she got out of jail, Isabel Alvarez de Toledo (that is her name) was much more interested in talking about the women who were still in jail than she was in talking about herself. Very simple, very well informed, thanks in part to her social contacts, she tells how she met Juan Carlos one day in Puerta de Hierro, one of the favorite high-society spots. Franco's designated heir said: "They've been boring me all day with talk about politics. I'm going to see if I can shake all that off by playing a game of polo." A fine training for kingship.

The duchess is in favor of whatever regime the Spanish people want to choose for themselves, which is to say, in favor of the republic, and she does not even accept the distinction that I made earlier between father and son. "People forget," says the duchess, "that the father, Don Juan, when the Spanish War began, offered his services to Franco. For me, all Franquists are alike, and those two are both Franquists." She does not believe that, if Juan Carlos should become king, his reign would develop peacefully even at the beginning. "The army," she notes, "in spite of all its internal divisions, is loyal to Franco. But it is not loyal to Juan Carlos."

In any case the fighting youth, seconded by the old anti-Franquists of all tendencies, were making ready, as the writing of this book approaches its end, to frustrate the monstrous attempt to prolong the interminable dictatorship of Franco with another dictatorship in which Juan Carlos would be a false front and a docile instrument. A happy coincidence was regrouping the boldest elements of the opposition around movements like the FRAP (Anti-Fascist and Patriotic Revolutionary Front) with this basis: what happens in Spain must not be like what happened in Portugal, that when Salazar died everything went on just the same. A double battle: against Franco and against the monarchy.

The government replied with a policy of aggravated repression. Franco might have appeared physically diminished but he recovered his vigor when there was a chance to go on killing workers, as in his native city, El Ferrol del Caudillo. The idea was to strangle in embryo any rebellious movement that might develop in the passage from one regime to another, from the Franco regime to the Juan Carlos regime. To jail all those who might interfere with the carrying-out of that semi-tragic farce that was in preparation.

I, who had been a specialist in illegal journalism, wrote for the clandestine press of Spain an article entitled: "Can All of Spain Be Put in Jail?" If one could not jail all those who were opposed to Franco's plan to outlive himself by means of a king who was just one more Franquist, then the whole maneuver was destined to fail. Around those whom they had not been able to jail would form the new resistance against the monarchy and in favor of the republic, a republic more progressive and more capable of self-defense than the romantic and frustrated Republic of 1931.

This mobilization of youth and all the anti-fascist elements was the basis on which would be built the truly democratic Spain of tomorrow. And on this basis I was preparing my return trip to Spain, determined to aid in every way I could and with no political ambition beyond that of serving the people.

I used to hear some of my comrades of the long exile: "At least we can go back to die in Spain." That is not my program. I shall go back to live fully the wonderful moment of the liberation of Spain, of the victory of the people. I shall throw myself into the fight with joy, zest, and determination. I shall call for battle.

I do not share the worry of some so-called leaders of the opposition about the problems that are awaiting us. Of course there will be problems, serious problems. But I remember 1936, when Franco rebelled. The legitimate government was found to be without an army, without a police force, without diplomatic or administrative services, with most of the machinery of the State in the hands of the enemy. And the Spanish people with its enthusiasm and its ingenuity filled the vacuum and half-way through the war the Republican army, born out of the first voluntary militias, was capable of winning battles like that of the Ebro, and we would have won the war if it had not coincided with the panic of the democracies confronted with Hitler and Mussolini.

NINETEEN

Gauchisme

Jean-Paul Sartre and Simone de Beauvoir were walking down the street; I followed them at a distance in order to observe them better. They were distributing copies of a Maoist newspaper that had been outlawed. Sartre, the philosopher, dramatist, and novelist, is one of the great intellectuals of our time. Even General de Gaulle, who was so careful in selecting titles for people whom he addressed, began a letter to Sartre: "Mon cher maître." He was awarded, and he rejected, the Nobel Prize for Literature. Simone de Beauvoir is famous in Europe and America as an early champion of women's rights. Neither of them is a Maoist. But in the name of freedom of expression they felt themselves obliged to protect, with the prestige of their names, little leftist papers that without their support would have even more difficulty in staying alive.

Sartre is today the incarnation of a collective political personage that has been the subject of impassioned controversy for some years and that will provoke even more controversy in the years to come. What the French call *gauchisme* — leftism — is present almost everywhere, from one continent to another. In Uruguay the Tupamaros have changed the most tranquil democracy in the world, the "Switzerland of Latin America," into a land of constant agitation. In Turkey the "Dev-Gene," the organization of the "Revolutionary Young Turks," on March 30, 1972, in the face of a threatened attack by the Turkish army, blew up the house of the Mayor of Kizildere, where they had taken refuge with their hostages, one Canadian and two British technicians. All were killed in the explosion except one young Turk, who was then used by the police as an informant.

Because of the political interest that it has for me, I am in frequent touch with *gauchisme*, and I shall outline its various activities and the most representative people involved in it. At times I shall give names but at other times I shall withhold them to protect those involved.

277

In the final analysis the present spread of *gauchisme* is the result of the disillusion in progressive ranks caused by the *volte-face* in the Soviet Union that followed the death of Stalin and especially Khrushchev's rise to power. Many of those who felt disheartened by the new direction were far from being Stalinists, quite the opposite, but they remained faithful to the enthusiasm awakened by the October 1917 Revolution. For a long time, whether they were Communists or leftist Socialists or simply leftists, they had been looking to Moscow as if from there came the most authentic revolutionary inspiration.

I had met Khrushchev in New York, at the United Nations, and later in Paris at the time of the abortive Big Four Conference. He was a likable man, a character, with nothing of the rigidity of the usual Eastern Communist leader, excessively talkative, and that was one of the reasons for his fall. But it will be hard for tomorrow's historians to deny the consequences for the unity of the Communist and Socialist movement (using this word in its widest concept) of Khrushchev's report to the Twentieth Congress on the purges, the trials, and the life of the Party under Stalin.

Khrushchev's report was the beginning of a series of internal crises within the Communist parties and allied movements, crises that went on for years and that led to resignations and expulsions and that prepared the ground for a worsening in the relations between the two giants in the Socialist camp, the Soviet Union and China. It led many people, up to then supporters of the U.S.S.R., to doubt her ability to continue as the leader of world revolution. This was especially so when Khrushchev's rise to power, following his report to the Twentieth Congress, was accompanied by anti-Stalinism, and by the concept of peaceful coexistence, not peaceful coexistence per se but the way of conceiving it and practicing it, which for many meant turning one's back on Revolutionary Russia and instead supporting Russia as a great power.

In the period of skepticism, bitterness, and reciprocal accusations that developed in the 1950s, to be critical of the Soviet Union exposed one to being accused of being anti-Communist and of giving arguments against the Communists to the right. I remember a discussion in Paris about the film *The Confession*, with a script by Jorge Semprún, a fine novelist and a Spanish political refugee. The film starred Yves Montand and Simone Signoret, two actors whose past was certainly not anti-Communist. Our discussion was in private. One of those present said: "Let's be careful not to let ourselves be swept into a position that will favor the reactionaries." *The Confession* is about a trial in Prague. And it was precisely the occupation of Czechoslovakia by the Soviets that had produced the second great crisis in the Communist movement, after the first one precipitated by Khrushchev's report on Stalin.

It is a fact that *gauchisme* is nourished in part by disillusion with respect to the Soviet Union and more immediately, more locally, with respect to the national Communist parties that are thought to be following the Moscow line. It is nourished by revolutionaries who no longer want to have anything to do with the great old parties and who, at the same time, cannot resign themselves to being neutral or indifferent to the great political and social struggles of our time.

Gauchisme is very much in the forefront now, but it is not an invention of today. It goes all the way back to the French Revolution. In the Revolutionary Parliament, the radicals sat to the left and the moderates to the right of the president. Robespierre was a *gauchiste*, and with some justice Sartre, in referring to Lumumba, the leader of the Belgian Congo assassinated by the neo-colonialists, called him "the Black Robespierre." The "Jacobins," members of the Jacobin Club, were the spearhead of the left, although their claim to that title was disputed by other groups, members of the "Club des Cordelliers" and the followers of Babeuf.

From the French Revolution to the Paris Commune of 1871, *gauchisme* kept renewing itself in France. Its leaders were Robespierre, Saint-Just, Marat, and, at the time of the Commune, Blanc, Blanqui, and Proudhon.

The Jacobin flame took on a universal radiance. In Czarist Russia it shone in 1825 with the Decembrist Movement, the revolutionary aristocrats of Russia at that time executed or sent to Siberia, accompanied by the grandes dames of St. Petersburg society. It gleamed in Spain, where reactionary attacks always found a response in the ranks of the common people.

Everywhere, amid the failure of the various attempts at revolt, strong personalities picked up the flag and renewed the fight. After the Revolution of 1848 Alexander Herzen, the inspirer of Russian Populism, and its most brilliant theoretician, Nikolai Chernyshevski, whom Lenin called "the only really great Russian writer between 1850 and 1888," called to the farmers to resist with violence the authority of the czar. There is *gauchisme* in Nechayev, the implacable Nihilist who inspired Dostoevski's *The Possessed*. It is the *gauchiste* tradition in the farm movements in various parts of the world that leads Herbert Marcuse to maintain that only in the farmers, not in the factory workers, lies the hope for revolution and leads him to present China as the one place today that is witnessing a genuine attempt to plant true socialism.

I have a long list of famous and anonymous leftists, strong personalities at the top or at the bottom, whom I have interviewed over the years and who can serve to reconstruct *gauchisme*, a movement that is the object of furious attacks by traditional parties, but which has the immense potential strength of attracting the young people into political action, an important event of the last third of this century.

I shall begin with Bertrand Russell. I interviewed him on one of the most critical days in the war in Vietnam. That afternoon I had been in the House of Commons talking with the half-dozen leftist Labor members who were faced with a conflict of conscience. To vote against Wilson, against their own Government, which had only a very precarious minority, was to risk causing it to fall. To follow Wilson in his policy of unconditional support of Washington on the Vietnam question was torture for them. If at that time Michael Foot, the member whom I admired most, had had the courage to oppose Wilson even at the risk of toppling the Government, Foot might have been the next leader of the Labor Government, which will be returned to power within a couple of years. But he felt that such an action would be putting his personal ambition above the interests of the Labor movement. Finally one of the members advised me: "Go and see Bertrand Russell. He is in London today. He's the youngest one of us all."

Lord Russell was already ninety-three and he told his friends that he would reach a hundred. He almost did. That same afternoon he had led a delegation of British pacifists who had gone to the United States Embassy to deliver a document protesting the war. He welcomed me and asked if I smoked. I said No. Might he smoke? "You can do anything," I answered. He was a very moderate eater but he allowed himself two whiskeys a day. Talking with him, so alert, so lively, so amusing if the occasion was amusing, I thought of American journalists' fondness for the word "aging" whenever they refer to a well-known person who has reached a certain age. In the case of Bertrand Russell, "aging" was senseless. Only a few Americans, like Walter Lippmann, John Kenneth Galbraith, Senator William Fulbright, and Ernest Gruninge, had such a keen sense of or deep penetration into the historical importance of the Vietnam War and of the obstacles that the various American governments had placed in the way of a possible end to the war.

Bertrand Russell was especially fearful of the influence on the average American of widespread and ill-founded remarks from their leaders. In the case of Vietnam the most dangerous statement was President Nixon's remark that the United States had never lost a war and that any American President was justified in declaring that he didn't want to be the first President to lose one. To express oneself this way was, for Lord Russell, to be completely ignorant of the characteristics of a people's revolutionary war. The average American did not understand how a small country, poor, subjected to daily air bombardment of unprecedented intensity, could continue to oppose the United States, the most powerful nation in the world.

But, added Bertrand Russell, no matter how many people the American bombers kill, no matter how many fields and crops and cities they destroy, it would be impossible to kill all the Vietnamese, and among the survivors new guerrilla fighters will spring up and neither the United States nor anyone else can put an end to them.

The famous British philosopher had undergone a great evolution from his first writings, works of classic liberalism, to his recent position, dominated by his belief in the inevitability of the triumph of socialism. This process, in his opinion, would be slow and difficult, on the one hand, because the tendency for Labor parties to become more conservative, either to stay in power or to reach power, gave a great respite to capitalism.

There was a way to escape from that degradation of opportunist socialism. It was to appeal directly to the masses over the heads of their leaders. Russell was already thinking of setting up a people's tribunal to judge the Vietnam War crimes, a tribunal that was set up soon afterwards under the leadership of Sartre. "Whether we are many or few," Russell repeated, "we who think alike must act." The idea of the "grouplet," more effective than the "party," was already in his mind. It was *gauchisme* justified by a man of his long experience, shaken to the depths of his being by the degrading sight of the Labor prime minister, Harold Wilson, giving his blessing to the American aggression in Vietnam.

When Sartre assumed the presidency of the "Russell Tribunal Against American War Crimes in Vietnam," he continued his political involvement, which in the course of time was to become more precise and more radical. He rejected the simple leftist intellectual, the classic intellectual, who was content to give his name to a document condemning imperialism and aggression and then to return calmly home to go on with his literary work, believing that with that declaration of a single day he had fulfilled his duty to the people. "It is no longer a question of testifying but of acting." While the traditional left was content to call for a negotiated peace, Sartre placed the opponents of the Vietnam War face to face with genocide and he asked them what they thought not of war in general but of killings that are thoroughly documented. In May of 1968, during the student revolt, Sartre went to mingle with the students. He practiced not solidarity from a distance but solidarity in the midst of defiance of the authority of the state in the barricades. Some time before he had written that "the street has become again as it was in '89, as in '48, the great ephemerides of the French Revolution, the theater of great collective movements and of social life."

In the street *gauchisme*, free from the restraining discipline of political and syndicalist organizations, today opposed to agitation and revolution, can reveal itself without fear of being repressed, although sure of being attacked. At the time of the funeral rites for Pierre Overney, a Maoist worker killed in a demonstration by a private agent of the Renault factory, thirty thousand *gauchistes* from different groups on the fringes of the parties came together to put on a show of force that was impressive. Sartre himself went to the factory to talk with those who were criticizing the Maoists for having organized commando groups against the factory in order to force the workers to adopt a more revolutionary position.

Sartre would be the last man to let himself be pushed into a systematically anti-Communist position. He basically believed in the old formula: "You can't do anything with the Communist Party, but you can't do anything without it." Others express it: "Nobody can be a Party-line Communist, but the anti-Communist is a dog." In the course of his many differences with the Communists, Sartre has always tried to keep in touch with them. But, he commented: "I am convinced that within ten years all the present leaders of the Left will not represent anything, and I do not see what danger there can be in having a revolutionary movement take shape outside the Communist Party and to its left. I believe this is inevitable and that it is the only thing that can change the politics of the Communist Party and help the true revolutionaries who are still in it to impose a new orientation of the Party."

This feeling is one that I have found widespread as I have talked with important and long-time members of the French Communist party, today in favor of *gauchisme* and whom I shall not name.

For some of those who had fought in the Communist party for many years, leaving it, forcibly or voluntarily, was heartbreaking, as if part of their flesh had been torn away. They had resisted as long as possible until they found themselves one day in the tragic situation of being Communists without a party in which to continue to function. For one of them, the limit of endurance came in May 1968. He said to me: "It is enough that many believe, whether or not they are objectively justified, that if it had not been for the brake applied by the Communist party and by the C.G.T. (*Confédération Générale du Travail*), the Union with Communist sympathies, the May Revolution would have succeeded, and the spectacle of the official Communist leadership taking a stand against the students who were fighting in the streets against the police turned out to be something I couldn't swallow. Even worse, the Party leadership was operating at that moment with an eye to the elections, no matter how far away they were. Our Communist party, the French Party, has been changed into an electoral party. To win elections, to form part of a democratic-front government, or whatever they call it, that is its main goal. Therefore it has to make itself respectable, and condemn all agitation."

My informant feared that the possibilities for changing the party from within were practically nonexistent. He continued: "The chances are slight because the remoteness of the party from the revolution is parallel to the remoteness of Moscow from the revolution. The prospect of Brezhnev with five years ahead of him as the number one leader of the Soviet Union (after his personal victory in the Twenty-fourth Congress of the Soviet Communist Party in April 1970), is not one to give hope of a return to revolutionary positions by the world Communist Parties that follow the Moscow line, although under pressure at certain moments, in Czechoslovakia, for example, they may try to assume a position of independence or of tepid criticism. But the youth of May 1968 and the youth of 1972 and of 1975 do not accept that the interests of the Soviet Union or the electoral calculations of the national Parties should prevail over their deep desire to see changes in a society that young people detest."

My friend did not underestimate the difficulties that dissidence brought in its wake. To abandon a party that is, from a distance, the second most important in France, with a powerful organization and unmatched propaganda strength, to join one of the leftist grouplets, fighting among themselves, was not an easy choice. But he insisted that one must not ignore the fact that, despite quarrels and rifts, there was a common strength of conviction and purpose among all the leftist groups. But *gauchisme*, he said, would be nothing if it did not have the youth behind it. And he reviewed the youth movements in the United States, in Latin America, in Germany itself, where one could not have expected ten years ago that they would become so widespread.

For many years to come, in a struggle against a society that has no answer to its problems, youth will dominate the scene in the Western world. Young people, Spaniards or foreigners, are for me talkers of constant interest. The university is one of the places which one must watch with great care if one wishes to follow closely this great historic crossroads between a world that is disappearing and a world that looms up stormy and untamable, one that will make the next decade one of great convulsions.

"Historical reality, in the past as in the future, is born of an ocean of possibilities," is a true observation of Roger Garaudy, one of the dissidents in the French Communist party who is being much discussed now. And this tumultuous but promising entry of youth into today's politics is in keeping with the Marxist concept, because what is essential in the Marxist inheritance, even more than Marxism, is perspective: a science and an art of inventing the future, one that will allow us to foresee the role played by youth in Europe, in the United States, in Latin America, everywhere.

It is not just a question of making *futurologie*, as the French say, now very much in fashion, in books such as that of Herman Kahn, *The Year 2000*. It's a question of trying, on the basis of analysis of present events, to see which way the world is moving. It is a fact that, contrary to what many of the politicians of the past have maintained, young people, far from being uninterested in politics, have erupted into political life, and at times chaotically, not as a passing fad but in an irreversible process.

"Don't say anything to my parents, but I'm up to my eyebrows in '*la bagarre*' [the brawl]," said a twenty-year-old, very intelligent and attractive daughter of some French friends who had made a quick and large fortune. An only child and therefore a great heiress, she fought, at the university, on the side of the Maoists. We were on the eve of the return to classes. I asked her how she thought the coming school year would shape up. She answered that of course one could not count on another May 1968, the year of the frustrated revolution, "frustrated," she said, repeating what I had heard so many times, "because the French Communists, the 'Muscovites,' afraid of the masses, abandoned us." She was at the time a first-year student. "But even if it won't be a May 1968, the path on which we are starting out will be an emotional one, not only for us students but for the workers. The struggle for better wages will continue in spite of the attempts of Pompidou's government to stifle it. So there are new possibilities opening up of a student-labor front. As for the university, all the claims of reforms since 1968, introduced only through fear of us students, are not enough for us. So the '*bagarre*' is the order of the day."

Like other French students, she questioned me with great interest about American students. She was convinced that students in the United States would go on struggling, even after the Vietnam War ended. "I have learned English to be able to make contact with them. I go to the American Center on the Boulevard Raspail." This was the Center created during the most acute period of the Vietnam War, one of whose inspirers was the indefatigable Marie Jolas, an ageless American and one of the most stimulating conversationalists that one could meet in Paris. In that Center I heard, among other Americans, Arthur Miller and Ira Morris, who showed, a few months before he died, a moving documentary film on the bombing of Hiroshima.

My friend, this young French student, considered the student movement in the United States one of the most important and promising in the whole world student movement. "Of course it has its ups and downs, just as it does here. But I've been impressed by the firmness and clearness of students' ideas, even though people say that the United States is the fatherland of confusion. But that's not true of the American students that I've met. They're not confused. Just the opposite." With her and with the other students of the group, all leftists, but of divergent tendencies, we talked about Marcuse. I wanted to know what they thought about him after the events of May. In 1968 Herbert Marcuse, for French and German students, was a revelation. Later, this University of California professor took part in a Congress organized by UNESCO to commemorate the hundred and fiftieth anniversary of the birth of Karl Marx. Marcuse said that university students had an important part to play in the political future. The students reciprocated in esteem for Marcuse. To the "official" Communists, those who follow the Moscow line, Marcuse is a danger. He sows confusion among young people whom the Communists feel to be already too confused.

The young people to whom I spoke were split in their judgments on Marcuse. For some of them his great contribution to the revolution is his double criticism of American society of today and the Soviet Union of today. But his criticism of the Soviet Union is not of today. His *Soviet Marxism: A Critical Analysis* was published in 1958.

One of the students with whom I talked reproached the workers for lack of faith. "They believe in us students. This is good. But they do not believe in the workers. This is false. This goes against Marx. Marx assigned to the working class the vanguard role in the Revolution." The young student adds: "It is true that in 1968 the working class failed. Not so much the ordinary workers — remember the Renault factory — as the managers. But those are transitory periods. In his time Engels himself criticized the shift of the English working class to the middle class." But this student was in agreement with Marcuse that Russia today suffered from an excessive tendency to compromise.

The sad thing, observed another of the young men, is that the same thing that happens today in the Soviet Union has now become the rule in Communist parties in each of the industrial countries, the preference for parliamentary collaboration with other parties, not only the Socialist ones but those that continue to believe in an advanced neo-capitalism.

At this moment the discussion became quite lively, especially when it touched on the relationship between Marxism and psychoanalysis, the kind of illustration promoted by Marcuse of Marx, Freud, and Heidegger. Of the books of Marcuse those most read by French youth were *Eros and Civilization* and *One-Dimensional Man*. In the second of these Marcuse develops his theory, with which these young people that I talk to are more or less in agreement, that advanced industrial society succeeds in lulling the revolutionary forces with the promise of a higher scale of living. In Spain this is the promise of the Opus Dei ministers, who tell Spaniards that they will get their average income up to a thousand dollars a year. This sounds like a lot of money to the Spanish farmer. To get it, he must promise to be calm and to give up strikes and violence. This is the strategy of technocrats everywhere. They think they have found the secret that will eliminate revolution from the world. What happens is that after a period of increased wages the rise in the cost of living wipes out the increase.

My young friend spurns an attempt to compare Marcuse with Georg Lukács, who was one of the great European Marxists, a Hungarian born in Budapest in 1885 and who just died while still hard at work on his *Esthetics*. My friend denounced the revisionists (she spoke of Brezhnev and his associates only in those terms) who on the death of Lukács had devoted to him only a few lines in *Pravda*. "If it had been the Marxist Georges Marchais [the French Communist leader for whom these students had nothing but scorn], there would have been a page and a half. But nevertheless," she continued, much moved, "Lukács has written *History and Class Consciousness*, a great book. And when he was defending Stalin, who had tried to have Lukács shot, and someone reminded him of this, he answered that it had been a personal incident, that it could not influence his opinion of Stalin, that Lukács was opposed to Stalin for other reasons and not because Stalin had had him jailed." No one could deny that Georg Lukács had been not only a great Marxist theoretician but a man of action. He had taken part in the Hungarian Revolution and had stayed on in Vienna, after the defeat of Béla Kun, in whose government he had been. At times excluded from the Communist party for his independence and for his refusal to accuse himself falsely, he had returned to the ranks at the first propitious moment. He was as formidable a fighter as he was a thinker.

Marcuse felt obliged to leave Germany; as a Marxist and a Jew, he would have ended up in a concentration camp. After a brief stay elsewhere in Europe he came to the United States. He had an opportunity to continue his university career. He was shocked to see the low state of socialism here and the lack of spirit of the working-class movement in general. This could not help but increase his tendency to see in advanced industrial societies a constant threat to the role of revolutionary vanguard that Marx considered the privilege and the duty of the working classes.

From the discussion of that afternoon it was clear that for most of the students who had been in the May Movement Marcuse continued to be an important influence. But for me the most important thing was to see that, three years after the May Movement, the passion for politics in these students was in no way diminished. This contradicted the stories that the spring '68 failure had demoralized the youth, removing them from the struggle.

Ten days before the May explosion, the dominant opinion in Paris, even in leftist circles, was that French youth was interested only in sports, the good life, free love, and, eventually, drugs. No one was expecting that students would put up barricades around the Sorbonne. And to suppose that the movement could acquire a force and a breadth that would oblige de Gaulle to transfer the French Headquarters in Germany in order to be sure of the support of the army — this would have seemed insane. Just as three years later people would have been completely wrong who maintained that May 1968 had been a temporary epidemic and that the young people, cheated, had lost interest in the answer and in the revolution.

All this, in addition to future orientation, served me as an argument to fight the despair that had overcome some Spanish exiles, weary of waiting thirty-four years for the fall of Franco. Deciding that there was nothing to be done, in some cases they returned to Spain to die. This was sad, for to go on struggling in secret would have been noble. At the risk of being attacked I repeated again and again that Franco's strength came, even more than from the American aid that kept him in power, from the weakness of his opposition. I maintained that the dictatorship can and will be destroyed.

In the rest of Western Europe the movement of youthful rebellion had not been beaten down by police repression in spite of its harshness. From the University of Florence, where I had spoken about Spanish student activities, they sent me leaflets that had been handed out in the most recent riots in Italy, a country that never calms down. The students there could count on the backing of the young workers. They even got support from some of the leaders of the unions, who showed more initiative than did their French comrades. Italy's verve and temperament were always vehemently expressed in the streets.

The "wild strikes" in all of Western Europe, from Spain to bourgeoise Switzerland, are the clearest proof of the divorce between the workers and their union leaders. In Italy the strikes acquired an unexpected dimension: they were supported by the students. This spontaneous alliance between workers and students was upsetting to the parties that formed the Leftist-Central governments. It was described to me by one of the young Italian militants who had gone to Geneva to make a report to the Swiss students. Another of the impressive recent developments is this kind of student international, which has even managed to include peaceful Switzerland, thereby shaking the habitual tranquility of the Swiss universities.

One of the most interesting young German Marxist writers, Hans Magnus Enzenberger, confronted Marcuse in a controversy that was discussed at length in those days. Marcuse raised the question: Could one still classify as a proletarian the laborer who came home from his job to a comfortable apartment, who had a car in which to take his family on weekend trips? Enzenberger answered that if one wanted to measure the life-style of today's laborer with that of the laborer of 1850, one could indeed speak of the deproletarization of the proletariat. But it was false to deduce from this that the laboring class had everywhere disappeared as an element interested in radical social change, or that a new kind of laboring class was emerging that would turn its back on the revolution. First, he did not believe in the increasing and inevitable shift to the middle class of the laboring class; second, even if one admitted that this was the tendency, the duty of a revolutionary was to try to recapture the workers for the revolution. Otherwise, who would control it, Enzenberger would ask.

Marcuse would answer by stressing the importance of the student movement in the struggle for social justice. Enzenberger would reply that in Federal Germany the university population was drawn mainly from the bourgeoisie. The working class was represented by a maximum of about 6 to 8 percent in the universities.

For Marcuse many of Enzenberger's points of view were "Popular Marxism." Naturally one has to go to the factories and win over the young workers to political action, not with clichés about capitalism and the proletariat but with a valid explanation of the prospects open to today's capitalism. One has to work with the intellectuals and with the housewives. It is the housewives, insisted Marcuse, who are the basis of the movement in the United States against the Vietnam War. Agreed, Enzenberger would say, but you can't build socialism on intellectuals, students, and housewives alone, excluding workers.

Gauchisme developed in Germany through the activities of student leaders, who succeed one another and thus assure the continuity of the movement. Among them were a few leaders with strong personalities, like Rudi Dutschke. He made a careful study of Karl Marx and "the new men of our time," his preference going to "Ché" Guevara and Frantz Fanon. Dutschke had a highly internationalist sense of the task that the years ahead would set aside for youth. He was much interested in Spain, where "students and workers march together," and in the Vietnam War, whose outcome is going to strengthen the movements of rebellion, of national independence, and of liberation throughout the world.

Basing himself on the declarations of McNamara and other American statesmen, Rudi Dutschke identified as the principal objective of the United States in Vietnam to forestall the entrance into action of the masses at a worldwide level. According to him, the United States intervened in Vietnam not in answer to Communist aggression from outside but to discourage the guerrilla warfare from spreading in different forms from one continent to another. The American War in Vietnam is an anti-guerrilla war. And the failure of the United States in Vietnam, proving that the best equipped army in the world is incapable of winning in a people's revolutionary war, cannot but serve the cause of the revolution everywhere.

Dutschke foresaw, for the next ten years, harsh struggles between the fringe revolutionary movements (those on the edge of the traditional Communist and Socialist parties) and the Establishment, with reaction and neo-fascism rushing to the defense of a capitalistic order that feels threatened by the people's revolution. He rejected all dogmatization of

Marxism, "this critical science that, based on dialectics, permits a confrontation with everything that reality presents again." He also analyzed the causes of the failure suffered by the labor movement in his own country at the end of the First World War. Rudi Dutschke took for himself the expression of Rosa Luxemburg "the collapse into barbarism," with the success of the revolution disastrously threatened, more than by the direct force of the bourgeoisie, by the lack of socialist clarification, of clear and precise objectives from the proletariat.

As for the future, Dutschke's recommendation is "to revolutionize the revolutionaries, the condition necessary for the revolutionization of the masses." He considered that Georg Lukács was, with Lenin, the theoretician who during the 1920s had given most support to a radical interpretation of Marxism. Lukács' major practical contribution to saving revolutionary socialism from the tendency of official Communist parties to fall under the influence of the system and of bureaucracy was his determination to fight from within. In spite of excommunication and anathema Lukács took advantage of the first opportunity that he was given to renew his ties with the Party.

To his prestige as a Marxist thinker with scarcely an equal in his time Georg Lukács added that of a first-rank literary critic, one of the few who found more pleasure in emphasizing what was good in a work than in seeking out the weaknesses of an author in order to destroy him. To him we owe some of our most interesting studies on the novel. He was one of the earliest critics to discover in Thomas Mann one of the greatest novelists of this century. Lukács saw in *The Magic Mountain* the beginning of a great realism in the novel that would become a school. Later he compared *The Magic Mountain* to the novels of Alexander Solzhenitsyn, and the interest that Lukács showed in getting him the Nobel Prize was another reason why Lukács brought on himself the hostility of official Soviet circles. Lukács' opinion of Solzhenitsyn was nevertheless quite balanced. He admired the way in which he presented the gravest crisis through which socialism had passed in his country. But he did not put him on the level of Tolstoi: He saw in the author of *A Day in the Life of Ivan Denisovich* a narrator of unusual force but not a great Communist narrator of the Stalin era. This judgment may have had some political conclusions, but they were indirect. Unless his future works showed him exceeding the quality of his present production, Solzhenitsyn would be considered no more than a talented novelist. It was not that Lukács was trying to diminish Solzhenitsyn's historic merit. Together with having written the novel that won the Nobel Prize, the cause of so much controversy in his country, he is in the heritage of writers who created the greatness of Russian literature.

Georg Lukács has dedicated a whole book to Solzhenitsyn, which bears his name. In it he writes: "It is not enough to make clear that these novels represent a dramatization throbbing with interest, with what was the high point of Socialist realism, to conclude that they may resolve the problem of giving a deep meaning to the time in which we live. It would be quite inconceivable not to wonder whether these novels have a political character, and if so, to what extent. If there is no question that the bitter enemies of Solzhenitsyn attribute to him political criteria and conclusions that are simply false, it would, on the other hand, be groundless to think that he should imagine that his books offer an answer to the questions created by the crisis of Socialism."

The personality of Georg Lukács made it difficult for the bureaucrats of the party to which he had belonged for intermittent periods to run down his reputation. This was the situation with Louis Aragon in France. I had known Aragon very well ever since the Spanish War. He has, as the French say, "un talent fou." He can do everything with exceptional brilliance: poetry (the verses to "The Eyes of Elsa," Elsa Triolet, his late wife and his lifelong inspiration), the novel *Holy Week*, journalism. He is the most important intellectual of the French Communist party. And he can allow himself to criticize Soviet policy, he can defend dissident writers in the Socialist camp, he can do anything. The Party would never dare to exclude him from its ranks.

Gauchisme knows no limits of frontier or of age. In the new state of Bangla-Desh, born out of the explosion in Pakistan, the old peasant leader, Maulana Bhashani, ninety-one years old, in April 1972 harangued fifty thousand persons in the Dacca stadium with a vigor that roused the enthusiasm of his audience. Like the famous Italian Renaissance monk Savonarola, the chief of the Awami national party, of Maoist background, cursed the corruption of the supporters of Mujibur Rahman, yesterday's conqueror. He spoke of those who had exchanged their huts for splendid houses and of those who, never having seen a car before, now traveled about in luxurious automobiles. And each one of his paragraphs was greeted with cries of "Shame, shame!"

But, in general, *gauchisme* belongs to youth. To youth Roger Garaudy dedicates his latest book *L'Alternative*. He is, in fact, one of the most prominent old members of the French Communist party, expelled from the direction of the party and from the party itself because of his criticisms of the party and of the foreign policy of the Soviet Union. I met Garaudy years ago in the book fair of *L'Humanité*, the party journal, when he was still considered by his comrades to be one of the most approved Marxist theoreticians.

Roger Garaudy looked to the future. And the future was, for him, the young people. The worldwide uprising of youth meant the appearance of a new power. "The future," he wrote, "has already begun. The young people remind us of it every day with their rejections and their anger."

290

Under different forms these young people, who make up half the world, are in rebellion. They reach the point of creating the bases of a new society, with its unwritten laws, its customs, its choices, which are not those of established society.

The characteristic trait of today's youth is rebellion. In China, the Cultural Revolution, at first without any restrictive bonds, later reoriented toward the consolidation of the conquered positions, with the courts that Mao Tse-tung judged to be necessary, and which were made possible thanks to his authority, has given to youth all possibilities and a secure future. In France, in May 1968, the young people felt themselves for a moment on the eve of victory. But the Parties and the syndicalist organizations blocked their path. Nothing was solved. Four years after May 1968, it took a single death, the worker killed in the Renault factory, to make the streets of Paris once again the setting for the rebellious will of the young people.

For Roger Garaudy this political behavior of the young people, in spite of the diversity of the conditions in each nation, presents two fundamental common characteristics: that the political activity of young people should develop outside the party framework, and that the clichés that the accommodating currents of official communism would like to impose, trying to discredit *gauchisme* and the "revolutionary venturism," have ceased to be a strong dissuader. Garaudy justifies the space that he devotes to the Chinese Cultural Revolution in relation to the problem of today's rebellious youth and he declares that it is far from his intention to suggest that one follow the Chinese path. But he follows it because the Chinese Cultural Revolution is "the only historical example of an attempt to change the ends and the means of culture, to conceive a new project of civilization." When the Sorbonne students, in May of 1968, wrote on the walls of the Paris streets "Power to the imagination!" they were denouncing the lack of logic and realism in the solutions that the regime in power was offering them, not only in the field of education but also the field of politics.

It is interesting to stress the fact that, together with Rosa Luxemburg, the revolutionary thinker from the 1920s who is read and studied by European students and young *gauchistes* of today is Gramsci. Antonio Gramsci, the great militant theoretician of the Italian Communist movement, creator of the concept of the new "historic bloc." Gramsci's notion of a "historic bloc" was tied to the present controversy about the use of outlines and slogans of social analysis that have become too old for the taste and the uneasiness of today's youth.

In each epoch the definition of the "historic bloc" demands: 1) a scientific analysis of the relations between the "base and the superstructures" and as Gramsci boldly writes in his *Notes on Machiavelli*, an analysis of the unity between nature and spirit; 2) a corresponding analysis of social classes; 3) the "adequate initiative," to give to the bloc a consciousness of their unity and their ability to carry out a possible unpublished history.

A basic principle exists around the problem created by the antagonism between the traditional parties, today substantially suspected of *gauchisme* and of "the adventurers of the revolution," and the action groups, whether called Trotskyites, leftist Communists, leftist Socialists, or Maoists. The principle is that there is no passive liberation, in the face of the threats of reaction and of a neo-fascism that are revealed with greater or lesser force everywhere pushed by panic toward revolution. For it is only in the constant struggle for liberty that the exercise and the future of that liberty can be achieved.

TWENTY

Revolution and the Arts

Films, theater, literature are for many people *"au-dessous de la mêlée"* (above the squabble), as Romain Rolland said one day, even though he later got involved in the squabble. Through the years, as a matter of fact, I have frequently noticed their enormous effectiveness as political weapons. This effectiveness is bound to increase in the coming years in the historic conflict between the forces of the past that are struggling to outlive themselves and the forces of the future that refuse to be intimidated or to withdraw.

Speaking of films, Bernard Shaw was right in saying that they had produced only one genius, Charlie Chaplin. Many talents but only one genius. I once sat next to Chaplin at a political dinner in New York and I took advantage of the opportunity to talk to him about the Spanish War. Later I was tempted to go to visit him in his Swiss home, but I respected his need to be left alone. The movies really began with Chaplin. His first movies have a responsive message, in today's language. He continues to appeal to the masses more than anyone else. On his return from his triumphal journey to Hollywood, a journey that was in itself a political triumph over American reactionary forces that had kept him away from there, he reached the Geneva airport on Sunday, April 16, 1972, on his eighty-third birthday. A young Swiss student, known for his leftist opinions, shouted: "He's one of us!"

I have often gone to working-class districts in various cities to watch simple people looking at the early pictures of Charlie, which again and again draw immense crowds. It was clear that, even some sixty years after they were produced, they still had an undeniable current importance. It was not just through the joy of seeing them, it was also that they had an egalitarian message. Whether or not their creator so wished, Charlie Chaplin's films are political films. The stunning mimicry of *The Kid* shows that gestures called burlesque can take on a philosophical value and can shake the spectator who came merely to be amused. When sound came to the movies Chaplin was able to adjust rapidly to the new demands. He worked hard and patiently to produce *A King in New York*.

Movie actors and actresses have often entered the political arena in protest against war and dictatorship. The Vietnam War, the Fascist dictatorships in Spain and Greece, offer frequent opportunities to stage demonstrations. At the head of the list of activists is Jane Fonda. She has everything it takes to be an agitator for a good cause, capable of mobilizing drowsy consciences. Beautiful, well-dressed, speaking excellent French, Jane Fonda for a whole hour held the attention of a crowd that filled the vast hall of the Maison des Centraux in Paris. Her French was not just social, party French; it was good enough for a political speech filled with facts and passion. It was quite a linguistic tour de force. Jane Fonda and Melina Mercouri are two famous actresses who have warmly embraced noble causes, Melina, the struggle of the Greek people against the dictatorship of the colonels, Jane, the fight against the war in Vietnam. With bold gestures accenting her words, Jane Fonda that night introduced the testimony of former American fighters in Indochina about war crimes. She was surrounded by American and Vietnamese witnesses who had contributed to the report of a commission of inquiry that met in Detroit. But the person who had everyone spellbound was Jane Fonda. Especially when she kissed the last person to reach the platform, a black who came to tell what he had witnessed.

This meeting took place at a moment when French public opinion, opposed to the war, but lulled for some months, like the parallel movement in the United States, by the supposed magic of Vietnamization, was beginning to wake up to the danger of greater future complications in Asia. One of my French newspaper friends, an authority on the war in Indochina, Jean Lacouture, had used a very drastic phrase to define Vietnamization, the *"jaunissement des cadavres"* (the yellowing of the corpses), by which he meant that giving some other color than white to the men and women and children killed in the war showed that they did not count.

Jane Fonda, at that meeting in Paris, was not intimidated by the intelligence officers who were undoubtedly present. She called a spade a spade. She called a crime a crime. She denounced, as those responsible for the mass assassinations of My Lai, the government of the United States, the Pentagon, and the C.I.A. "What courage!" said some French students sitting beside me as they followed her words with shining faces. The effect of her words was heightened by the French fear that "the disaster of Cambodia and Laos" (that's how the French military expert described it; would at some point lead the Americans to bombard the whole area. And the bombardment of Haiphong and Hanoi in April

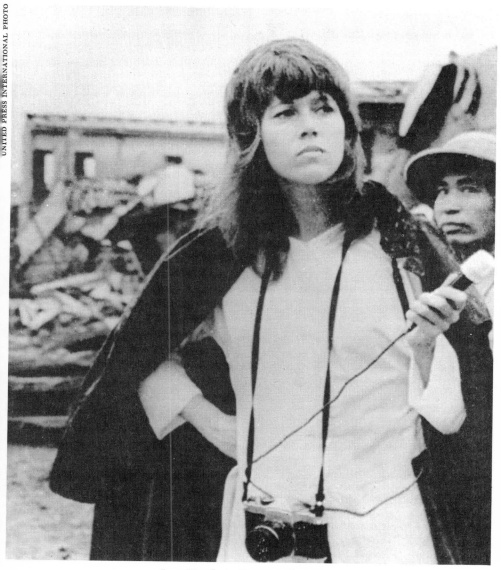

Jane Fonda in Hanoi, July 1972

1972 showed that such fears were justified. My Lai was not an isolated incident. "In fact, on a lesser scale, it occurs quite frequently."

I leave to Jane Fonda the responsibility for what she said. Her comments may sound exaggerated. They sound less so when we hear Johnson's attorney general, Ramsay Clark, describe what he saw of American bombardment of the dikes in North Vietnam.

Jane Fonda was chosen by Jean-Luc Godard for his latest picture, *Tout va bien*. A perfectly logical combination, the revolutionary film maker and the politically conscious actress. Since *La Chinoise*, which gave him a certain reputation as a Maoist, Godard has insisted on using films in the revolutionary struggle. *Tout va bien* is not, according to its author, a film about politics but a political film. The difference is important since in the second case all the elements that give life to the film are organized and move forward as a function of the political analysis, which is basically the confrontation of the social forces, the class struggle, after May 1968.

Of all the French film makers who give their production a revolutionary aim, Godard is the most effective. His film-making methods are highly original. He uses the camouflaged camera better than most film makers, and this allows him to capture the expression, the attitudes of those who, without being aware of it, are going to be part of one of his films, thus assuring a maximum degree of spontaneity. He shoots scenes in the street, in the middle of a crowd unconscious of being observed. He is a great enthusiast about states of mind, and he never fails to capture them. He is an excellent maker of documentary films, for which he writes shrewd analyses of the pictures that he has collected. He has humor, irony, faith, and a sound analysis of today and tomorrow. Godard's main virtue is his rejection of all artificiality, whether narrative or dramatic. In May 1968 he put a sudden end to his cinema career, which had gone from success to success. He concentrated on the production of films of revolutionary information composed of fixed shots, of pamphlets scattered around the Sorbonne, of pictures that came right out of the barricades. His fighting spirit even caused some suspicion in leftist circles, where people asked why a film-maker with an assured position in bourgeois society would place his whole career in jeopardy. Godard has discovered, to use his own words, "that there is no art outside the class struggle. It would be pretentious," he says, "to claim that a film can make people take to the streets, but one *can* try to make films that will make people think about the need for taking to the streets." He is one of those who have read Mao and understood him.

Married to a daughter of François Mauriac and having much of his polemical temperament, Godard maintains that, in the case of films, the thing to do is to adopt an attitude of maximum offensiveness, not the defensive attitude that, for example, would lead the French Communis<!---->

party to conclude that by casting Jean Gabin, the very popular French actor, as a metal worker, they were advancing the cause of the working man. Godard was almost killed in an automobile accident. Fortunately he recovered and, though he is still on crutches, he continues on the road that he has mapped for himself with a clear vision of the moment in which we live.

André Malraux made only one picture, *L'Espoir* [Hope], but it had great political value. Together with *To Die in Madrid, L'Espoir* brought to the screen the war in Spain. The scene of the procession of the farmer-soldiers carrying down from the mountains the bodies of the dead Loyalist aviators could have been signed by Eisenstein.

It was, in fact, my friendship with Eisenstein that helped me most in seeing clearly the importance of films in advancing political action. I had met him in Berlin, but it was in Mexico that I had the fullest opportunity to talk with him about art in general and about the movies, especially during the week that we spent together on the farm where he was shooting part of his film *Viva México*. I was able to be of help to him in his dealings with the Mexican authorities, and when the shooting was over I was able to show the whole film in the Spanish embassy before it suffered the cuts that resulted from Eisenstein's difficulties with his American producers.

Sergei Mikhailovich Eisenstein was so skilled a talker that he held his listeners fascinated no matter what he was talking about. He told me a lot about his childhood and adolescence, which gave me a tableau of czarist Russia. His father was Jewish, his mother a Russian society lady. He was studying to be an architectural engineer, like his father. But the revolution came and he enlisted in the Red Army. When he was demobilized he decided to devote himself to the theater. He worked with Meyerhold and staged, in the Proletkult, a work adapted from Jack London, *The Mexican*. From that time on he had a desire to go to Mexico. Then his films *The Strike* and *The Battleship Potemkin* made him the most successful of Russian film makers.

In Mexico Eisenstein had as helpers Tisse and Alexandrov, who were very enjoyable. Tisse and Alexandrov, who were known only by their last names, were Eisenstein's principal photographers and technicians. I sometimes acted as interpreter when he would talk with the farmers on the estate. In spite of the agrarian reform, that estate, located in a fabulous landscape, still had many features of the prerevolutionary epoch. We all ate at the table of the owner, who was much interested in hearing from Eisenstein how the Russian landowners were getting along after their lands had been confiscated and turned over to the farmers. During the meal the owner was constantly fanned by a young Indian girl to chase away the flies. This amused Eisenstein very much. He lost no opportunity to observe the farmers as he went back and forth to work.

Eisenstein was a master of film making, a specialist in the interpretation of detail. In *October* it was the headlight of the train that was bringing Lenin to Petrograd, the gesture of his hand imposing silence on the thousands of workers and soldiers who kept shouting to him, and his pledge: "The Republic of the Soviet workers and farmers throughout the country, from top to bottom."

There was the amusing gesture of Kerenski beside the statue of Napoleon. Kerenski, a man who found himself in the position of leadership but without the ability to lead. The half-empty glasses of coffee of Kerenski's ministers, slouched in their seats after Kerenski had abandoned them to go to wage a final imaginary battle. The balalaika interrupting the speech of one of the opponents of the Bolsheviks in a meeting just prior to their taking over power. Eisenstein got his inspiration for this symbolic shot from a sentence of Lenin: "Kerenski plays at playing the balalaika to distract the workers and farmers." The shining face of Antonov-Ovseyenko, who laid the foundation for the insurrection, announcing that the provisional government had been overthrown. Antonov, a former officer of the Imperial Army, had been condemned to death for insubordination in 1905. I knew him during the war in Spain. He died a victim of the purges.

October cannot be compared to any other film. It had a hundred thousand actors and extras, forty thousand yards of film, soldiers who refused to fight against anyone, workers who wanted to work with dignity, farmers who claimed their rights to the land, and a revolutionary giant, Lenin. *October* may not have perhaps the majesty of *The Battleship Potemkin* or the polish of *Alexander Nevsky* or the tragic and tormented toughness of *Ivan the Terrible*, but it is my favorite Eisenstein film. It was the marvelous staging, filled with strength and humor, of the "ten days that shook the world," in the classic definition of the great American journalist John Reed.

With *October* in 1927, as Eisenstein explained to me, a new phase began in the films. The revolution dominated everything. The old narrative and melodramatic concepts were finally rejected. The language of the film was capable of expressing all by itself any class idea, any political or tactical slogan, without the need to have recourse to the trickery of psychological interpretations. There was no need for bad literature, no need to exalt the movie star. The revolution was its own star. The revolution became the protagonist of the film. When Kerenski's government, after the shooting in Nevski Avenue, decided to close off the bridges to halt the march of the workers, the bridges refused mechanically to obey, showing the futility of trying to stop the forward march of a revolution.

Eisenstein told me that he felt so sure of his revolution in film techniques, so sure of having found the way of bringing triumphantly to the screen works that seemed least suited for it because of their abstraction that he thought one of his next films would be Karl Marx's *Das Kapital*. The important thing was to know how to use images as words and through the clash of images to succeed in giving a human dimension to ideas that might seem least susceptible of being filmed. *Das Kapital*, that herald of the presence of the proletariat as a guide for humanity struggling to put an end to injustice and inequality, seemed to me excellent material for a film. Unfortunately Eisenstein never made the film. He died of a heart attack in 1948, shortly after his fiftieth birthday.

The last time that I saw Felix Greene, the British writer and film maker, his dream was to return to China. He has fulfilled it by now. He was in Peking after the bombardment of Haiphong and Hanoi and the interview that Chou En-lai granted him, and which was transmitted over one of the American networks, was one more proof that on the Vietnam question China's position was unchanged: complete support of Hanoi and the Vietcong. This was in mid-April 1972.

Felix Greene, like our friend Wilfred Burchett, the Australian journalist, is well acquainted with North Vietnam and its leaders. He covered for British television the funeral rites for Ho Chi Minh. A very impressive broadcast, it came from Greene's conviction that all the destructive capability of the United States Air Force, without which Thieu's regime in Saigon would have disappeared long ago, would not succeed in destroying the will to victory of the successors of Ho Chi Minh. Among these successors the man who represents better than any other leader that will to victory is Vo Nguyen Giap. He and Pham Van Dong, the politician, and Truong Chinh, the theoretician, are the nucleus of the unbreakable men trained by Ho Chi Minh. Jean Lacouture, to whom we owe the most exciting biography of Ho, has also done the portrait of General Giap, the conqueror of Dien Bien Phu, the leader of the April offensive, who adds to his brilliance as a strategist the equally great asset of being a man of ideas. One has only to look at his forehead. "If Beethoven had been a Vietnamese," writes Lacouture, "I thought absurdly, he would have had that head."

The amazing resistance fighters of Hanoi are succeeding through teamwork. That handful of men, inheritors of the goals of Ho Chi Minh, held firm after the death of their teacher and leader. They carried on his wishes. That spirit of firm cooperation was what Greene stressed in his account of the funeral of the man whose life and example would make it impossible for his successors ever to capitulate. And so this patriotic war will continue for as long as necessary and in spite of all the bombs that are dropped.

Felix Greene had already made a film on Vietnam. I saw it in New York and watched the reactions of the audience. I was told that a few days before, Walter Lippmann had seen the film and had been horrified by the cruelty of a war that he knew his country could never win. Greene makes political films. When I saw him he was finishing a film on the Cuban Revolution. He is not blindly opposed to imperialism. He has taken the trouble to study it closely. The result is *The Enemy*, his latest book, a profound and fighting book.

Imperialism is also the theme of one of the most successful political films *¿Qué hacer?* (What Can We Do About It?), which describes Chile at the moment of the election in 1970 of Salvador Allende, whose experiment of revolution through democratic means has the whole leftist world hanging on each incident.

The political film made an unexpected appearance in Spain in the 1950s. In spite of the Franco censorship, Luis García Berlanga and Juan Antonio Bardem managed to produce *Bienvenido* (Welcome) *Mr. Marshall*, a fine satire on American aid. A small Spanish town is fascinated by the prospect of being able to get dollars thanks to the Marshall Plan. It is really more a village than a town. There is enormous excitement. The mayor, played by an excellent actor, José Isbert, is instructed by a representative of the Franco government on how to prepare for a great reception for the American visitors. Everything has to be renovated and tidied up in the space of a few days. It is emergency, shoddy reconstruction, pure false front. It recalls the famous constructions the Potemkin Villages, built by Potemkin, the minister and lover of Catherine the Great. They were not much more than cardboard, set up to impress Catherine as she rode past them.

The mayor of the Spanish village is deaf. The explanation of the enormous advantages of the Marshall Plan becomes complicated and amusing. When the Franco emissary insists on the importance of having the Americans carry away a good impression of the visit, the mayor asks in surprise: "Carry away? I thought they were coming to bring!" The village is all dressed up. Hundreds of streamers and little American flags have been made to welcome the guests. The great moment arrives. Everyone gathers at the station, and the official train approaches and then thunders through the station without stopping. No welcome for Mr. Marshall. At the end we see streamers and banners floating in the river like lost election posters. Bardem later made *La muerte de un ciclista* (Death of a Cyclist), the story of the "worldly men," the bourgeois filled with egotism and hypocrisy. Berlanga, Bardem, Carlos Saura, and other less well-known young film makers surely have in reserve projected films to be made as soon as the dictatorship ends.

It is to be hoped that some of them will concern themselves, as soon as it is possible to do so, with a magnificent theme for a film: Franco and the world. The world that has forgotten that the name of Franco is linked with the death of millions of men and women killed in the Second World War. He is the only survivor of the leaders of international fascism who caused a loss of human lives in numbers up to then unheard of. The United Nations, before it was poisoned by the Cold War, passed resolutions, in 1946 and in following years, saying that Franco was a war criminal placed in power by Hitler and Mussolini and that Franco Spain had no place in the international organization. The bartering of corpses for strategic advantages, the forgetting of those who fell for the cause of liberty, could be the theme of a harsh, implacable film that would be a lesson for future generations.

Meanwhile we have a picture of Spanish society that results from thirty-four years of Franco rule thanks to the penetrating and marvelously ironic camera of Luis Buñuel. If he had produced nothing more than *Tristana*, Buñuel would have been a landmark in film history.

Tristana is taken from a novel by Benito Pérez Galdós. When I was a college student in Madrid, I used to help him to climb the stairs as he mounted the platform at meetings, for his sight was failing. He is the greatest Spanish novelist after Cervantes, and he has much of the realism of the author of *Don Quixote*. He had a sharp perception of types and authentic scenes. About his own life and work the best that has been written are his own *Memorias de un desmemoriado* [Memoirs of an Absent-Minded Man]. In them he tells how he used to write "by fits and starts, a bit at a time," sometimes beginning a page without knowing how it was going to end. His enormous output begins with *Los episodios nacionales*, which is the fictional history of rebellious and patriotic Spain. *Gibraltar* told the terrible and heroic adventure of the Spanish fleet. Other *Episodios* were *La corte de Carlos IV*, *El dos de mayo*, the Spanish people rising up against Napoleon in the beginnings of a guerrilla warfare that is a very current event in Latin America today.

Galdós later turned to pure fiction in such works as *Fortunata y Jacinta* and *Ángel Guerra*. In *Nazarín* he attempted a portrait of Christ. His play *Electra* was an extension and dramatization of his novelistic skills. The novel *Tristana* is laid in Toledo. Galdós was born in Las Palmas in the Canary Islands, but he came to love Madrid and Castile. *Tristana* was written in 1892; it could have been written today. Although modern buildings, in Madrid more than Toledo, have replaced the big old houses, the soul of the Spanish bourgeoisie and all that surrounds it have not changed.

Buñuel portrays this soul in a provincial café. His protagonist, an elderly bourgeois, dyes his beard every morning (this is one of the unforgettable scenes in the film) before going to have chocolate with his friends, the friars. He seduces a young girl to whom he has offered the protection of his home. And of course, he supports and defends that social filth, the inevitable and "worthy" Civil Guard.

Seeing Buñuel's film one can get a better understanding of current Spanish problems than by reading all the books written about the Spanish War and the Franco dictatorship. Arthur Miller agreed with me about the virtues and importance of *Tristana* when I visited him in 1971 in Connecticut where he was working on a new play. Miller told me that Buñuel's film has made such an impression on him that for the first time in his life he had written, just for himself, for his own pleasure, a movie review.

It is interesting to note that two of the top dramatists in the United States, Arthur Miller and Lillian Hellman, are both politically involved. Miller behaved admirably before the House Committee on Un-American Activities, when others were evasive. Lillian Hellman, whose memoir *An Unfinished Woman* is a marvel of style and grace, was on our side during the Spanish War, as was Barbara Tuchman.

I was involved in the various attempts to create a revolutionary theater in Europe, revolutionary in content and in staging. Piscator was my friend from my Berlin days in the early 1920s when he was staging the Russian Revolution, and I saw him later in New York where he had to flee when Hitler came into power. At the parties that I used to give in the Berlin office of *La Nación* of Buenos Aires I gathered the most advanced directors, actors, and actresses of those times.

In the 1920s the theater experienced a great renovating prosperity everywhere. The strongest impulse came from Paris, from an actor of extraordinary talents, Jacques Copeau, equally brilliant in the role of Dostoevski's Ivan Karamazov or as an interpreter and director of Shakespeare. It was he who created the Théâtre du Vieux Colombier, breaking with traditional formulas and giving to the stage all its revolutionary potential.

Copeau's success was extraordinary. People fought for seats to see *The Night of the Kings* and it can be said that thanks to the patient work of a cast intelligently chosen by Copeau, who believed not in temperamental improvisation but in the actor's discipline and in his total understanding of and sympathy with the work that is being performed, Shakespeare began to be popular in France. This disproved the theory that the public in general favored, instead of works of Shakespeare, Dostoevski, or Claudel, the frivolous comedies or melodramas that packed the boulevard theaters.

Copeau had a rare sense of dramatic development. The rehearsing of a work under his direction was an exercise in patience that went on until a perfect interpretation was achieved. He made the actor speak and move without ever losing sight of the total effect. He never let an actor impose himself as a star at the expense of the other actors. The actor's voice must be heard from every corner of the theater, but it must never take on an artificial intonation. The actor must always be simple and natural. His mission was to transmit the poetry, the spirit of the work, to the audience. He was a singularly human theatrical creator, going directly to the heart of the public without cheap effects, without concessions.

The Vieux Colombier remains as a proof that it is not money but genius that makes good theater. Copeau began with very little money. He used a subscription system, founding patrons, devotees of good theater, until he was assured of an initial sum of three hundred thousand (old) francs, enough for a start. He had the enthusiasm of a company of actors who would not have gone to any other theater even at three times their salaries. At the heart of the company was another great actor, Louis Jouvet.

Copeau gathered around him some of the best young writers of that time, Roger Martin du Gard, Georges Duhamel, and established playwrights, including André Gide, in whose *Saül* Copeau himself played the title role. He was inspired by Claudel in his concept of the theater as poetry. The Vieux Colombier triumphed equally well abroad, in Germany, Switzerland, Holland, and England.

This innovative theatrical venture attracted to Paris great artists from everywhere. Copeau was delighted to welcome Chaplin, who was introduced by Waldo Frank. They all went off to the Cirque Medrano, where the famous Fratellini clowns were delighting all Parisians, old and young. The audience discovered Chaplin, and the staff of the circus had to be mobilized to protect him from admirers amazed and delighted to have him among them on that evening.

The Vieux Colombier filled its stage with flowers to honor the presence of the greatest actress of that time and perhaps of all times, Eleonora Duse. The magic name of the Italian tragedienne was a triumph of personality over age. La Duse rejected the attempts of makeup artists to hide the wrinkles brought to her face by the disappointments of her life, her experience of the ingratitude of those whom she helped forward on the road of glory. Her pale cheeks and expressive lips were equally used to expressing suffering on or off stage. Her existence was marked by love and jealousy. But she reigned in triumph on the stage of Copeau's theater, in defiance of approaching death.

In the classical theater, as in the modern theater, there are many works with a clearly revolutionary content. Calderón exalted the conflict between the power of the king and the power of the people represented by a mayor in *El alcalde de Zalamea* [The Mayor of Zalamea], a drama of universal fame. I saw it performed in Yugoslavia. And Lope de Vega's *Fuente Ovejuna* immortalizes the people of a town who put to death their rapist overlord. When the king sends a judge to discover who murdered him, the townspeople say that it was Fuente Ovejuna that killed him. It would be risky to stage this play in Madrid today because of

Bertolt Brecht, 1940

its rallying cry: "Fuente Ovejuna, todos a una!" (Fuente Ovejuna, all together), which would provoke shouts of "long live the people" against Franco.

The Russian dramatist Alexander Ostrovski, a contemporary of Chekhov, less well-known abroad but almost as great a dramatist as the author of *Uncle Vanya*, sketched the portrait of the Russian businessman. The businessman best-known to theatergoers outside of Russia is Lopakhin, the masterly creation of Chekhov in *The Cherry Orchard*. But the characters of Ostrovski have more satirical strength and they are more politically involved. The *kouptsy*, the Russian business class, were an element of Russian society under the czar, not on the same level with the nobility and the clergy, but very representative in their way, dressed in their long black coats that reached to their knees. They were among the exploiters of the people and were therefore a legitimate target for revolutionary satire.

One could mention several dramatic works based on the great social convulsions, the French Revolution, the Paris Commune, or revolts as recent as the one of May 1968. And one could mention the "theater of ideas" of Ibsen and Shaw. But the real revolution in the theater between the two World Wars and afterwards was made most vigorously by Bertolt Brecht. He was a revolutionary in content and in technique.

I met Brecht at the climax of his dramatic production, which was inseparable from his poetic production. He was in exile. The fate of man and the world inspired his clear words, his determination to sing even during the dark years of Hitler and fascism. "In a time of darkness," he asks himself, "will people still sing? Yes, people will sing the song of darkness." And "in me there is a confrontation between the exaltation of seeing apple trees in bloom and the horror produced in me by the tirades of the house painter, but it is the horror that forces me to write." Brecht's work is filled with apple trees in bloom, and the house painter, of course, was Hitler.

Like other markedly political poets — for example, Pablo Neruda singing the heroism of the people during the Spanish War — Brecht in his poetry and in his plays became logically, in the course of his literary development, a Socialist poet and dramatist. The theater of Brecht was patronized by a part of the bourgeoisie that had a snobbish fondness for what was new, but it was deeply understood and shared only by the revolutionary sector of the public. His strength was in his determination to rouse the spectator's conscience, to make him politically active through art.

Althuser is one of the Marxists who has the greatest influence on the youth after the deaths of the Austrian Ernst Fischer and the Hungarian Georg Lukács. Althuser observes that Brecht wants to make the spectator be the actor who concludes the drama, but in real life. It is a too-limited conception of Brecht's theater to refer to him as the genius of theatrical technique (which he is), forgetting his moral strength, his fighting opposition to reaction and mediocrity.

There is a good reason for saying that Brecht basically followed the advice that Engels gave to Lassalle, to "Shakespearize," to follow the path of Shakespeare, not to "Schillerize," or follow the path of Schiller. For Engels, to "Shakespearize" meant to dramatize, giving to the stage where heroes appear the historic dimension of the class struggle; it was the dramatization of history. In *Arturo Ui*, ridiculing the Fascist executioners, Brecht presented them not as the strong men that they believed themselves to be but as wretched neurotics. And he did not think that the neuroses of some murderers could ever be explained by history.

West Germany, which, in part through the fault of the Western Power swayed by anticommunism, never really broke with its nationalist and military past, was cool to Brecht. There was no formal censorship, but all kinds of obstacles were placed in the way of producing his plays. Even Chancellor Adenauer went so far as to deny that Brecht had any literary importance. But the progressive movements, the Disarmament Movement, the Union of Socialist Students, succeeded in overcoming that resistance.

After Brecht died I kept in touch with his theater through one of his most gifted interpreters, Ernst Busch, who had been with us in Spain during the war. An actor and musician, he composed the war songs that even today delight foreign friends of the Spanish Republic and that are sung in some commemorative gatherings: "Hans, the Commissar," "The Four Generals," "Madrid, Capital of the World." He frequently came to my house in Barcelona, where the piano was always waiting for Busch, the great songwriter of the war. I saw him again in Paris one evening when they were performing Brecht's *The Caucasian Chalk Circle* in the Théâtre des Nations and Busch was reading the text that accompanied the play. We spent that whole night together, my wife and he and I. He told me, as so many others did, that the Spanish War had been the greatest experience of his life.

The Brechtian theory about the strong bond between the author, the artistic creator, and the public, was based on a long and continuous experience. Only the other day in Paris, Maia Plisetskaya, the great star of the Bolshoi Ballet of Moscow, said that she felt more at ease dancing in the Palais des Sports than in the Opera. In the first, the audience was the people of Paris. In the Opera there was only high society.

In China I saw the revolutionary ballet "The Red Women's Detachment," with its prodigious leaps by young Chinese girls who were great athletes. This was the new theatrical form consecrated by the Cultural Revolution and replacing the opera of the emperors and their concubines. The audience was the common people, wildly enthusiastic.

We are moving toward a form of theater in which the author and the audience merge into a single expression of feelings and ideas. The talented Latin American dramatists and the Mexican Carlos Fuentes are oriented in that direction. It is in the spirit of the times and it confirms the political mission of the theater.

Among today's young painters Eduardo Arroyo is considered by respected critics to be one of the best. To the list of Spaniards who have played a major role in the development of modern art in Paris his name can unquestionably be added. This young man from Madrid has come rapidly to prominence as one of the most original painters of our time. Arroyo was born during the convulsion that followed the war in Spain, which may explain his liking for conflict. In his case, moreover, literary training preceded pictorial expression. That is why, at first, some technical weaknesses were noted that might suggest a certain naïveté in style. But by the time of the Third Biennial in Paris in 1965, Arroyo had defined his style boldly. He was part of the group "L'Abattoir I" (Slaughterhouse I), with Brusse, Camacho, Pinnencelli, and Zletykamien. That same year he won the Gold Medal of the Captains Regent in the Biennial at San Marino, even though the contestants included such established artists as Jorn, Hundertwasse, and Pasmore.

Aggressive painting, scornful of the aesthetic choices that occupied the forefront of the scene in the past twenty years and which found their inspiration in sources other than those of Anglo-American pop art, has coincided with the end of a cycle and the advent of "new figuration." Arroyo feels the same scorn for legends that falsify historic truths as far as the artificial values enshrined by the history of art.

There is no doubt that he became a painter because in our age a printed pamphlet does not have the effectiveness of a picture. And the pictures of Arroyo are crammed with characters that come back. His favorite model is Napoleon. Here is one of his paintings: a square with four medallions in which appears a character representing Napoleon in profile. In the first medallion Napoleon has his mouth shut, in the second, his mouth is open, in the third, the tip of his tongue appears, in the fourth, it is hanging out.

Historic fiction-making, for which the artist shows such a strong fondness, serves as a springboard for a very Spanish fantasy carried to a morbid extreme. Arroyo has not succeeded in freeing himself completely from the influence of artists whom he denounces violently in his imitations: del Mazo, son-in-law and pupil of Velázquez, David, Grosz, among others. At first, one still senses that he is torn between desecration and making a furtive sign of the cross as he turns to the old idols. But his demonstrated talent is impressive. He can play with the division of the canvas into small squares or large triangles. He also has the recourse of the systematic shifting of the main character. When, by necessity, the background of the composition is a landscape, the expanse, the emptiness, and the space cease to be abstractions. All this with a very sure sense of adjustment.

Someone has called Eduardo Arroyo the revolutionary Bonaparte of young contemporary painting. His two big shows, "Twenty-five Years of Peace" and "Thirty Years After" are the most conclusive accusation that has been made on canvas against the Franco regime since Picasso's "Guernica." And the second of the shows included a "Guernica 1970" by Arroyo. His painting justifies the comment of a North Vietnamese leader: "A painting or a poem can become also a weapon." It is in the area of political caricature that Arroyo reaches his greatest effectiveness. He evidently keeps in mind Unamuno's remark: "Nothing is more dreadful than an idiot." A critic, Alain Jouffroy, wrote: "One fact is clear: Arroyo, whether or not one understands him, whether his paintings make one think more of Mozart than of American imperialism, whether he paints to make you laugh or to make you brood, is today one of the few painters who dares to take a position, publicly and at the very center of all his paintings, against one of the most repressive regimes in the world, and without sparing anyone."

In fact, in "Thirty Years After," Eduardo Arroyo strikes hard, not only against the cruelty and the inhumanity of the Franco regime, but against its idiocy and its mediocrity. And also the American presence in Spain, as a support for Franco, is harshly upbraided. In "The Billiard Table: A Map of the American Bases in Spain," the billiard cushions have the colors of Franquist Spain and the obstacles are painted in star-spangled colors, one of them shaped like an ice-cream cone. Nobody is around the table. The American occupation speaks for itself and it is seen as destined to lose in the long run.

Arroyo has no pity for the other painters of his country who have been insensible to the suffering of the Spanish people and who, in one form or another, have shown deference for the Franco dictatorship. So in his show "Thirty Years After," which was a great success in Paris, in Frankfurt, and in other European cities, there is a portrait of "The Dwarf Sebastian Mora, Court Buffoon, born in Cadaques in the first half of the twentieth century." It is one of his most absurd paintings, drawing on the famous painting of Velázquez, and it is easy to identify Salvador Dali. In his catalogue Arroyo quotes several passages and among them this statement by Dali: "Franco is the leader who has restored clarity, truth and order to the country at one of the most anarchistic moments in history."

Arroyo's satire is not confined to the pillars of the Franco regime — the upper middle classes, the typical playboy with his variety of moustaches, the gypsy tourist guide, the diminished number of the Catholic hierarchy that go on supporting Franco, the generals. He also attacks all those who believe that Spain can be liberated by gentle and evangelic means.

With Ailland, an excellent French painter, marvelous with birds, and with others, Arroyo has contributed to the war of the Vietnamese patriots by selling his paintings for their benefit. Modest, ironic, amusing, he knows that he is a great painter. He did me the honor, in that show of his, to do a portrait of me as a symbol of the resistance and as a world wanderer, roving from continent to continent to beg for justice for the Spanish people. He generously quotes me at length. He has painted me with five legs, one each continent. One of them clearly points to China and another to Spain. It is a kind of announcement of my next journey to a liberated Spain.

TWENTY-ONE

My Next Journey

My next journey will not be my last journey, for I am planning several, but it will be the most sensational from the planning point of view, because the planning has been going on for nearly thirty years. At the end of the Second World War, I could see myself already on the road back to Madrid. It was a logical expectation. The fall of Hitler and Mussolini should have been followed by that of their partner Franco. All the Western political leaders with whom I talked at the time shared this opinion. It did not turn out that way, for reasons often stated. So, thirty years behind time, I am getting ready for my journey to Madrid.

In this long exile, in my determination not to abandon the struggle for freedom, I have been sustained by the example of bravery given by those who struggled inside Spain, them above all; and also by the encouragement of a lively sense of conscience outside of Spain which, in spite of all the time that has gone by, has acquired new vitality each time that there was a sharpening in the conflict between the Spanish people and the Franco regime, as on the occasion of the Burgos trial.

In Brioni President Tito told us that in the long run we would be the winners, and he added: "You may have lost in 1939, but you have contributed greatly to the crushing of Fascism. In some ways, Yugoslavia was born in Spain." He was referring to the fact that, at the time when we went to see him, twenty-eight generals and ten Yugoslav ambassadors had fought on our side in Spain in the International Brigade. The current prime minister of Albania, Shehu, also fought in the Brigade. I have already written of how Nehru never missed an opportunity to praise the Spanish people he had seen during the war. I have spoken of André Malraux's attitude. Even later, on a Mediterranean cruise in 1972, when the ship docked at Cádiz, he refused to set foot on Spanish soil. He said: "Too many Spanish comrades of mine are lying under that soil. I am not a casual tourist."

But the millions of tourists, beginning with the French, who supply the bulk of the annual financing of Franco, continue to be heedless of the appeal addressed to them by Jean Cassou, standing next to the widow of Grimau, the Communist leader executed in Spain. Cassou said: "Remember this murder! Don't go vacationing in Spain!"

So I say again that we were not alone. And as I make ready for my journey to Spain, I call the roll of all those loyal friends. I am going to Spain to meet my new comrades-in-arms, the youth of Spain.

The same spread of discontent provides the basis for a democratic

Del Vayo and other Spanish exiles in Paris, 1972, planning for their "next journey"

alternative. In fact, by February 1973 it was clear that, aside from the people who benefited from Franquist corruption and from those who placed the defense of their money above the interests of the nation, no one now identified his own future with the future of Franquism. The great majority of Spaniards had either turned against Franco or against the prospect of a monarchy under Juan Carlos.

The discontent was not limited to the Church, whose opposition to the regime was in itself a very significant step in a Catholic country. During the war we Loyalists had had the support of Catholic writers as famous as Mauriac, Bernanos, and Maritain, but in general the Catholics were then for Franco. But not now. The bar associations, very influential in Spain, are against Franco and call for the end of the use of military tribunals in trials that do not fall, even under Franquist laws, under their jurisdiction. They publicly denounce torture and mass arrests without specific motive. The university professors, by a great majority, identify themselves with the rebellious students. They find it incompatible with the dignity of their profession to have to hold classes in lecture halls under the surveillance of the police. And the same attitude is developing in all the other liberal professions.

Forces that had been with Franco during the war and after it, like the Carlists, now declared themselves "firm in their democratic attitudes and committed to the people who struggle for liberty in the face of repression." This was the language of the traditional Carlist Assembly that met in Montejurra in Navarre on May 7, 1972, in defiance of the government's prohibition. In that assembly the Carlist party pointed out the following events which had occurred during the current year: the Church was breaking with the State; the solidarity of the workers was getting stronger in the face of the capitalist and Fascist activities of the regime; there was a great acceleration in the political and moral awareness of the youth; the Spanish people were eager to smash myths and taboos that once seemed sacred; the regime is the only factor that prevents the possibility of fulfilling the European objectives that it claims it is pursuing; opposing the attempt to achieve an agreement among Spaniards is the attitude of those who cling to the concept of two distinct Spains and who intend to bring about, through violence and repression, the elimination of all those who express themselves democratically; there is a belief, beginning to spread through the ranks of the young officers, that the army must fulfill its institutional mission and not be a mere instrument at the service of privileged groups who are opposing the nation. This is what was said in May of 1972 by the Carlists who fought side by side with Franco.

All of this confirms the existence of an ample potential basis for the establishment in Spain of a democratic regime. The so-often-talked-about "fear of the vacuum" was only the fear of those who did not have a clear conscience. Others spoke of "chaos" if Spain should re-establish elementary human liberties. But an important Madrid industrialist, on his way through Paris, said to me: "What greater chaos than that created by Franco, who refused to settle the problem of his successor some years ago, and who now wants to settle it by naming as his successor a prince who inspires neither confidence nor respect?"

Some foreign commentators return again and again to the theme of the fragmentation of the opposition. But the opposition in many countries and in some cases even the ruling party, as in France and in Italy, is divided, which does not prevent it from having a very civilized political life.

Around a minimal program that includes the fulfilling of the aspirations of Catalans and Basques, Agrarian Reform, nationalizations, an independent foreign policy, an equitable social policy that will give satisfaction to workers, university reform, and a few other reforms, there is a possibility for the now-divided forces of the opposition to unite behind a government of broad anti-Fascist and democratic unity.

For me, the problems presented by the change from a dictatorship to a truly progressive republic in Spain are not frightening. I am counting the hours until I can return to a Madrid without Franco. I shall go with hope. I shall go with joy. I shall not miss this rendezvous with Spain.

Index

(1936), 155; political decay of (1920s–1930s), 156; policy of, toward Spain, 159, 160, 167, 186; fall of (1940), 138, 165, 166; approval by, of Italian aggression, 211; difficulties facing, 268; Maoist workers in, 281–282; Communist party in, 282–284, 290. *See also* "May 1968" revolt

Franco, General Francisco, and Franco regime, 127, 158, 166, 167, 173, 175, 179, 206, 210, 269, 274, 315; and UN, 109–110, 303; supported by Hitler and Mussolini, 147, 185; Churchill's sympathy with, 160; last years of, 179, 258; U.S. policy toward, 184, 185, 190; threatened by Negrín plan, 191; and Asturian miners, 209; and intellectuals, 253; young people under, 271–274; and Juan Carlos, 272–274; loyalty of army to, 273; source of strength of, 287; Catholic opposition to, 316–317; successor to, 317

Franco-Prussian War, 21
Frank, Leonhard, 46, 48, 58
Frank, Waldo, 305
Franz Ferdinand, Archduke, assassination of, 27
FRAP (Anti-Fascist and Patriotic Revolutionary Front), 273
Fratellini clowns, 305
Freedom's Battle (del Vayo), 164, 174
French Revolution, 86, 279; women in, 250. *See also* "May 1968" revolt
French-Spanish treaty of commerce, 164
Freud, Sigmund, 285
Friedrich II, 21
Fuentes, Carlos, 215, 309
Fulbright, William, 190, 280
Furmanov, Dmitri, 82

Gabin, Jean, 299
Galbraith, John K., 260–263, 280
Galdós, Benito Pérez, writings of, 303
Galsworthy, John, 14
Gamelin, General Maurice, 139
Gandhi, Mahatma, 89
Garaudy, Roger, 261, 262, 283, 290, 291
García Lorca, Federico, 128, 134, 206
Gasperi, Alcido de, 197
gauchisme, 277–292; origin of, 279; in China, 279; and youth, 283, 290; in Germany, 288
Gazette and Daily (York, Pa.), 105, 111
Genoa Conference, 41, 106, 143, 199
George IV, 130
"German century, the," 28
German militarism, 19, 20, 22, 23, 28, 46, 51, 52, 146, 204; constituting act of war, 49

German-Soviet pact, 118
Germany: unity of, 20, 21; foreign policy of, 21, 26; resurgence of power of, 21, 121; "art of imitation" in, 22; prosperity in (1910–13), 22–23; in League of Nations, 118; *gauchisme* in, 288; Social Democrats in. *See* Social Democrats
Gide, André, 305
Gil Robles, José María, 156n
Giner de los Ríos, Francisco, 3
Giral, José, 192
Gitt, J. W., 105, 111
Gladkov, Fedor, 82
Gladstone, William E., 5
Gleichheit (periodical), 31
Godard, Jean-Luc, 298–299
Goethe, Johann W. von, 20, 33, 166
Gogol, Nikolai, 81, 89, 96, 258; his *The Inspector General*, 92
gold shipment from Spain to Russia, 184–187, 189
González Martínez, Enrique, 192, 206
Gorki, Maxim, 81, 82, 94, 259; writings of, 92, 96
Gorvin, Captain John, 78
Gramsci, Antonio, 161, 291–292
Grand Tournant, Le (film), 159
Great Britain. *See* England
"great leap" (China), 232, 235, 237
Greene, Felix, 301; his *The Enemy*, 302
Grimau (Communist leader executed in Spain), 316
Gromyko, Andrei, 110
Grosz, Georg, 23, 61, 309
Gruninge, Ernest, 280
Guesde, Jules, 37
Guevara, Ernesto ("Ché"), 221, 288
Guevara, Sra. Ernesto, 221
Guilbeaux (French Socialist), 65
Guillain, Robert, 242
Gullón, Francisco, 99
gypsies, 127–134; in Spain, 128–132; in Switzerland, 127; origin of, 128; customs of, 129–134; in Russia, 129, 132; fortune-telling of, 130

Halifax, Lord, 123
Hammarskjöld, Dag, 110
Hammerstein, Baron von, 26
Han Dynasty, 238
Hanseatic League, motto of, 22
Han Suyin, 242, 242n
Hardekopf, Ferdinand, 58
Hardie, James Keir, 7
Hari, Mata, 57
Harriman, Averell, 148
Harting. *See* Hechelmann
Hauptmann, Gerhart, 25

Hauser, Richard, 261
Hauser, Mrs. Richard (Hephzibah Menuhin), 261
Heath, Edward, 9
Hechelmann (Russian secret agent), 24–25
Heidegger, Johann, 285
Heine, Heinrich, 25
Hellman, Lillian, 304
Hemingway, Ernest, 270; writings of, 188
Hennings, Emmy, 58, 59
Herr, Lucien, 155
Herriot, Edouard, 118, 123, 158, 159, 212
Herstein (painter), 55
Herzen, Alexander, 279
Hess, John, 156
Hidalgo de Cisneros, Ignacio, 187
Higgins, James, 111
Hilferding, Rudolf, 35, 161
Hindenburg, General Paul von, 55, 120
Hitler, Adolf, 12, 106, 115, 116, 118, 122, 148, 156, 160, 161, 165, 167, 171, 185, 187, 268, 274, 303, 307; violates Versailles Treaty, 138; supplies arms to Franco, 147; concept of state of, in *Mein Kampf*, 166; invades Austria, 211; and youth, 271; fall of, 315
Hoare, Sir Samuel, 211
Hobson, John Atkinson, 35
Ho Chi Minh, 301
Hohenzollern Empire, 20
Homme enchaîné, L', 54
Homme libre, L', 54
Hoover, Herbert, relief organization of, 73
House, Colonel E. M., 48
Hsuan Tsung, 238
Huang Chen, 148
Huang Hua, 148, 243
Hugo, Victor, 7, 82, 153, 247
Hull, Cordell, 149
Humanité, L' (party journal), 290
Hundertwasse, Fritz, 309
Hungarian Revolution, 286
Hyde Park, London, 3–4, 13

Ibarruri, Dolores (*La Pasionaria*), 99, 193, 249
Ibarruri, Rubén Ruiz, 99
Ibsen, Henrik, 7
Ickes, Harold, 110
Iglesias, Juana, 183
Iglesias, Pablo, 26, 182–184
"Ilyich" (Lenin), 145. *See also* Lenin
Indochina War, 263, 267
Industrial Revolution, 8

Institute of Foreign Affairs, Peking, 226, 229, 231, 232
International, Second, 31, 62
International, Third, 62, 80, 192
International Brigade(s), 187, 190, 193, 268, 269, 315
Isabella I, 129
Isbert, José, 302
Iskra (Spark) (Lenin's newspaper), 65, 143
Italy, in Ethiopia, 211. *See also* Mussolini
Ivan IV (the Terrible), 24
Izvestia (Moscow), 88; on Spanish armed forces in Russia, 102

Jacob, Mathilde, 40
Jacobin Club, 279
Jacobins, Société fraternelle des, 250
James, Henry, 46
Janco, Marcel, 59
Japan: withdrawal of, from League of Nations, 143; in China, 238
Jara, General, 206
Jar Ptitsa (art magazine), 259
Jaurès, Jean, 28, 38, 53, 153, 155, 163
Jewish question in Russia, 144
Joffe (Russian suicide), 145
Jogichès, Léon, 31, 33
Johansen, F. H., 71
Johnson, Lyndon B., 298
Jolas, Marie, 284
Jorn, Asger, 309
Jouffroy, Alain, 310
Jouhaux, Léon, 110, 174
journalism in U.S., 46, 261
Jouvet, Louis, 305
Juan (of Spain), 273
Juan Carlos, Prince, 167, 256, 272–274, 316
Juárez, Benito, 214
"July Oath," 158
"Junius" (Rosa Luxemburg), 38
Junta de Ampliación de Estudios, 3

Kahn, Herman, his *The Year 2000*, 283
Kandinsky, Wassili, 59
Kapp *Putsch*, 105, 106
Kaufman-Pasternak, Rosa, 96
Kautsky, Karl, 26, 33, 36, 62, 161; journal (*Die neue Zeit*) of, 27
Kautsky, Louise, 26, 33, 38, 40
Kazantzakis, Helen (Mrs. Nikos), 271
Kennedy, Joseph, 184
Kerenski, A. F., 62, 63; film portrayal of, 300
Khrushchev, Nikita, 76, 97, 225, 230, 278
"Khrushchev, the Chinese," 239
Kierkegaard, Sören, 52, 253

Kirchwey, Freda, 105, 108–110, 111
Kirov, Sergei M., 145
Kissinger, Henry, 20, 261
Klee, Paul, 59
"Klim" (Molotov), 145. See also Molotov
Klossovska, Elsa, 57
Klossovski, Balthus, 57
Klossovski, Eric, 57, 108
Klossovski, Pierre, 57
"Koba" (Stalin), 145. See also Stalin
Kolchak, Admiral, 75
Koltzov, Michael, 268–270; his Memories of the Spanish War, 269
Konchalovski, P. P., 81
Korfanty, Deputy Wojciech, 46
Korolénko, Vladimir, 38
Korzeniowski, Teodor Jozef Konrad. See Conrad
Kraft, Joseph, 112
Kremlin buildings, 79
Kreuzzeitung (Conservative party newspaper), 26
Kropotkin, Prince Peter, 23, 183, 247
Krupp Syndicate, 22
Kuang Wu-ti, 238
Kun, Béla, 286
Kuomintang regime, 234, 235; former generals of, 239

Lacouture, Jean, 260, 261, 296, 301
Lamoneda, Ramón, 183
Lamprecht, Karl, 20
Lange, Oscar, 110
Lansier, Henri, 264
Lansing, Robert M., 57
Largo Caballero, Francisco, 160, 163, 179–182, 184, 186, 189
La Rocque, Colonel Jean, 158
Laski, Harold, 13
Lassalle, Ferdinand, 27, 308
Laval, Pierre, 138, 158, 211
League of Nations, 49, 50, 164, 173, 190, 211; Nansen at, 69, 71, 72; Russian suspicion toward, 72–73; Czechoslovak crisis in (1938), 115; Germany enters, 118; Spain returns to, 120; defeatism of, 138–139; Russia admitted to, 140; Preparatory Disarmament Commission of, 141; Japanese withdrawal from, 143; weakness of, against Hitler, 147; Fascist pressure on, 171; Mexico in, 211; Ethiopian crisis in, 211; Pact of, 212
Léance (gypsy), 130
Leclerc, General Jacques, 101
leftism. See gauchisme
Leftist Socialists. See Bolsheviks
Léger, Alexis, 118

Leipzig, University of, 19
Leipziger Volkszeitung, 31
Lena Goldfields mines, strike at, 23
Lenin, Krupskaya, 62
Lenin, V. I. (Vladimir Ilyich Ulyanov), 38, 39, 62, 63, 65, 79–80, 82, 88, 89, 94, 142, 143–144, 145, 197, 263, 270, 289; on Rosa Luxemburg, 28; War of, 35; in Switzerland, 58, 61–63, 65; "April Theses" of, 62, 63; return of, to Russia (1917), 63; in The State and the Revolution, 63; New Economic Policy (NEP) of, 79; portrait of, in China, 146; illegal newspaper (Iskra) of, 143
Leningrad, siege of, 99
León, Maria Teresa (Sra. Rafael Alberti), 222, 269
Leonidov (actor), 88
Lerroux, Alejandro, 156n, 209
Levi, Paul, 39, 40, 65
Lewis, Anthony, 112, 261
Liberal, El (Madrid), 46, 49
Liebknecht, Karl, 38, 39, 40–41, 56, 61
Liebknecht, Sonia, 33
Liebknecht, Wilhelm, 36
Lilienthal, David, 264
Lin Piao, 223
Lippmann, Walter, 261, 280, 301
Lister, Enrique, 193
literature. See arts and literature
Litvinov, Maxim, 116, 118, 120, 137–149, 268
Liu Shao-chi, 222, 226, 239, 241
Lloyd George, Countess, 8
Lloyd George, David, 3–9, 50–51, 143, 160
Locarno Treaty, 118, 138
Lockhart, R. H. Bruce, 143
Lodge, Henry Cabot, 52
Lombardo Toledano, Vicente, 206
London, Jack, 299
London, 3–15
London Daily Mail, 4
London School of Economics, 11, 13, 19, 35
Long March (China), 148, 237
Long March, students', in Cultural Revolution, 241
Look magazine, 184
Loriot (French Socialist), 65
Loudon, John, 142
Louis XIII, 131
Ludendorff, General Erich von, 55, 106
Lukács, Georg, 12, 145, 225, 289–290, 307; writings of, 285–286
Lumumba, Patrice, 279
Lunacharski, Anatoli V., 81, 85–89, 97
Lusitania, torpedoing of, 48, 49

Lutovinov (Russian suicide), 145
Luxemburg, Rosa, 28, 31–42, 55, 56, 61, 65, 80, 263, 289, 291; correspondence of, 33; writings of, 34, 35, 38, 39; imprisonment of, 38, 40; assassination of, 40–41; trial and death of, dramatized ("The Blue Blouses"), 86

Macaulay, Lord, 14
Macciocchi, Maria Antonietta, her De La Chine, 242
MacDonald, Ramsay, 118, 120
Machado, Antonio, 270
MacLeish, Archibald, 110
Madrid, Alliance of, 270
Madrid, attack on, 122, 180, 268, 269
Maiski, Ivan, 143, 147, 161
Malaysia, relations of, with China, 224
Malraux, André, 55, 97, 156, 187, 315; loyalty of, to Spanish Republic, 188; film of his L'Espoir (Hope), 299
Manac'h, Etienne, 148
Manchester Guardian, 105, 111, 112
Manchukuo, "independence" of, 238
Mann, Heinrich, 56, 259
Mann, Thomas, 259; his The Magic Mountain, 289
Manuilski, Dmitri, 110, 192–193, 193n
Manzini, General, 270
Mao Tse-tung, 89, 148, 198, 210, 219, 221, 222–223, 225, 226, 234, 237, 239, 241, 242, 269, 271, 291; "thoughts of," 224; devotion of workers to, 230; falsely interpreted, 240; workers of, in France, 281–282
Marat, Jean Paul, 250, 279
Marchais, Georges, 286
Marcuse, Herbert, 279, 284–288; writings of, 285
Maria Theresa, 132
Marinetti, Emilio, 198
Maritain, Jacques, 317
Marosov Modern Art Gallery, 80
Marshall Plan, satiric film about, 302
Martí, José, 214
Martin, Kingsley, 11, 111–112
Martin du Gard, Roger, 305
Martínez, Manuel, 101
Martínez Báez, Manuel, 192
Martínez Barrio, Diego, 191, 192
Marx, Karl, 8, 27, 263, 285, 288; portrait of, in China, 146; Das Kapital of, considered as film, 301
Masaryk, Jan, 193
Mateo Sagasta, Práxedes, 183
Matesa, 256
Maura, Antonio, 183, 187
Mauriac, François, 155, 187, 298, 317
Maurras, Charles, 166

Maximilian, Archduke, 207
Mayakovski, Vladimir, 81–82, 86, 97, 99, 259
"May 1968" revolt (France), 158, 167, 248, 282, 286
McNamara, Robert, 288
Meany, George, 13n
Medellín, battle of, 187
Medina-Sidonia, Duchess of (Isabel Alvarez de Toledo), 273
Mehring, Franz, 34
Meir, Mrs. Golda, 159
Mendès-France, Pierre, 158, 226, 230, 260, 261, 262, 263, 265–268; on Chou En-lai, 267
Menuhin, Hephzibah (Mrs. Richard Hauser), 261
Menuhin, Yehudi, 261
Mercouri, Melina, 296
Mérimée, Prosper, 132
Mexican Revolution, 204, 205–209
Mexico, 186, 203–215; Agrarian Reform in, 204, 213, 214; relations of, with Spain, 204, 210–211; in League of Nations, 211; oil companies in, 213, 214
Meyerhold, Vsevolod, 86–88, 299
Miaja, General José, 269
Michel, Louise (The "Red Virgin"), 247–258
Michelet, Jules, 248
Miller, Arthur, 284, 304
Millerand, Alexandre, 37
Ming Dynasty, 238
Mirabeau, Honoré, 249
Mirbach, Count Wilhelm von, 79
Mitre, General Bartolomé, 105
Mitre, Jorge, 105, 106, 108
Mitterand, François, 158
Moch, Jules, 158–159, 193; in Rencontres avec Léon Blum, 161
Modesto, Juan, 193
Mola, General Emilio, 182
Molière, Jean Baptiste, in Le Malade imaginaire, 130
Molotov, V. T., 145, 146, 192–193
Mommsen, Theodor, 28
Monde, Le, 176, 242
Monnet, Jean, 155
Montand, Yves, 278
Montgomery, Viscount, 236
Montherlant, Henry de, 188
Morris, Ira, 284
Moscow, University of, 99
Moscow Art Theater, 88
Moskvin, Ivan, 88
Mujica, General, 206
Munich Pact, 115, 116, 122, 138–139, 165, 171
Mussolini, Benito, 123, 138, 158, 166,

Saltykov, Mikhail E. *See* Stchedrin
Sangerkrieg Intirol, Der (Dada publication), 61
Santo Cretchuno, feast of, 132
Sarraut, Albert, 138
Sartre, Jean-Paul, 52, 175, 277, 281, 282
Satie, Erik, 58
Saura, Carlos, 302
Savonarola, Girolamo, 290
Scheidemann, Philipp, 33, 40
Schikele, René, 58
Schiller, Johann von, 25, 308
Schubchukin Modern Art Gallery, 80
Scott, Charles Prestwick, 105, 111, 112
Scott, Robert F., 14
Sebastiani, Horace, 39
Second International. *See* International, Second
Second World War: Spanish contribution to Allied cause in, 99, 122, 160; Spanish Civil War "first battle" of, 137, 174
Seeckt, General Hans von, 106
Selassie, Haile, 211
Semprún, Jorge, his film *The Confession*, 278
Semyonov, N., 89
Serner (Dadaist painter), 58
Serrati, Giacinto M., 198
"Seryozha" (Sergei M. Kirov), 145
Shakespeare, William, 254, 304, 308
Shaw, George Bernard, 11, 295
Shehu, Mehmet, 315
Shen Ping, 148
Sholokhov, Michael, 97
Shultz, Lillie, 110
Sierra, Manuel, 192, 206
Signoret, Simone, 278
Silva Herzog, Jesús, 192, 206–208, 210, 212, 214, 215
Simon, Sir John, 211
Simon and Schuster, 13n, 111
Slaughterhouse I. *See* "Abattoir I, L'"
Snow, Edgar, 112, 220, 241, 242
Social Democrats (Germany), 26–28, 31, 33, 35, 37, 39, 40, 56
Socialista, El (Madrid), 183
Socialist International, 37, 159
Socialists: victory of, in Potsdam, 26; party of, in France, 37; the duty of, 40
Solzhenitsyn, Alexander, 94, 289–290
Soviet Academy of Sciences, 99
Soviet Embassy, Peking, 222
Soviet Union. *See* Russia
Spain: armed forces of, in Russia, 99–102; policy of, before Second World War, 122, 123; returns to League of Nations, 120; U.S. embargo against, 184; relations of, with Mexico, 204,

210–211; young people in, 271–274; U.S. bases in, 310
Spanish Civil War: Nehru on, 123; as "first battle" in Second World War, 137, 174; revolutionary climate of, 156; international significance of, 160; weapons for, 164; Azaña's interpretation of, 173; as symbol, 176; Government of, 189
Spanish Republic, 106, 112, 173, 274
Spanish Republican Army, 122, 269, 274
Spanish Squadron, organization of, 187
Spartacus (party), 40
Spellman, Cardinal, 184
"Spider, the" (fellow prisoner of Silva Herzog), 208
Stalin, Alliluyeva, 144–145
Stalin, Joseph, 12, 268, 286; his definition of writers, 97; his respect for F. D. Roosevelt, 139; foreign policy of, 141, 146; on Jewish question, 144; his wife's death, 144–145; statesmanship of, 145–146; portrait of, in China, 146; on U.S., 146; supports Chiang Kai-shek, 225; results of death of, 278
Standard Oil of New Jersey (in Mexico), 212–213
Stanislavski, Constantine, 87, 89
Stchedrin (Mikhail E. Saltykov), 88
Stein, von, household, 19–20
Stendhal, Marie Henri, 14, 85
Stone, Izzy, 110, 112
Stresemann, Gustav, 118, 120
strikes: in England (1911, 1912), 9; in Russia (1912), 23; theory of, first put into practice, 34; as political weapon, 35; in France (1936), 155
student movements. *See* young people in politics
suffragettes (England), 9
Sung Dynasty, 238
Sun Yat-sen, Mme., 249
surrealism, 61

Tabouis, Geneviève, 115
Taft, William Howard, 49
Talleyrand-Périgord, Charles de, on diplomacy, 203
Tang (interpreter in China), 222
Tang Dynasty, 238
Tardieu, André, 120
Taylor, A. J. P., 5
Tchen Tche-pang, 148
Tedeschini, Cardinal, 133
Thackeray, William Makepeace, his *Vanity Fair*, 128
Théâtre du Vieux Colombier, 304–305
Thiers, Louis, 248
Thieu, N. V., 148–149, 265, 301

49; his biography of George Washington, 50; foreign policy of, 50; on Lloyd George, 50–51; on future militarism, 51; his *Leaders of Men*, 51; failure of, 52

women, political activities of, 9, 247–250
Women's Lib movement, American, 249
working class in England, 8, 9
World War II. *See* Second World War
Wrangel, General P. N., 75
Wuang Chao Treuen, 232
Wu Hoan Hsing, 236
Wu Hou, 238

Yao Teng-shan, 240
Yasnaya Polyana (home of Tolstoi), 85, 89–90, 91
Yesierska, Miss (friend of Rosa Luxemburg), 56

young people in politics, 284–288, 290–291
Yugoslavia, 141, 305
Yugoslavia, King (Alexander) of, assassinated, 156
Yung Lo, 238
Yung Lung-kuei, 233, 235

Zanko (gypsy chief), 134
Zapata, Emiliano, 206
Zassulich, Vera, 64
Zetkin, Clara, 35, 80
Zickler, Arthur, 40
Zinoviev, Gregory, 200
Zletykamien (painter), 309
Zola, Emile, Heinrich Mann's essay on, 56
Zugazagoitia, Julian, 183